The Business School in the Twenty-First Century

Questions about the status, identity and legitimacy of business schools in the modern university system continue to stimulate debate among deans, educational policy makers and commentators. In this book, three world experts share their critical insights on management education and new business school models in the US, Europe and Asia, on designing the business school of the future, and how to make it work. They look at how the business school is changing and focus in particular on emergent global challenges and innovations in curricula, professional roles, pedagogy, uses of technology and organisational delineations. Set within the context of a wider discussion about management as a profession, the authors provide a systematic, historical perspective, analysing major trends in business school models, and reviewing a wealth of current literature, to provide an informed and unique perspective that is firmly grounded in practical and experimental analysis.

HOWARD THOMAS is Dean and LKCSB Chair in Strategic Management at the Lee Kong Chian School of Business, Singapore Management University. He was Dean of Warwick Business School (2000–10) and, prior to this, he was Dean of the College of Commerce and Business Administration at the University of Illinois at Urbana-Champaign (1991–2000).

PETER LORANGE is President of the Lorange Institute of Business, Zurich, and is one of the world's foremost business school academics. He is Professor of Strategy at IMD, Switzerland, and was the President of IMD (1993–2008). Prior to this, he was President of the Norwegian Business School (BI) in Oslo.

JAGDISH SHETH is the Charles H. Kellstadt Chair of Marketing in the Goizueta Business School at Emory University, Atlanta, where he won the school's Global Innovation Award in June 2008. Professor Sheth is an internationally recognised business consultant and has been an educator for more than forty years.

The Business School in the Twenty-First Century

Emergent Challenges and New Business Models

HOWARD THOMAS

PETER LORANGE

JAGDISH SHETH

CAMBRIDGE
UNIVERSITY PRESS

CAMBRIDGE
UNIVERSITY PRESS

University Printing House, Cambridge CB2 8BS, United Kingdom

Published in the United States of America by Cambridge University Press, New York

Cambridge University Press is part of the University of Cambridge.

It furthers the University's mission by disseminating knowledge in the pursuit of education, learning and research at the highest international levels of excellence.

www.cambridge.org
Information on this title: www.cambridge.org/9781107013803

© Howard Thomas, Peter Lorange and Jagdish Sheth 2013

First published 2013

Printed in the United Kingdom by CPI Group (UK) Ltd, Croydon CR0 4YY

A catalogue record for this publication is available from the British Library

Library of Congress Cataloguing in Publication data
Thomas, Howard.
The business school in the twenty-first century : emergent challenges and new business models / Howard Thomas, Peter Lorange, Jagdish Sheth.
    pages   cm
Includes index.
ISBN 978-1-107-01380-3 (Hardback)
1. Business schools. 2. Business education. 3. Management–Study and teaching. I. Lorange, Peter II. Sheth, Jagdish N. III. Title.
HF1111.L668 2013
650.071'1–dc23   2013013775

ISBN 978-1-107-01380-3 Hardback

Additional resources for this publication at www.cambridge.org/9781107013803

Contents

Figures

Tables

Preface: Tipping or tripping? The business school and its dilemmas

Even the most cursory perusal of this book will reveal that it deals with an industry that, if not actually in crisis, is certainly suffering from a bad case of existential angst. The industry in question is the education of managers and the subjects are business schools, the main purveyors of management education.

As this book attempts to explain, business schools are in the line of fire of many critics and stakeholders for many reasons. It is an odd position for them to be in. Business schools are in the main fairly august institutions that can trace their origins back a long way (many celebrated their centenary just a few years ago, though with remarkably little external fanfare).

So what are they allegedly doing so wrong? Well, according to their critics, just about everything.

For example, they are said to be far too driven (for an academic institution) by the need and the desire to make a profit. They are accused of pursuing a spurious academic rigour that leads to esoteric research that has little relevance to the real practice of management. Indeed, it is argued that attending a business school programme never actually made anyone a better manager. Some maintain that management is an art and not a science and is not even a profession since it has no widely accepted body of knowledge that has to be mastered, unlike in 'real' professions such as accounting, medicine and law.

That such criticism comes after what has been a Golden Age of some four decades for business schools is surprising. In the latter part of the last century business schools enjoyed enormous financial and reputational success. It disappeared in the crashes of the early twenty-first century. First there was the dot.com boom and bust (which was never the fault of business schools and in which they suffered considerably from potential students ditching MBA programmes in favour of crazily excessive entrepreneurial start-ups) and then the financial disaster of 2007–8, in which, some argue, business schools were more directly involved through advocating market populism rather than stakeholder capitalism.

So it may not be too much to say that management education and business schools are both at a tipping point. More seriously, they may also be at a *tripping* point, either about to stumble ungraciously to the floor and possibly knock themselves out or ready to collect their wits, pick up their feet and recover their poise. This book catches them, so to speak, in mid-air. Can they reinvent themselves and regain a new sense of identity and legitimacy among their key stakeholders? (What the outcome will be must remain to be seen.)

Acknowledgements

This book would not have come about without the background of the long friendship between the three authors who have known and trusted each other for several decades.

Peter's career in management education has covered such schools as Sloan (MIT), Wharton, Norwegian Business School (BI) (Dean), IMD, Switzerland (President), and the Lorange Institute of Business (President), whereas Jagdish's illustrious research career in consumer behavior and competitive strategy has embraced schools such as Columbia, MIT, Illinois, the University of Southern California and Emory University. Both of them have huge experience of management education. Howard's career has also involved experience in management education, gained in three continents (North America, Europe and Asia). He has been a distinguished strategic management scholar in such schools as London Business School, MIT, University of British Columbia, Northwestern, HEC Montreal and Warwick Business School. He has also held three deanships, at the University of Illinois at Urbana-Champaign (US), at Warwick Business School (UK) and most recently in Asia at the Singapore Management University.

Paula Parish was a key catalyst for this project. Through her role as a Senior Publishing Editor for Cambridge University Press, she already had published books on management education by Peter Lorange and Howard Thomas. She encouraged the book's focus and the author line-up. We are very grateful to her for her tireless efforts to bring this project to fruition.

We are also grateful to many colleagues for their advice and insight. There are so many that picking particular individuals is an invidious and impossible task.

However, we would like to thank our colleagues and researchers at Emory, the Lorange Institute and Singapore Management University. In the latter case President Arnoud De Meyer of SMU deserves special mention.

Finally, our sincere appreciation goes to the set of researchers, secretaries and editors who provided considerable support and understanding for this project. Therefore, we thank Gillian Goh Cheng Cheng for her excellent research assistance and Susan Chong Oi Yin for her highly professional and splendid competence in typing various drafts of the book. We further thank Andrea Zlobinski (Peter's PA) and Dorasen Khoo Ban Yie (Howard's PA) for organising Peter's and Howard's time and schedule so effectively and Michelle Lee Pui Yee, Associate Professor of Marketing, for her insight and for her ability in co-ordinating a number of research assistants.

Our Consultant Editor, George Bickerstaffe, is also owed considerable thanks for the high quality and professionalism of his work in making the final manuscript readable and accessible to our readers.

However, we alone are solely responsible for the quality of the final product. We sincerely hope you enjoy this book.

SMU, Singapore   *Howard Thomas*

Lorange Institute, Switzerland   *Peter Lorange*

Emory University, US   *Jagdish Sheth*

I The business school: history, evolution and the search for legitimacy

INTRODUCTION

Since the 1960s, young, ambitious managers have regarded attending a programme at a high-quality business school as almost a prerequisite for business success and eventual promotion to the executive suite.

More recently, despite business schools being one of the acknowledged success stories of higher education over the past forty years, there has been a wide range of comment and criticism and a growing sense of concern about the value, purpose, role and academic stature of business schools.

There is, for example, criticism about them being too market-driven (Bennis and O'Toole, 2005), about the impact and relevance of business school research (Pfeffer and Fong, 2002) and some doubt about whether attendance at a business school actually makes anyone a better manager (Grey, 2005: 106; Mintzberg, 2004). It is argued that management is an art and not a science (Mintzberg, 2004) and that it is not even a profession since it has no widely accepted body of knowledge, unlike accounting, medicine or law (Spender, 2007).

This chapter, therefore, poses the following questions:

(1) What is a business school? How did it become a commonly accepted model? What is its espoused role and purpose?
(2) How did the business school concept develop?
(3) How has the business school evolved from an historical perspective?
(4) What is the evidence of both success and failure of the business school?
(5) What is its current positioning and strengths/weaknesses?

It starts with some background on the evolution of the business school concept followed by a brief historical examination of its development. This is complemented by a discussion of the evolution of the business school from a social constructionist perspective (e.g. Porac and Thomas, 2002). The argument is that, through a social process involving the 'selling' of alternative visions of what a management school should be, the concept of the modern business school was created.

BACKGROUND: THE 'BUSINESS SCHOOL' CONCEPT

How did the term 'business school' become the commonly accepted shorthand term for a school of management? There have probably been four main spheres of influence (France, Germany, the UK and the US) in the development of business and management education. They exerted their influence mainly in the late nineteenth and early twentieth centuries – the period of the late Industrial Revolution, which is often dated from 1870 to 1914 (the advent of the First World War).

These four major industrial powers developed forms of educating managers in the practical aspects of management such as finance, accounting, management control and operations, and distribution and sales in a highly vocational manner. The material was very practical and focused on increasing the basic skill levels of managers. The French called their vocational schools 'écoles de commerce', the Germans 'Handelschochschulen', the British 'schools of commerce' and the Americans 'business schools'.

Educators in all four countries discussed, debated and recognised their differing viewpoints about the conduct of management education in various conferences and via other channels of communication.

In the US, 'product champions' such as Edmund James at the Wharton School of the University of Pennsylvania were, for example, well aware of the philosophy of the German schools and had studied them in forming their models of the US 'business school'. Indeed,

Wharton and Harvard, founded in 1881 and 1908 respectively, were very much influenced by the German Cameralist education system.[1]

Largely because of private donations (e.g. Joseph Wharton to Wharton, Amos Tuck to Dartmouth), the business school concept grew very quickly in the US, much faster than in France, Germany and the UK. By 1936 there were nearly 200 business schools in US universities.

Accompanying this fast growth, the US business education industry also invested heavily in generating textbooks (the Richard D. Irwin publishing company, for example, grew rapidly by publishing focused business texts) and case study material (Harvard Business School Publishing) that facilitated the development of a wide range of curriculum innovations.

Using the principles of competitive advantage, it is clear that these complementary assets (textbooks, cases etc.) along with sample curricula were, in due course, the benchmark assets adopted by French, German and British schools as exemplars of best practice and modern trends in business education. Through this process the term 'business school' became the socially constructed and accepted term for an institution of commerce, management training or management education. The 'business school' thus became the basis for a cognitive and learning community describing the institution in which management education takes place.

> It is important to recognise that the development of business and management knowledge within higher education originally started in Europe, not in the US.

---

[1] According to Richard E. Wagner (2012) the Cameralists have been described as 'consultant administrators'. They were engaged in real-world administration (e.g. managing mines and glass works) and also academic administration. They were partly economists, political scientists, administrators and lawyers. The first Chairs of Cameral Science were established in Halle and Frankfurt (in commercial economics) and there were over twenty Chairs by 1800. These Cameralist Chairs were not titled Professors of Business yet their syllabi were essentially those adopted by Wharton and Harvard in the early twentieth century (Spender, 2007).

Although 'business school' became the generally accepted term, this did not mean that all the business schools in different countries developed in exactly the same way. It is clear in examining the history of the development of business schools that while the US model provides a basic framework, a wide range of local, regional, cultural and educational differences have led to adaptations of the US-style business school model.

HISTORICAL REVIEW OF THE EVOLUTION OF THE BUSINESS SCHOOL

Business schools became recognised institutions in the US from the early twentieth century and have expanded worldwide since then, stimulated by the growth of US multinationals and the investments of leading American private business schools. Formidable competitors sensitive to local market needs have also since emerged in Europe, Asia and Latin America.

As noted already, it is important to recognise that the development of business and management knowledge within higher education originally started in Europe, not in the US. The main purpose was to improve the relatively low societal and professional status of business managers, although impetus also came from military sources who pioneered the study of logistics, operations and operations research.

In France, the Paris-based Ecole Supérieure de Commerce was founded by the Paris Chamber of Commerce in 1819–20 with the aim of complementing the quality of engineering education and with the laudable ambition of developing a superior education to secondary technical education. The mid-nineteenth century also saw the foundation of a school of commerce in Anvers, Belgium, in 1852. In Italy, a school of commerce was founded in Venice in 1867. In the late nineteenth century, similar schools appeared in Austria (Vienna, 1856), Germany (Aachen, Leipzig, 1898; Cologne, 1901; Frankfurt am Main, 1901; Berlin, 1906; Mannheim, 1907; Munich, 1910) and Switzerland (St Gallen, 1898).

However, despite this initial burst of activity, business school education in Europe developed slowly and on a national, rather than regional, basis. The main reasons were the shortage of good management faculty able to enrich the efforts of the original university pioneers. This was on top of the consistent and very strong resistance to the development and incorporation of the field of business administration as a formal university discipline by university professors in other areas of study.

In the UK, for example, there was little development of research or theory after the foundation of schools of commerce at the universities of Birmingham (1902) and Manchester (1904). As Larson (2003: 2) notes: 'The London School of Economics and the universities of Birmingham and Manchester experimented with "business", "commerce" or "industrial administration" curricula throughout the first half of the twentieth century [...] There was no academic research done to drive these courses and the lack of a theoretical framework hurt their reputation.'

The post-war recommendation of the British Institute of Management (BIM), created in 1947, that business schools should be developed in the UK was not implemented.

> BIM's enthusiasm was fuelled by admiration for the quality of America's logistical and management expertise in the military and the Department of Defense during the Second World War, which bred a considerable respect for American management culture.

BIM's enthusiasm was fuelled by admiration for the quality of America's logistical and management expertise in the military and the Department of Defense during the Second World War, which bred a considerable respect for American management culture (Locke, 1996; Locke and Spender, 2011). It was only much later, as a consequence of the Franks Report in 1963 (commissioned by the UK government), which had a similar policy rationale to the reports by the Ford Foundation (Gordon and Howell, 1959) and the Carnegie

Foundation (Pierson, 1959) in the US, that the business school model was accepted in the UK.

Franks' policy recommendations led to the creation, with strong government backing, of two elite (indeed, at the time only) 'business schools' in the UK, London Business School and Manchester Business School, both loosely integrated into their parent universities.

As we have noted above, the development of schools of management education in the US was heavily influenced by European models and, particularly, the Cameralist traditions of German universities such as Halle and Berlin (Spender, 2007). This development was consolidated in the twentieth century. The spread of this type of institution across America was rapid, with the development of both independent and university-based business schools.

By the early 1900s, a range of private schools such as Wharton (endowed by Joseph Wharton, owner of Bethlehem Steel, and built up by Edmund James after he had studied economics at Halle), Chicago, Harvard (formed by Edwin Gay in 1908 after he had studied economics at Berlin), Columbia and Dartmouth had already started to gain recognition.

Formalisation of degree-level business education progressed quickly. Wharton launched a bachelor's programme in business in 1881 influenced by the so-called scientific management principles developed and promoted by Frederick Taylor and often known as Taylorism. Interestingly, Taylor was an employee at Joseph Wharton's Bethlehem Steel.

The rather mechanical management training stage of business school development in the US from the turn of the twentieth century until the late 1950s has been described as the 'trade school' era.

Dartmouth offered the first master's degree in business in 1900 and Harvard launched the Master of Business Administration (MBA) degree in 1908. A number of business schools were created later but tended to rely initially on the educational philosophy of the earlier models.

In 1916, a group of leading US business schools set up the Association to Advance Collegiate Schools of Business (known as AACSB International and sometimes described as the American Association of Collegiate Schools of Business) with the objective of bringing scientific rigour to the study of business. They mandated the knowledge base required in business schools in order to establish quality standards and certify management as a legitimate profession. The signatory schools were: University of California, University of Chicago, Columbia University, Cornell University, Dartmouth University, Harvard University, University of Illinois, University of Nebraska, New York University, Northwestern University, Ohio State University, University of Pennsylvania, University of Pittsburgh, University of Texas, Tulane University, University of Wisconsin, Yale University.

The rather mechanical management training stage of business school development in the US from the turn of the twentieth century until the late 1950s has been described as the 'trade school' era, which Nobel Laureate Herbert Simon has typified as a 'wasteland of vocationalism'. Roger Martin, Dean of the Rotman School of Management at the University of Toronto in Canada (Moldoveanu and Martin, 2008), has characterised it as 'Business 1.0'. 'Trade schools' typically catered for undergraduate students (with some practically based masters' programmes), did not undertake much research and taught from a 'descriptive' viewpoint.

This 'trade school' orientation changed rapidly, following the very influential reports on the state of management education from the Ford and Carnegie Foundations in 1959. These reports formulated a number of policy prescriptions that drove the development of business schools towards a research and discipline-led focus.

For example, Gordon and Howell (who wrote the Ford report) advocated the study of all business operations and functions from a broad, integrated managerial perspective and championed education about the political, economic and social environment. They stressed analytical rigour and problem-solving ability, scientific method, research and knowledge creation, and placed a strong focus on graduate and doctoral education in business.

Pierson's Carnegie report further emphasised the scientific rigour element by endorsing the innovative quantitative methods (including statistics, simulation and operations research) of the GSIA (Graduate School of Industrial Administration) at Carnegie-Mellon University.

Following on from the two reports, in the early 1960s the Ford Foundation committed over $50 million to promote business education and research, initially in five business schools: namely, Carnegie-Mellon, Chicago, Columbia, Harvard and Stanford. UCLA, University of California, Berkeley, and MIT were added at a later stage (Augier and March, 2011).

Subsequent investments by these and other management schools led to the growth of scholarly, discipline-based academic research anchored firmly in the economic and social sciences. Those business educators who argued for a 'clinical' and 'practical experience' research imperative in business schools that focused on relevance through understanding and improving management practice felt disenfranchised and disillusioned.

To this day, these tensions between rigour (scientific logical positivism) and relevance (practical, applied research) in management still exist. Indeed, Bennis and O'Toole (2005) ask why 'business schools have embraced the scientific model of physicists and economists rather than the professional model of doctors and lawyers'. Nevertheless, the positivist model of management education became the dominant design from the 1960s to the 1990s.

However, there has been persistent and growing criticism about the nature and value of business schools, particularly those who have followed the US-dominant design embedded in the discipline-oriented prescriptions of the Ford and Carnegie reports.

Some critics accuse business schools of producing arcane, academic research, doing a poor job of preparing students for management careers, pandering to the market and the rankings, and failing to ask important questions. And, in the process of responding to demands from their environment, losing claims of professionalisation as they 'dumb down' the content of courses, inflate grades to keep students happy and pursue curricular fads.

> Critics stress that business schools do not encourage managers to incorporate an integrative, team-based philosophy and do not provide sufficient ethical and professional guidance.

Others argue that contemporary management education does a disservice to the profession by standardising content, being too analytical and not action-oriented, focusing on business functions (instead of the process of managing) and training specialists (rather than general managers). They also criticise business schools for being too parochial and not global in their thinking and values, and for not fully integrating experience, theory and reflection into group (rather than individual) decision-making processes.

Finally, these critics stress that business schools do not encourage managers to incorporate an integrative, team-based philosophy and do not provide sufficient ethical and professional guidance.

But many academics stoutly defend the research traditions in business schools developed in the years following the Ford and Carnegie reports. For example, Cooley (2007) argues that '[t]he research mindset brings a unique and powerful focus to business education. It is forward looking rather than backward looking. It moves education away from teaching students a collection of facts to teaching them how to think. It moves them from a stultifying "best practice" mentality toward developing analytical ability.'

Grey (2005), in contrast, notes that this analytic positivistic research tradition, particularly as practised in US business schools, has created 'norms' of what 'good' research is and has developed the bulk of textbook knowledge. Yet, in Europe the consensus of US-based researchers that social science and business research should follow an essentially positivistic route has been questioned, particularly by critical management theorists, who stress the value of action-based qualitative research embedded in management practice.

By the early 1990s Continental European business schools had developed strongly and their growing stature in the field was being recognised. Indeed, both Professor Pedro Nueno (1995), a pioneer activist in both the Spanish business school IESE and EFMD (European Foundation for Management Development) in Brussels, Belgium, and Claude Rameau (1995), a pioneer at INSEAD, stated that European schools are more international than US schools ... and that their international character should be a catalyst for transformation and change in management educators.

How did these European models evolve and prosper? Were they defined in local or regional terms or by reference to international prototypes (e.g. the US model) or in terms of a mix of national role models and international prototypes (Thomas, 2012)?

To help our discussion, Table 1.1 provides a partial 'map' of the management education landscape in Europe, which demonstrates the breadth of the marketplace and its heterogeneous nature.

European schools are generally regarded as eclectic and flexible. Europeans have never been very comfortable with the North American model's focus on shareholder management, market populism and entrepreneurial capitalism (Hubbard, 2006). Rather, they have advocated the need for stakeholder management and a more social democratic form of capitalism. (See Currie et al., 2010 and the work of EABIS (European Academy for Business in Society) and GRLI (the Global Responsible Leadership Institute).) This is apparent in the much more direct influence of governments, and regulation, in continental Europe on both public-sector and private-sector management. Consequently, across Europe, it is not surprising that there is a range of leadership styles and cultural influences on business schools.

European schools are generally regarded as more eclectic and flexible. Europeans have never been very comfortable with the North American model's focus on shareholder management, market populism and entrepreneurial capitalism.

Table 1.1 *A partial 'map' of European management education*

Country	Representative schools
Austria	Wirtschaftsuniversitaet, Wien (Vienna)
Belgium	Vlerick School of Management (Leuven/Ghent)
Czechoslovakia	CMC Postgraduate School (Prague)
Denmark	Copenhagen Business School (Copenhagen)
Finland	Handelschogskolan: Helsingors (Helsinki); Aalto Business School (Helsinki)
France	INSEAD (Fountainbleau); HEC; ESCP/EAP; ESSEC; EMLyon; Sciences PO (Paris); Grenoble; Paris/Dauphine; Audencia, Nantes; Bordeaux, ESCEM-Tours; Toulouse
Germany	WHU (Koblenz); EBS (Frankfurt); ESMT (Berlin); Mannheim; GISMA (Hanover); Leipzig; WHU (Munich); Cologne; Frankfurt am Main
Netherlands	NIMBAS/Tilburg; Erasmus (Rotterdam); Nijenrode (Breukelen)
Hungary	Central University Business School (Budapest)
Ireland	Smurfit/Quinn Schools UCD (Dublin)
Italy	SDA Bocconi (Milan)
Norway	Norwegian Business School (BI) (Oslo); Norwegian School of Economics and Business Administration (NHH) (Bergen)
Poland	University of Warsaw Postgraduate Management Centre (Warsaw); Koszminski School (Warsaw)
Russia	Moscow State University; Skolkovo (Moscow); St Petersburg
Slovenia	IEDC/Bled School of Management (Bled)
Spain	IESE./University of Navarra (Barcelona); ESADE (Ramon-Llull) (Barcelona); Instituto de Empresa (Madrid); EADA
Sweden	Stockholm School of Economics (Stockholm)

Table 1.1 (*cont.*)

Country	Representative schools
Switzerland	IMD (Lausanne); Geneva; Hochschule St Gallen (St Gallen); Lausanne; Lorange Institute of Business (Zurich)
United Kingdom	London Business School; Warwick Business School (Coventry); Saïd (Oxford); Judge (Cambridge); Manchester Business School; LUMS (Lancaster); Imperial (London); Cass (London); Edinburgh (Scotland); Cardiff (Wales); Henley; Cranfield; Ashridge

Sources: Financial Times (FT ratings); *The Economist (Which MBA?)*, EFMD, AACSB, AMBA, Antunes and Thomas (2007: 389)

In France, for example, INSEAD, self-styled as 'The Business School for the World', a private school based in Fontainebleau outside Paris, is a continental European 'outlier' in that it competes strongly with the major US schools, whereas HEC, ESCP/EAP, ESSEC and EMLyon are the so-called French 'grandes écoles', the French elite (i.e. the most prestigious and, perhaps, more theory-driven) schools, with HEC having a strong international reputation. Bordeaux, ESCEM, Grenoble, Nantes (Audencia), Skema, Toulouse and others, on the other hand, are exemplars of around twenty-five 'écoles supérieures de commerce' (a mix of theory-driven and practice-oriented schools). All are linked institutionally with the training and education needs of local chambers of commerce (as are the elites) and are anchored in their local regions where companies provide significant financial support.

In Germany, business schools have been relatively slow to adopt separate institutional forms despite the long German heritage of management education. This is partly because of the historical German traditions in education, with five-year first-degree courses in business and the Diplom-Kaufmann as the dominant educational model. In addition, the heavy technological and scientific orientation of German industry produced conservatism and scepticism about management education. For example, in Germany, managers generally have lower status than engineers do and management education is not generally well-regarded or seen as practically relevant.

However, with the advent of the Bologna Accord in 1999, which sought to harmonise the framework of higher education degrees in forty European countries, there has been a clear trend towards the development of first-rate MBAs in German schools. These include Cologne (a university-based school), WHU (Koblenz; a private school), Mannheim (a university-based school), EBS (European Business School) in Wiesbaden and ESMT (the European School for Management and Technology – a private school in Berlin).

For a relatively small European country, Spain has gained a very distinctive position in the business school field with three highly regarded and influential business schools. Two schools have grown significantly in Barcelona – IESE, supported by the Opus Dei (and developed with academic assistance from Wharton and Harvard) and ESADE, supported by the Jesuits – whereas Instituto de Empresa in Madrid is perhaps a more professionally oriented business school.

They have all expanded geographically and, in a very strategic fashion, have developed strong linkages with growing Latin American business schools. Their global footprint has been recognised through strong ratings in the *Financial Times* (*FT*) ranking of global MBA programmes.

In the UK, according to the Association of Business Schools (ABS), there are around 100 MBA programmes available from a wide range of schools. London Business School (LBS), like INSEAD in France, follows a US-style business school model and attempts to compete strongly and internationally with the major US schools. Henley Management College (now part of the University of Reading) and Cranfield School of Management, however, focus much more on executive education programmes (plus small MBA programmes) whereas university-based business schools such as Cass (City), Imperial (London), Judge (Cambridge), LUMS (Lancaster), Saïd (Oxford) and WBS (Warwick) offer a wider range of programmes from undergraduate to post-experience.

Scandinavia and Northern Europe have a widely regarded range of 'national champions' in management education in Stockholm, Oslo, Helsinki and Copenhagen and a Scandinavian approach to management exemplified in such journals as the *Scandinavian Journal of Management* and the *Scandinavian Journal of Economics.*

Interestingly, business schools developed very slowly in Scandinavia because the established schools jealously guarded their pioneer positions (Engwall, 2000). They also followed the pathways offered by German schools, with which they had a strong cultural affinity. Although these schools were absorbed into existing institutions, professors in other parts of those universities questioned the development of an applied field such as business education. Scandinavian schools have consequently grown and expanded much more slowly than their counterparts.

Switzerland, on the other hand, is home to a small but internationally prestigious school, IMD (Lausanne), and a 'national champion', St Gallen, alongside other strong schools in Lausanne (HEC) and Zurich.

Finally, Eastern Europe has developed its own business schools over the past fifteen to twenty years with schools such as IEDC in Bled, Slovenia, and Kozminski University in Poland and many others throughout the region leading the business school revolution in the transition economies.

These schools, too, have been heavily influenced by the US model (many US schools provided financial and advisory assistance in their early days) but perhaps tend more to the eclectic European model (see below) with clusters of a variety of school 'types'. They also in general reflect a strong belief that there is a recognisable 'CEE' (Central and Eastern Europe) approach to management education that differs from all the existing traditional models. In particular, they point to the emphasis on combining a liberal education background with management education and an unusual (and for some intriguing) mixing of the arts (visual, musical and dramatic) with their teaching curricula.

The snapshot provided by Table 1.1 indicates the diversity, quality and range of cultural offerings provided by European business schools. For example, as pointed out in the historical review, in the

UK there is clearly a range of schools and models. LBS and, to some extent Oxford, base themselves closely on the elite US model such as Chicago, Columbia, Harvard, Northwestern, Stanford and Wharton. Stand-alone schools such as Ashridge, Cranfield and Henley have a professional focus on practically oriented MBA, DBA and executive programmes and do not always emphasise basic research. Bath, Lancaster and Warwick, on the other hand, combine strong undergraduate and graduate programmes with an emphasis on strong social science-based research.

The Open University, Henley and WBS have also pioneered distance learning MBAs, whereas schools such as University of Leicester, with its focus on a critical school of management and a critical MBA, stress linkages between the humanities and social science research. Imperial College Business School has adopted a more science-based, technology and knowledge focus for its school, stressing research on finance and technology-based management. The Cass (City) school has an emphasis on economics, finance and insurance, given its close proximity to the City, London's financial district.

The evidence, therefore, suggests much greater diversity and niche behaviour in UK schools than the perhaps somewhat greater institutional conformity that exists in the US market. As a result, the UK demonstrates that a range of schools – namely, quasi US-model schools, professionally oriented schools, social science-based schools, and specialist schools in finance or technology – can co-exist in the same marketplace.

> The evidence suggests much greater diversity and niche behaviour in UK schools than the perhaps somewhat greater institutional conformity that exists in the US market and demonstrates that a range of schools can co-exist in the same marketplace.

Similar clusters and patterns can be identified in other European countries such as France, where INSEAD is seen as the 'US elite' model, the grandes écoles as the key social and management science

Table 1.2 *Asian business schools in top 100 of the UT Dallas rankings (2007–11)*

Rank	University
17	HKUST (Hong Kong)
42	NUS (Singapore)
52	SMU (Singapore)
60	Hong Kong Polytechnic University
66	Chinese University of Hong Kong
69	City University of Hong Kong
72	NTU (Singapore)
86	Korea University
88	Hong Kong University

schools and national elites, the écoles supérieures as containing some of the more professionally, practically oriented schools and Paris/Dauphine or Sciences Po as specialist schools. Indeed, it is probable on the basis of these two examples that some of the other countries in the European 'map' will follow a similar pattern of clusters involving internationally elite schools, national role model schools, practically focused schools and specialist schools.

In a similar fashion, the twenty-first century has already witnessed the rapid growth of business schools in fast-growing emerging markets and economies such as Asia and Latin America.

For example, in Asia there is now a wide range of MBA programmes in Hong Kong and nearly 250 in China. Five or six Asian schools are now ranked in the top 100 global MBA programmes by the *FT* and around four are in the top 25 schools. In the recent highly regarded research rankings published annually by the University of Texas at Dallas, nine Asian schools are in the top 100 in the world. Very few were present in the same rankings five years ago.

Table 1.2 shows the Asian business schools listed in the UT Dallas research rankings for the period 2007–11.

Although Asian schools stress the different cultural and other factors associated with Hong Kong, Singapore and Korea, they show a clear emphasis and focus on top-tier research publication in high-quality journals as cited in the ISI Web of Science set of journals (so-called A-journals).

Following this broad review of the evolutionary global landscape of business schools, we now examine in some detail the social constructionist perspective, which provides an insightful explanation of the historical evolution of business schools.

Business schools and business education as a social construction process

We use a social construction theoretical approach as a framework to understand and explore the creation of business schools and the business school 'industry'. We argue that industries, such as business schools, are essentially 'cognitive communities' – that is, 'social constructions that emerge from the interplay of cognition and action over time' (Porac and Thomas, 2002; Fraguiero and Thomas, 2011). As social interactions gradually occur and accrete within the business school cognitive community, a language and a nomenclature evolve to capture the 'industry belief systems' that consistently shape the strategies and actions of members of the community.

The different stories and 'models' of business education that are shared and interpreted through conversations among members and participants in a community are key components in the creation of 'industry beliefs'. Once they are widely shared, a range of institutionalising processes such as imitation of other organisations, the search for legitimisation and the powerful influence of legal and regulatory environments reinforce these beliefs, which then become incorporated into the routines and operating strategies of members of the business school community.

To explain the evolution of the business school, the social construction model consists of three elements or belief types.

- The first element argues that there are early beliefs about the boundaries of markets and competitive interactions. As we have seen in our brief

Table 1.3 *Evolution of business schools as a social construction process*

Generation and time period	Behavioural characteristics and causes	Implications and consequences	Legitimacy providers
First generation (nineteenth century to early twentieth century) Emergence of alternative business school models 'Trade school' Vocational era	Different knowledge structures, frames of reference and cognitive maps Different beliefs about management education but mainly vocational trade-type models focusing on commercial and administrative practice	Beliefs about market boundaries vary across countries Differential rates of growth and adoption across countries Influence of culture, regulations, country characteristics, and languages evident at local and national level Size of schools tends to be nationally determined	• The creation of managerial employment by industrialists, entrepreneurial individuals and the state to cope with larger organisations • Institutionalised managerial systems (e.g. accounting practices) • Establishment of AACSB (1916) and subsequent accreditation systems for business schools • National governments • Universities • 'Feeder' disciplines (economics, psychology)
Second generation (early twentieth century to 1970s) Clearly shaped national schools	Strategic reference points established in countries – US model is key reference point Imitative behaviour at a local/national level The image and identity of a business school becomes clear	The identification of national role models and a dominant industry recipe means that differences exist among the key drivers of: • governance • funding and endowment • international mindset	

	Institutionalising processes		
Third generation (1970s–1990s) Dominance of US business school model Growing strength of national champions	Industry recipe is established – dominant design/role model is evident Reputational structures and clear identities formed Internationalising processes Organisational adaptation and interpretation Benchmarking processes	• innovation • knowledge transmission • corporate linkages Issues of image and reputation become important Social capital is built up long-term Rankings and league tables become indicators of success International alliances form to enhance reputations of leading schools in the US and Europe	• Research rankings and citations • Globalised performance measures and rankings • National performance measures • International accreditation bodies (e.g. AACSB, EFMD AMBA)
Fourth generation (1990–2005) Strong emergence of European business school model	Mounting criticism of US business school model European industry recipe is established (mimicry of US model challenged) Emphasis on internationalisation and public management Clear European identity sought (EU etc.)	Recipe includes: • Largely one-year MBA model • Strong executive education focus • Push for softer skills and linkages to the role of business and government in society • Competing on high-quality research as per US model,	The Bologna Accord in higher education (common degree structures and credit transfer) Role of EFMD • Founding of EQUIS accreditation system as European accreditation

Table 1.3 (*cont.*)

Generation and time period	Behavioural characteristics and causes	Implications and consequences	Legitimacy providers
	Executive education and corporate relevance/linkages important Strong decline of state funding of higher education in general and management education in particular Strong reputations/identities developed for European schools INSEAD IMD LBS etc. Little private/endowment funding	but strong focus on impactful research • INSEAD opens campus in Singapore – slogan 'The Business School for the World'. Other schools follow international expansion approach • EFMD launches CEIBS as a business school in Shanghai in partnership with City of Shanghai	High rankings for European schools (HEC, IESE, IMD, INSEAD, LBS) in *FT* rankings
Fifth generation (2005 to present) Strong range of global models	Shift of global economy from West to East Increasing criticism and blame attached to business schools for the	• Adaptation of the business school models to different cultures, political and economic systems	CEEMAN develops accreditation for schools in Eastern Europe Increasing number of business school associations:

Globalisation in emerging markets (Asia, Eastern Europe, Latin America) global financial crisis (teaching ambassadors of market capitalism)	• Clear strategic reference points (business schools) emerge	• CLADEA (Latin America) • AAPBS (Asia Pacific) • AIMS (India)
• Issues of ethics, corporate social responsibility and sustainability become central to business schools	• CEIBS (Shanghai) • FUDAN (China) • HKUST (Hong Kong) • NUS (Singapore) • Getulio Vargas (Brazil) • IIM (India) • ISB (India) • IEDC (Slovenia) • Skolkovo (Moscow)	Role of EABIS (Europe) PRME/GLRI (EFMD), UN Global Compact and Aspen Institute in promoting ethical/societal values
• Questioning of market capitalism – search for a broader stakeholder view of management	• Continued questioning of the role and purpose of business schools	Strong ranking of Asian schools (CEIBS, HKUST and ISB) in *FT* rankings
• Influence of governments in Asia on business school development very strong (e.g. Singapore, Hong Kong, China)	• Is it a professional school? • Alternative models?	

historical overview, a range of very early commerce and business school models emerge with different frames of reference, such as 'We are a commerce school' or 'We are a trade school'.

- The second type or component of industry belief systems is where industry recipes or norms emerge.
- At the third level, as the social and intellectual capital of a business school emerges, reputational and status orderings of business schools develop. Interorganisational performance differences also manifest themselves.

This typology of social construction views the process of development of business schools as a long-term social process that builds up the reputation or 'social capital' of the institution. Over time, we also see various forms of business schools emerging, starting with the 'trade schools' of the early twentieth century to the current broad set of business school models. These diverge, and adapt, from the earlier US-dominant design (1960s–1980s) in terms of reputation, regional or local cultural differences.

However, it is clear that boundary beliefs about the business school industry, industry recipes such as the US model and reputational orderings and rankings (e.g. the *FT*) represent some of the strong cognitive foundations that are the essence of the business school cognitive community. Indeed, the formation of these industry beliefs and cognitive foundations can also be explained in terms of Kuhn's (1962) paradigm shift model of evolution.

The *first generation* – which covers the early twentieth century – is the period during which different business or commerce schools, typically in national contexts, began to create their unique product positions to achieve legitimisation for management as a discipline. Through a process of developing and sharing their visions between them, they defined frames of reference or boundary beliefs about the nature of such a school usually with definitions such as 'We are a school of commerce' (UK schools). Each of the schools (such as the German Handelshochschulen or the French écoles supérieures de commerce) was also influenced by the set of cultural, legal and regulatory characteristics in their home country, which also determined factors such as the rate of adoption and size of those schools.

Throughout the 'rump' of the twentieth century, and at the *second generation* of our model, the different 'industry' logics and beliefs about business schools became much more widely shared. The rapid standardisation of the US-style business school model, focused around the MBA, established that model as a strategic reference point and, ultimately, as a dominant industry model or recipe, which is self-reinforcing and taken for granted. During this process, at the national level, locally defined schools tended to imitate each other and adapted to each other's norms and practices and then explored and embraced the promising practices from key reference points and countries, such as the US-style model.

Such institutionalising processes involving imitation and legit-imisation of business schools occur across the entire global business school domain and argue that adaptation to consensual models or recipes is likely to occur. As a consequence, therefore, national – or, perhaps, key regional – players become the immediate role models, such as the grandes écoles in France, but with the elite US business schools (such as Chicago, Harvard, Wharton and Stanford) as the global role models or recipes.

As business schools evolved from the 1970s until the 1990s, the *third generation* of our model – the powerful reputational elites and structures – become well developed with clear identities, leaders and national and regional champions established. Harvard, Chicago, Stanford, MIT and so on became the leaders in the US with LBS in the UK, HEC in France, IESE in Spain and Bocconi in Italy similarly identified as the leading national schools in Europe. The pressures of consumer-ism (i.e. reputational and status rankings from the *FT* and others and accreditation processes such as AACSB International) have also enhanced the reputations of national champions and the industry leaders through the regular publication of league tables and strong social recognition of their values. In essence, the reputational

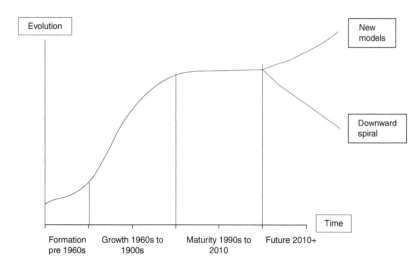

FIGURE I.I   The rise and fall (?) of the 'business school industry'

rankings that emerge over time develop from the social codings and interpretation of business school differences in performance.

At the *fourth and fifth generations* of our model from the 1990s to the present day, we see the emergence, respectively, of clear forms of the European model and the Asian model, which are clearly different from the US model. The European model, for example, derives its legitimacy from the international outlook of Europe, the role of EFMD and the development of its distinctive accreditation model, EQUIS. Clear elite European schools HEC, IESE, IMD, INSEAD and LBS have also emerged.

On the other hand, in the Asian case, the shift in the global economy from West to East, the global financial crisis and the strong role of governments (such as China, Hong Kong, Singapore) have contributed to the important and significant growth of Asian business schools such as Fudan and CEIBS in China, HKUST in Hong Kong, NUS and SMU in Singapore, and ISB and IIM in India.

To summarise, the model of the evolution of the business school industry represented diagrammatically in Figure 1.1 suggests that industry beliefs, industry recipes and reputational rankings together represent the cognitive foundation of the business school communities, leading to the present somewhat mature social construction of the business school 'industry'. The Asian and European schools of today, therefore, rely on insights drawn from a mix of national and regional models as well as key high-reputation schools in the US.

However, future evolution will require the creative development of new, frame-breaking models or perhaps lead to a 'muddling through' around existing models and a 'downward spiral' as shown in Figure 1.1.

We now provide, through a more detailed examination of the social construction model, a discussion of how the differences between Asian, European and American styles of management education have been formed.

Differences between Asian, European and US business schools

Table 1.4 provides a 'map' of the key drivers of differentiation between US business schools and schools in Asia and Europe. It identifies three sources of difference:

- *institutional differences*, which are associated with the first phase of our social construction model, in which different viewpoints and interpretations of business schools are debated and shared in a national context;
- *competitive differences*, which correspond to the second phase of the social construction model, in which markets and a dominant US recipe form, strong competition develops, and the key drivers or differentiators between the US, Asia and Europe in management education become evident;
- *social capital differences*, which reflect the processes of maturity and growth of business schools at the third and subsequent phases of the social construction model, where national and international brands and school images are formed.

Here, we examine output and reputation measures for US and European schools. Figure 1.2 also provides a conceptual framing of the differentiation phase of the model, showing the processes of business

Table 1.4 Broad differences between Asian, European and US business schools

		Europe	US	Asia
Institutional differences	Language/ culture/ regulation	Many languages; twenty-seven nation states (EU) Multi-cultural Heavy regulation	Single language More homogeneous culture Low level of regulation	Many languages Mix of mature and newly emerging countries Multi-cultural Heavy government involvement (e.g. China, Singapore)
	Standardisation	Slower acceptance and institutionalisation of business schools	Fast acceptance and institutionalisation of business schools	Rapid growth of business schools since 2000
	Size	Small to medium size (c. 250 business schools)	Medium to large size (c. 800 business schools)	Generally small size (but growing number)
Competitive differences	Governance/ values	Predominantly public funding Strong public-sector linkages	Predominantly private funding Weak public-sector linkages (state governments)	Strong public funding
	Funding and endowment	Small endowments Weaker resource base	Large endowments Strong resource base	Some endowment funding Resource base strong in mature economies
	International mindset	International in outlook Students/faculty more international	Less international, more insular Students/faculty less international	Regionally focused Mix of local and foreign faculty (50/50)

Innovation	Practical, problem-based learning	Two-year model for MBA	Range of models but generally one-year
	Critical reflective thinking	Discipline- and research-based	Asian case development
	Range of models: one-year MBA, distance learning, action-oriented learning		Mix of US and local models
Knowledge transmission/ corporate links	Knowledge conveyed in books and practice-oriented journals	Knowledge conveyed in discipline- and research-based journals	Focus on A-journals, peer review and publications
	Greater reliance on executive education	Fewer schools promote executive education	Relevance to business and corporate linkages important
	Closer to business		Executive education growing
Social capital differences — Rankings	Lower overall rankings in league tables	Higher overall rankings in league tables	Six Asian schools in *FT* rankings
	Favoured for international outlook, career progress, value for money	Favoured for initial salary, salary progress, alumni and research quality	Strong on research quality, student quality
Reputation	Some strong brands but generally lower brand identity and reputation	Many strong brands – particularly private schools. High brand identity and reputation	A few strong brands but social/reputational capital growing

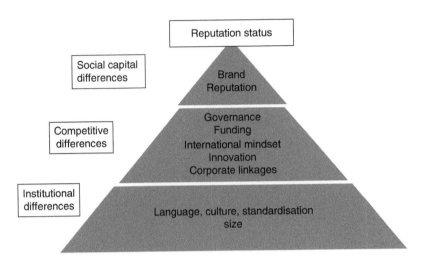

FIGURE I.2 Differentiation factors

school evolution 'funnelling' into the mature, established rankings, status and reputation measures. Baden-Fuller and Ang (2001) note, in a constructionist vein, that 'status and reputation are close allies, and reputation is typically defined as the expectation of a high level of quality as perceived by an audience'.

INSTITUTIONAL DIFFERENCES

While it may have been the case thirty or forty years ago that aspiring European and Asian managers seeking professional and academic career opportunities had to study at a leading US business school, the present situation in Asia and Europe (see Tables 1.1 and 1.2) is such that there is a range of very good alternative local schools that focus on Asia's and Europe's distinctive strengths. Such models, therefore, have adapted to the institutional frameworks and the many different *languages, cultures and regulations* that exist.

It is important to recognise, for example, that there is a new European order in management education as a result not only of the Bologna Accord (signed in 1999) but also the influence of processes for degree accreditation. The main accreditation agencies (AACSB

International in the US, AMBA and EQUIS in Europe), which provide confirmation of the quality of a school, have clearly different criteria and philosophies.

For EQUIS, there is a much broader focus, a clear examination of executive education and corporate links and a definite concentration on internationalisation. AACSB, on the other hand, does not currently require any extensive review of international or corporate linkages because it simply accredits the institutional range of degree and educational programmes and mainly focuses on the faculty inputs, curricula designs and assurance of learning.

As a consequence, EQUIS has a strong European flavour, which stresses the diversity and international theme as an important element in the design of management education and does not assume the primacy of a single unitary model – the US-based functional and discipline-oriented model – for management training.

Asian schools, however, have been strongly guided by the educational policies and investments of governments such as China, India, Hong Kong and Singapore. These governments have sent the best and brightest of their students to European and US graduate programmes in business and built up strong alliances with key elite schools such as Wharton (with Singapore Management University) and Northwestern (Kellogg with HKUST). They adopted some but not all of the norms (e.g. publication in top-quality journals and high-quality research-oriented faculty) of their international competition. They, however, have stressed the need to develop distinctive Asian case studies and databases and to focus their research on the needs of fast-paced Asian economies.

As noted earlier, the focus in the US on a single, somewhat insular educational model arose from a rapid institutional *standardisation* of business education. In the US, the standardisation of business education started very early and the founding of the AACSB in 1916 provided a significant building block for institutional development, since accreditation could improve the market recognition that various business schools needed. This drove a process of convergence towards similarity, homogeneity and mass production in business education. The best example of such convergence and standardisation is the successful market acceptance of the MBA degree, which quickly became the model for general graduate management education worldwide and became both an effective licence to practise management and an attestation of a high standard of business analysis.

The standardisation of business education in Europe, however, evolved at a much slower pace due to the diverse influence and importance of various national bodies and governmental policies. It was over eighty years after the AACSB had created a US system of accreditation and audit of business schools that in 1997 EFMD developed the European Quality Improvement System (EQUIS). This international system of strategic audit and accreditation was designed by the Europeans for the assessment of their own business schools (followed, more recently, by EPAS, the European Programme Accreditation System).

Five years earlier, AMBA had created an accreditation scheme in the UK focusing specifically on the growing range of UK MBA-awarding business schools but this had a much less international focus.

Thus, whereas the US-based business school environment achieved rapid standardisation, the European one was relatively slow to standardise; rather, there was a focus on 'national champions', which recognised the different educational, cultural, legal and language requirements of each European country. Since the 1990s, these national champions such as HEC, IESE, IMD, INSEAD and LBS have achieved quite distinctive and strong international reputations. Similarly, in Asia the rapid emergence of schools such as Hong Kong University of Science and Technology and the China Europe International Business School (CEIBS) in Shanghai attest to the similarly strong international footprint of Asian schools.

The *size* of business schools differs significantly in the US, Asia and Europe. Size, as a strategic variable, indicates that a school has achieved significant growth and a sound resource base. If a school is relatively small, its financial performance is margin-driven whereas with larger size performance is volume-driven. Therefore, size enables business schools to generate and exploit the potential of economies of scale and scope, including a broader resource profile, a wider range of programmes and courses, and the ability to attract and pay high-quality faculty in order to gain a sustainable, competitive advantage.

The Indian School of Business (ISB) in Hyderabad, which is ranked among the top twenty business schools in *FT* rankings, has gained the size advantage in its one-year MBA programme. It now admits more than 500 students per year and has a very large number of visiting faculty from North American business schools, especially Northwestern and Wharton.

As a consequence of standardisation and the early acceptance of the MBA model, and given their much larger markets and global recognition, some of the largest American schools (Harvard, Kellogg and Wharton) admit more than 500 MBA students per year whereas most European and Asian programmes tend to be much smaller and focus on national or regional norms (except for global alliance type EMBA programmes). However, it is important to note that in the competitive marketplace, high-quality niche strategies and pro-grammes offered by small business schools can be very successful.

Such is the case, for instance, of IMD in Switzerland, which specialises in international management development for large cor-porations and offers a small but highly ranked one-year full-time MBA programme.

In general, US business schools vary in size from medium to very large (particularly in large state schools, such as Texas and Ohio State), whereas the European and Asian schools vary from small to medium, reflecting the wide range of countries, resource bases and contexts in which they operate.

COMPETITIVE DIFFERENCES

The competitive differences in business school models reflect key drivers of management education and become evident as competitive recipes are shared and as imitative behaviour takes hold.

The system of *governance* is a clear difference between Asian, European and US business schools. We define governance as the type of financial and legal arrangements that structure the relationships of a school with governmental and private interests. These arrangements can be expressed along a continuum from a privately funded and owned institution to an institution almost entirely reliant on government and public funding.

In general terms, the present pattern in the US is of a competitive abundance of private schools (which have a very significant resource base) alongside public or state schools. In Asia and Europe there is a clear dominance of publicly funded schools (with more constrained resource bases) although in certain parts of Asia, such as India, Korea and Thailand, there is evidence of the growth of private schools.

For instance, following a detailed analysis of the *FT* rankings data, we show in Table 1.5 that, out of the fourteen business schools (eleven from the US and three from the EU) that consistently appeared in the top twenty positions over seven years in the *FT* MBA rankings, virtually all of them are *private*. Thus, the private funding of business education common in the US model is a phenomenon rather uncommon to their European and Asian counterparts. An exception is the ISB in India.

The *funding* and endowment of business schools is also a major difference between the US and Asia/Europe. Because of the ready acceptance in the US of the business school as an established institution and the recognition of the value of private education in the US, American business schools quickly started fundraising campaigns and, thus, generated financial resources from sponsors, corporations and loyal alumni. The success of this approach to business school development can be seen in the case of Harvard Business School, the best endowed of all, which has amassed more than $1 billion. (However, newer for-profit schools such as the University of Phoenix, which is owned by the Apollo Group, also have extensive financial resources.)

Table 1.5 FT *rankings of MBA programmes (1999–2005)*

Business schools	Governance	2005	2004	2003	2002	2001	2000	1999	Average ranking
Harvard Business School (US)	Private	1	2	2	2	2	1	1	2
Pennsylvania/Wharton (US)	Private	1	1	1	1	1	2	4	2
Columbia Business School (US)	Private	3	3	3	3	5	5	2	3
Stanford Graduate School (US)	Private	4	7	4	4	3	3	3	4
Chicago GSB (US)	Private	6	4	5	5	4	6	6	5
INSEAD (EU)	Private	8	4	6	6	7	9	11	7
London Business School (EU)	Private/public	5	4	7	9	8	8	8	7
MIT/Sloan (US)	Private	13	9	10	7	6	4	5	8
Northwestern/Kellogg (US)	Private	11	11	9	10	9	7	7	9
NYU/Stern (US)	Private	9	8	8	8	10	13	17	10
Dartmouth/Amos Tuck (US)	Private	7	10	11	11	13	15	9	11
IMD (EU)	Private	13	12	13	14	11	11	13	12
Yale/SOM (US)	Private	9	13	12	12	20	18	20	15
Duke Fuqua (US)	Private	18	20	15	19	18	17	15	17

In comparison with the situation in the US, European and Asian business schools have either relatively small endowments or none at all. This has made them much more reliant on annually acquired funds (often from government sources) and budgets and, particularly, the revenue stream from their MBA programmes to manage and develop their resources. In Europe, typically, if the MBA programme falters then so does the revenue stream.

Therefore a business model dependent on internally generated cash flows – as is the case in most Asian and European business schools – is likely to be able to cover operating expenses and generate small surpluses but much less likely to provide significant cash flow to fund new business opportunities or facilities investments in the school.

> Financial independence, autonomy and the capacity to deploy critical resources can reinforce and build a business school's image and strategic positioning.

The existence of private endowments clearly gives a school the financial strength to weather the effects of MBA programme downturns and to invest in future growth. This financial independence, autonomy and the capacity to deploy critical resources can, in turn, reinforce and build a business school's image and strategic positioning. More importantly, however, such 'slack' financial resources should ideally be directed towards the creation of new business models and opportunities.

Despite the relative lack of financial muscle in Asia and Europe, these business schools and their leaders have always possessed a strong *international mindset*. This mindset means that the Asian and European sensitivity to international business, languages, diversity and culture is a competitive advantage. They have learned how to deal with the complexities of international trade and, more importantly, have developed a strong motivation for success in international business and, with it, a distinctive approach to management education.

It is also clear from a further detailed 'variance analysis' of the *FT* rankings data that students attending European MBA programmes will be taught by a more international faculty and meet a more diverse set of students than equivalent US students. See the analysis, column 3, in Table 1.6, which shows EU schools perform better on value for money, career progression, and international diversity of faculty and students. As a consequence, students should be able to develop better language and cross-cultural skills and sensitivities during their business school experience that will help them to succeed in a world of international trade and globalisation.

For example, in the case of the alumni recommendation criterion, the average US school ranking is 173 per cent below that of the average of the top twenty schools, while the average EU school rating is 651 per cent below that of the average of the top twenty schools. Further, the EU average performance is 477 per cent below that of the US schools on this criterion. Clearly, when positive signs occur in the percentages, EU schools score better than US or top twenty schools. This occurs across criteria such as value for money, career progression, female faculty and internationalisation.

Flexibility and innovation are also key competitive advantages of Asian and European schools. They have experimented with, and adopted, alternative delivery technologies much faster than their US counterparts. For example, the Instituto de Empresa in Madrid, and Henley, the Open University Business School and WBS in the UK, are among the world leaders in distance and blended learning forms of the MBA, though joined much more recently by the 'one' MBA model of the University of North Carolina, Chapel Hill, in the US.

Europeans and Asians have also innovated with a much more flexible one-year MBA model (see Cass, Judge, Leicester, SMU and WBS, and ISB and IIMS in India) and have not slavishly followed the analytic, functional and discipline-oriented two-year US MBA model. These schools have also focused on a learning style of management

Table 1.6 *Relative performance of US and EU business schools*

Criterion	Difference of US business schools' average rating from top 20 average rating	Difference of EU business schools' average rating from top 20 average rating	Difference of EU business schools' average rating performance relative to US business schools' average rating
Salary-weighted	– 23%	– 42%	– 20%
Salary increase	– 14%	– 65%	– 51%
Value for money	– 6%	10%	15%
Career progression	– 16%	6%	21%
Aims achieved	– 3%	– 2%	1%
Placement success	– 6%	– 34%	– 28%
Employed at three months	– 2%	– 3%	– 1%
Alumni recommend	– 173%	– 651%	– 477%
Female faculty	13%	15%	2%
Female students	1%	– 3%	– 4%
International faculty	– 66%	0%	66%
International students	– 25%	40%	65%
Faculty with doctorates	– 2%	– 34%	– 32%
FT doctoral rating	– 5%	– 16%	– 11%
FT research rating	– 37%	– 296%	– 259%

(a) The criteria are those used in the *FT* ranking, which contains about 100 schools in its annual global ranking of MBA programmes (http:// rankings.ft.com/businessschoolrankings/charts).

(b) The top twenty schools are similar to those in Table 1.5

(c) The EU business schools are those in the *FT* rankings outside the top twenty and their averages are compared to either the average of the top twenty schools or the average of US schools in the rankings outside the top twenty over the period 1999–2002.

Source: Antunes and Thomas (2007)

education. They have adopted problem-centred, project-based learning in small classes with field studies, consulting projects, internships and an emphasis on practice and critical, reflective thinking. In other words, the aim is to understand the student's acquisition of knowledge and learning, and to pace the flow of understanding and logic with the student's manifest capabilities.

> The Instituto de Empresa in Madrid, and Henley, the Open University Business School and WBS in the UK, are among the world leaders in distance and blended learning forms of the MBA.

Europeans, in particular, also tend to *transmit knowledge* through books, media articles and practice-based journals and publish less frequently in the so-called 'A-journals' in the field, which have a primarily academic, discipline-based orientation. For example, of the forty-five top journals in the ratings in the *FT* MBA rankings, more than 75 per cent are US-based with discipline-based top journals and cutting-edge research. Few European journals are listed but, nevertheless, there is a strong, high-quality knowledge-development tradition in Europe. For example, the European Group of Organisational Studies (EGOS) has nearly 2,000 members at its annual conference, publishes the journal *Organisation Studies* and presents a European critical and interpretive perspective on the field of organisation studies.

European and Asian schools have also been extremely successful in establishing *corporate links* and partnerships, and have managed to translate that success to the classroom. With the absence of endowment funding in Europe and Asia, schools have developed creative ways to develop research and learning programmes with corporations that are directly linked to corporate problems and issues (e.g. SMU's i-Cities Labs in partnership with Tata Consultancy Services). As a consequence, European and Asian schools have focused more on solving relevant business (as opposed to academic) problems and have placed the solution of business problems and executive education as high priorities in their visions, missions and overarching strategic intent.

SOCIAL CAPITAL DIFFERENCES: REPUTATION EFFECTS AND BRAND LOYALTY

In aggregate, following the logic of the social construction model, the interactions of the institutionalising and market development processes over the longer term produce what we call 'reputation effects'.

Reputation effects can clearly influence the patterns of competition for resources in the business school market, since reputation hierarchies act as mobility barriers for the entry of new, upcoming schools into the elite, high-reputation category or strategic group (McGee and Thomas, 1986). Moreover, this elite category tends to form a 'closed system', which is difficult but not impossible to penetrate. In the case of business schools, as D'Aveni (1996) has argued, reputation across different audiences influences the ability to gather resources.

> Since reputation has self-reinforcing dynamics, (alumni) loyalty reinforces the reputation of the business school itself, facilitates the acquisition of new students and resources and produces a virtuous circle.

In parallel with these reputation effects, a high degree of brand loyalty also develops among a school's alumni. Those who invested their time and money to acquire a degree or qualification from a high-quality school want the symbolic value of this degree to be recognised and enhanced over time. Since reputation has self-reinforcing dynamics, this loyalty reinforces the reputation of the business school itself, facilitates the acquisition of new students and resources and produces a virtuous circle. Baden-Fuller and Ang (2001) describe this process as 'building a "charmed circle" of resources and benefits'.

We can further substantiate our argument for these reputation effects by re-examining the positioning of the 'top twenty' business schools over a seven-year period (1999–2005) of the full-time MBA ranking by the *Financial Times*.

Table 1.5, described earlier, shows that fourteen schools were present in this 'top twenty' for the whole seven-year period, with little change in their average ranking. Of these fourteen top business schools, only three are European (INSEAD, LBS and IMD – which are primarily private and tend to follow a US-style model), while eleven are in the US. It also shows the remarkable lack of mobility over the seven-year period in the top schools' rankings, particularly when recognising that the *FT* ranking covers more than 100 schools worldwide.

Further, the following business schools, all from North America, appeared in the top twenty in at least one year of the period. Although there are a number of public schools in this list, they receive very little public funding and are essentially private. They are colloquially described as Public Ivies (i.e. they mimic Ivy League schools).

Six times:	UC Berkeley (Haas); Virginia (Darden)	(Public schools)
Five times:	UCLA (Anderson)	(Public school)
Four times:	University of Michigan	(Public school)
Three times:	University of Western Ontario (Ivey);	(Public schools)
Two times:	University of North Carolina (Kenan-Flagler) Emory; Cornell (Johnson)	(Private schools)

Similar findings are obtained from the business school rankings of *Business Week*. Corley and Gioia (2000) report that only a very small elite group of schools consistently occupy the top positions and show that over the twelve years in their study only fifteen schools have ever been in the top ten. These data show a pattern in which a select, predominantly private (recognising the private nature of the Public Ivies) and well-endowed group of schools consistently score the top ranking positions and are labelled 'winners' by the media. Therefore, we believe that the schools in the 'top twenty' are likely to profit most significantly in terms of status from the brand and reputation effects they have developed over the period of their existence.

Overall, the combination of brand loyalty and reputation effects we referred to above suggests the existence of critical differences between the top twenty schools and those outside the top twenty. We suspect this could be particularly true relative to the main European and Asian schools. European business schools do not have the same strategic orientation as US schools and position themselves in the marketplace against criteria that more closely reflect the cultural and competitive characteristics of those markets. As pointed out earlier, a re-examination of the analysis in Table 1.6 shows that European schools rate much more highly on international dimensions, career progression and value for money but fall behind on the salary, research and alumni criteria. Note that the latter criteria reflect longer-established reputations. We would expect that, if similar data were available for key Asian schools, the same patterns would emerge.

Moreover, the perception of the quality of particular business schools held by high-paying employers is itself crucial in deciding the salary offered to new recruits. Those schools that are able to establish a reputation with such employers or place students into 'top flight', fast-track career channels are more likely to create a self-sustaining momentum for success in the 'rankings game'. Generally, the more established US business schools in terms of size and endowment clearly benefit from such reputation advantages.

> Those schools that are able to establish a reputation with employers or place students into 'top flight', fast-track career channels are more likely to create a self-sustaining momentum for success in the 'rankings game'.

It is also noteworthy that the fourteen schools that remained in the top twenty group for all seven years of the *FT* rankings (Table 1.5) are all, primarily, US-based (or -modelled) private institutions with large endowments. These well-endowed business schools, therefore, have had access for some time to greater financial resources with which to make strategic investments and hire high-quality, research-productive faculty. The somewhat lower, but increasingly competitive, Asian and European faculty salaries and their relative lack of funding opportunities for research contrast with the strong research orientation and heavy investments in research by top US business schools.

This makes it difficult for European and Asian business schools to bridge the research gap between themselves and the top US business schools. Nevertheless, the global crisis and the increasing stress on research in Europe/Asia, both for competitive and institutional reasons (e.g. the British research assessment exercises), may narrow this gap. Clearly, the European and Asian schools have an important opportunity to redefine the marketplace and pioneer the next generation of knowledge creation. However, European and Asian schools see such US-dominated rankings as a useful source of market information but not necessarily the ultimate standard to be targeted and scaled.

Indeed, in a recent article, Thomas and Li (2009) used *FT* data (up to 2007–8) to map global business schools into clusters (Table 1.7). This shows clearly that clusters of European and Asian schools are rapidly gaining significant reputations. More recently, the evidence from the *FT* surveys in 2010 and 2011 confirms the rapid swing towards Asian and European schools in the ranking of the top twenty-five schools.

Table 1.7 *Mapping of global business schools*

Name of clusters	Exemplar schools
1. Elite private schools	Harvard, Wharton, Chicago, Stanford
2. Elite European schools	LBS INSEAD IMD
3. Top US private schools	Duke Dartmouth Yale
4. Top European schools	IESE IE ESADE
5. Top US public schools	Michigan UCLA UC Berkeley Illinois ANC
6. Other top European schools	HEC Oxford Cambridge WBS
7. Top non-US public schools	HKUST UBC Melbourne
8. Second tier of US private schools	Rochester Rice Babson
9. Second tier of US public schools	Indiana Arizona State Texas A&M
10. UK schools	Bath Edinburgh

Source: Thomas and Li (2009)

In 2010, for example, eleven were from the US, eleven from Europe and four from Asia. Also, the recent UT Dallas research rankings show that around 20 per cent of the schools in the top 100 are from Europe and Asia compared to around 70 per cent from the US – again a significant movement towards European and Asian schools. Van Roon (2003) notes: 'the [European] schools see rankings as a valuable source of business intelligence, that can drive decision making aimed at developing the school's products and services. Schools, however, say they try hard to resist pressure to radically alter the school on a more fundamental level to cater better to the [FT] ranking's criteria, seeing this as a challenge to their identity and value system.'

In essence, European critics would argue that accreditation and rankings are forcing business school deans to focus on the wrong things: that is, image management at the expense of concentrating on, for example, narrowing the gap between theory and practice and providing sound advice to professional managers.

SUMMARY

The strengths of the leading US business schools (see also Tables 1.3 and 1.5) derive from the competitive advantages associated with their gains as 'fast first-movers' in management education. These advantages include product standardisation (e.g. MBA), business school legitimisation, strong and well-established brands and reputations (e.g. Harvard, Wharton) and, above all, significant financial strength and very large private endowments fuelling their strategic positioning in the marketplace.

In essence, as a consequence of rapid standardisation and rapid adoption of the business school in the US, money resources, in abundance in the leading schools, 'moved mountains' in establishing US business schools and their curricula, and in developing strong brand images and reputations internationally (see Tables 1.5, 1.6 and 1.7). Alongside these elite US schools, a cadre of other strong US schools developed in state universities and private schools.

As a consequence of rapid standardisation and rapid adoption of the business school in the US, money resources, in abundance in the leading schools, 'moved mountains' in establishing US business schools and their curricula, and in developing strong brand images and reputations internationally.

European and Asian business schools, on the other hand, have developed strength mainly over the past twenty years (and particularly over the past five years in terms of the *FT* Global MBA Rankings), with the fast development of business schools in higher education worldwide. The initial shortage of key faculty to staff the schools was solved by sending promising young faculty from European and Asian countries to leading US schools to complete their postgraduate studies.

In the Asian case, for example, the Singapore government provided appropriate scholarship and fellowship support. There were clear initiatives in the UK (via the Foundation for Management Development) and in France and other countries, through government-sponsored initiatives, to provide doctoral fellowships/scholarships for study in the US. These newly minted US-trained, but European, PhD students then returned to join home faculties and developed curricula defined and derived, initially at least, from their US experience. Another innovative approach is to invite faculty from well-respected schools to teach intensive six- to eight-week programmes as pioneered at ISB in Hyderabad, India.

Quite quickly, however, leading programmes in Europe and Asia developed their own identity as students and faculty sought to make them more relevant to the business practices and customs in their own countries. Consequently, 'national' champions and role models have developed since the 1980s (see Tables 1.1 and 1.2) with distinct identities and competitive characteristics, and have reinforced their reputational position over the past decade (see Tables 1.1, 1.2, 1.5 and 1.7). Since they never possessed the abundant financial resources of their US counterparts, the European and Asian schools have positioned themselves uniquely in their markets as niche, segmented players, targeting their distinctive national and regional characteristics and the requirements of their management audiences. However, they have also sought to establish strong research credentials and provide quality research output as clearly recognised by their growing importance and positioning in the UT Dallas research rankings (see Table 1.2).

> European and Asian schools have positioned themselves uniquely in their markets as niche, segmented players, targeting their distinctive national and regional characteristics and the requirements of their management audiences.

THE BUSINESS SCHOOL'S IDENTITY, LEGITIMACY AND POSITIONING

It is unquestionable that over the past 100 years business schools have become recognised globally as significant players in higher education, whether as part of prestigious universities or as stand-alone management education providers. The pursuit of their initial purpose – to upgrade management, building its own body of knowledge, rules and values – shifted from a combination of individual insights shared by savvy veteran managers and practical advice to a more scientific approach that encompassed several academic disciplines.

In addition to shaping management practices and knowledge and educating business leaders, their role as liaisons between the academic and business worlds afforded them great visibility and influence. As businesses expanded internationally and American management practices seemed to prevail, the demand for management education became more intense and new business schools in some European countries and, later, in Asia and Latin America joined the pioneering US institutions in a burgeoning industry.

Despite this impressive growth, business schools have faced criticisms from within business schools themselves, the broader academic community, management practitioners, and the press and media. Such critics do not recognise business schools as fully legitimate organisations. Therefore, gaps in the social construction of their organisational legitimacy can have negative effects.

Rather than a complete legitimacy gap, the criticisms of business schools signal that there are areas of ambiguity, conflict and uncertainty around their legitimate form. For example, business schools around the world soon found themselves trapped in the 'double hurdle' of delivering answers to relevant practical business dilemmas and simultaneously deploying scholarly research to expand and deepen critical management knowledge. As a result they occupy a controversial position at the interface between academia and practice. Arguably, the needs of neither are met! Crainer and Dearlove (1998: 48) caricature this predicament, with business schools portrayed as schizophrenic organisations that must demonstrate their capacity as *bona fide academic institutions*, improve knowledge to provide solutions to management problems and at the same time perform as businesses.

> Rather than a complete legitimacy gap, the criticisms of business schools signal that there are areas of ambiguity, conflict and uncertainty around their legitimate form.

To finesse their point, there are two sources of legitimacy with which business schools must interface.

- First, there is an academic component where business schools must demonstrate that they have a place in academe. Historically, for business schools, this has followed a 'scientific' model, oriented towards the intensification of knowledge about the theories of management to secure a legitimate position within the university system. This has entailed the activities of scholarly publication and also developing intellectual capacity through doctoral programmes.
- Second, there is a fundamental question about the purpose of management research; is it for, or about, managers? The tensions between theoretical

rigour and practical relevance in management research mark a potential conflict between legitimacy providers for business schools. Indeed, as noted previously, Bennis and O'Toole (2005) ask why 'business schools have embraced the scientific model of physicists and economists rather than the professional model of doctors and lawyers'. These positions have clear implications for what constitutes the legitimate activities of a business school. Indeed, 'consumers' of management education have already pushed hard for an increasing focus on practical relevance in research and teaching.

Business schools, we argue, have key sources of legitimacy that act as reference points for structuring and positioning.

The social constructivist perspectives on the evolution of business schools in Table 1.3 include sources of legitimacy in each of the five generations of business school development.

In turn, these multiple sources of legitimacy begin to explain contrasting organisational responses by business schools to their institutional setting. For example, in the second generation, national differences between business schools and the emergence of strategic groups among both business schools (Thomas and Li, 2009) and MBA programmes (Segev et al., 1999) indicate some of the organisational efforts to gain legitimacy in order to secure resources and long-term survival.

A legacy of the third generation (as characterised by the dominant US design) is the core activity of research production and the legitimating performance measures that stem from this activity, including citation measures, international rankings, national audits and accreditation standards. This is in stark contrast to the first-generation schools, where the emphasis was on providing administrative and commercial training for the then-emerging occupational class of managers.

Why is legitimacy important to business schools? First, an organisation must have (or appear to have) legitimacy for its long-term survival. The evolution of the business school illustrates how, in order to integrate and survive as part of the university system, an intense and rigorous approach to management education was adopted. But, as

Schoemaker (2008) stresses, this paradigm 'with its strong focus on analytic models and reductionism is not well suited to handle the ambiguity and high rate of change facing many industries today'.

Second, there are ramifications for performance. There is growing evidence that current university business school research serves increasingly as a commodity product, which is disjointed from the liberal pursuit of knowledge, a principle on which universities were founded (Willmott, 1995), and from the needs of managers to solve management problems. Indeed, the extent to which business schools compete for the highest rankings, the best cadre of students and faculty, the greatest number of citations in the highest-impact journals and to secure the largest possible slice of research funding suggests that schools exist in an era of 'hyper-competition' (Starkey and Tiratsoo, 2007). This presents a serious problem of maintaining organisational legitimacy.

> The business school has still not gained strong acceptance from business, has not made an impact on the management of universities and is often treated with scepticism and sometimes contempt by other university disciplines and academics.

Two possible strategies to help manage the conflicting sources of legitimacy can potentially be found in the consumption and performance measures of management research. First, there is much work to be done to improve the context of research, the engagement with managers and uptake of research through translating findings adequately. Second, the performance measures and mechanisms of business school research need to be critically appraised with regard to whether they demonstrably enhance the state of management disciplines or management practice.

CONCLUSION

The problem for business schools is their phenomenal expansion, which has made business schools a business in their own right (Pfeffer and Fong, 2002, 2004a, 2004b). The scale and continued growth of management education is remarkable and something that is unique compared with other academic disciplines. However, this growth has bought challenges, envy from other areas of study and other academics and, as noted earlier, criticisms about its role, meaning and purpose in both a university and a management context.

In short, the business school lacks identity. It has still not gained strong acceptance from business, has not made an impact on the management of universities other than through its strong financial contribution to the increasing commercialisation of university activities and is often treated with scepticism and sometimes contempt by other university disciplines and academics. We examine these challenges and issues in the next chapters.

REFERENCES

Antunes, D. and Thomas, H. (2007). The competitive (dis)advantages of European business schools. *Long Range Planning*, **40**(3): 382–404.

Augier, M. and March, J. G. (2011). *The Roots, Rituals, and Rhetorics of Change: North American Business Schools after the Second World War*. Stanford, CA: Stanford Business Books.

Baden-Fuller, C. and Ang, S. H. (2001). Building reputations: the role of alliances in the European business school scene. *Long Range Planning*, **34**(6): 741–55.

Bennis, W. G. and O' Toole, J. (2005). How business schools lost their way. *Harvard Business Review*, **83**(5): 96–104.

Cooley, T. (2007). The business of business education. *Stern Business*, Fall/Winter: 23–5.

Corley, K. and Gioia, D. (2000). The rankings game: managing business school reputation. *Corporate Reputation Review*, **3**(4): 319–33.

Crainer, S. and Dearlove, D. (1998). *Gravy Training: Inside the World's Top Business Schools*. Oxford: Capstone.

Currie, G., Knights, D. and Starkey, K. (2010). Introduction: a post-crisis critical reflection on business schools. *British Journal of Management*, **21**: s1–s5.

D'Aveni, R. (1996). A multiple-constituency, status-based approach to interorganizational mobility of faculty and input–output competition among top business schools. *Organization Science*, **7**(2): 166–89.

Engwall, L. (2000). Foreign role models and standardisation in Nordic business education. *Scandinavian Journal of Management*, **16**(1): 1–24.

Fragueiro, F. and Thomas, H. (2011). *Strategic Leadership in the Business School.* Cambridge University Press.

Gordon, R A. and Howell, J. E. (1959). *Higher Education for Business.* New York: Columbia University Press.

Grey, C. (2005). *A Very Short, Interesting and Reasonably Cheap Book about Studying Organisations.* London: Sage.

Hubbard, G. (2006). Business, knowledge and global growth. *Capitalism and Society,* 1(3): 1–10.

Kuhn, T. S. (1962). *The Structure of Scientific Revolutions.* University of Chicago Press.

Larson, M. J. (2003). Practically academic: forming British business schools in the 1960s. *Business and Economic History On-Line,* Vol. 1. At www.thebhc.org/publications/BEHonline/2003/Larson.pdf

Locke, E. R. (1996). *The Collapse of the American Management Mystique.* Oxford University Press.

Locke, E. R. and Spender, J. C. (2011). *Confronting Managerialism.* London: Zed Books.

McGee, J. and Thomas, H. (1986). Strategic groups: theory, research and taxonomy. *Strategic Management Journal,* 7(2): 141–60.

Mintzberg, H. (2004). *Managers, Not MBAs: A Hard Look at the Soft Practice of Managing and Management Development.* San Francisco: Berrett-Koehler Publishers.

Moldoveanu, M. and Martin, R. (2008). *The Future of the MBA.* Oxford University Press.

Nueno, P. (1995). Untitled article in *Training the Fire Brigade*: 53–5. Brussels: EFMD Publications.

Pfeffer, J. and Fong, C. T. (2002). The end of business schools? Less success than meets the eye. *Academy of Management Learning and Education,* 1(1): 78–95.

(2004a). The business school 'business': some lessons from the US experience. *Journal of Management Studies,* 41: 1501–20.

(2004b, 22 May). But can you teach it? *The Economist*: 61–3.

Pierson, F. C. (1959). *The Education of American Businessmen.* New York: McGraw-Hill.

Porac, J. F. and Thomas, H. (2002). Managing cognition and strategy: issues, trends and future directions, in A. M. Pettigrew, H. Thomas and R. Whittington (eds.), *Handbook of Strategy and Management*: 165–81. London: Sage.

Rameau, C. (1995). Untitled article in *Training the Fire Brigade*: 72–3. Brussels: EFMD Publications.

Schoemaker, P. J. (2008). The future challenges of business: rethinking management education. *California Management Review*, **50**(3): 119–39.

Segev, E., Raveh, A. and Farjoun, M. (1999). Conceptual maps of the leading MBA programs in the United States: core courses, concentration areas, and the ranking of the school. *Strategic Management Journal*, **20**(6): 549–65.

Spender, J. C. (2007). Management as a regulated profession: an essay. *Journal of Management Inquiry*, **16**(1): 32–42.

Starkey, K. and Tiratsoo, N. (2007). *The Business School and the Bottom Line*. Cambridge University Press.

Thomas, H. (2012). What is the European management school model? *Global Focus*, **6**(1): 18–21.

Thomas, H. and Li, X. (2009). Mapping globally branded business schools: a strategic positioning analysis. *Management Decision*, **47**(9): 1420–40.

Van Roon, I. (2003). Steer clear of B-school spin. *European Business Forum*, **15** (September): 39–40.

Wagner, R. (2012).The Cameralists: fertile sources for a new science of public finance, in J. G. Backhaus (ed.), *Handbook of the History of Economic Thought: Insights on the Founders of Modern Economics*: 123–35. Dordrecht: Springer.

Willmott, H. (1995). Managing the academics: commodification and control in the development of university education in the UK. *Human Relations*, **48**(9): 993–1027.

2 Business school identity and legitimacy: its relationship to the modern university and society

INTRODUCTION

In the modern university the business school is currently valued much more for its managerial expertise, cash-generation abilities and financial strength than its intellectual vigour and scholarship (Bok, 2003; Starkey and Tempest, 2008). Indeed, as indicated earlier, the legitimacy of business as a serious academic discipline is critically questioned by scholars in science, arts and the humanities (see, for example, Nussbaum, 1997). Further, with the mindset of the corporate university and corporate managerialism as fashionable metaphors for the commercialisation of higher education, many university critics (Bok, 2003; Angus, 2009; Menaud, 2010) have berated university presidents for abandoning the fundamental ideals and visions of universities as 'thinking institutions' and generators of knowledge.

They argue that university presidents have instead championed business schools and commercial relevance as criteria for university success and growth while ceding the values of the traditional, elite university to marketisation, market values and financial stability.

Clearly, these current university forces of commercialisation produce considerable challenges, tensions and stresses for business school academics and, particularly, business school deans as they position themselves and their academic strategies against those of the traditional disciplines (science, social sciences, arts, humanities etc.) and professions (law, medicine, engineering) commonly present in universities.

Should business schools allow themselves to be portrayed as, for example, 'cash cows' and necessary evils (Pfeffer and Fong, 2004a,

2004b) to fund a university elite and/or traditional disciplines? Or should they argue that management and business must be viewed as legitimate professions similar to those of law or medicine (Khurana and Nohria, 2008) and be recognised as such by traditional academics?

And there is, of course, the other side of the equation – namely, the top leadership of the university itself. It may simply have no choice but to treat the business school as a cash cow. The overall financial situation may dictate this.

It could be argued that this current situation represents both a 'tipping point' (Gladwell, 2002) and a turning point in the evolution of the business school. There will be increasing experimentation in approaches to educating managers. Here, several leading European schools that are not parts of classical universities – INSEAD, IMD and the Lorange Institute – come to mind. Also, for example, there seems to be increasing acknowledgement that change is necessary and an acceptance, at least in European contexts, of an alternative business school model that acts to provide a moral and ethical compass for students that transcends instrumental issues of status and salary.

Such a model has a focus on a broader stakeholder mission as a professional school that provides a conscience for business and contributes to a better world by examining issues such as ethics, health, poverty, corporate social responsibility, sustainability and the problems of globalisation, natural disasters, urbanisation and the growth of cities. This presents an interesting challenge for business schools: if more emphasis is placed on a broader set of core values, will the school attract a different kind of student and yet still be an attractive proposition? Would this focus be highly valued by future employers? What impact might this have on ratings and consequently income? Would these ideas be welcomed by university presidents and vice-chancellors?

The legitimacy and identity of the future business school is, therefore, bound up with the role, meaning and purpose of the business school in the context of the university and society. There are many competing arguments that raise important issues and ideas about identity. They include the following.

- Joel Podolny (2009), a former dean at Yale and now head of Apple's Corporate University, points out that many business academics allegedly are not curious about what goes on inside organisations. They prefer to develop theoretical models that appeal to academic audiences and obscure rather than clarify the way organisations work.
- Jeff Pfeffer's (2007) future dream for management research (clearly not yet realised!) includes greater impact on management practice, greater effect on policy debates in both the public and private sectors, and having as close an engagement with the 'management profession' as other professional schools such as law and medicine.
- Similarly, journalist Michael Skapinker (2011), in an article in the *Financial Times*, explores why business still ignores business schools. In an earlier article in 2008, he argued that business schools did not command the attention of managers and failed to engage energetically with the management practitioners. At the time, he noted that business school academics offered three reasons why managers ignored them.
  - Management was not a profession and not subject to the qualifications common in other professions.
  - Management was not a science and, given the unpredictability of human behaviour, management produced less compellingly clear-cut research.
  - Business schools wanted respect from other academic disciplines and needed to produce (A-journal) arcane research that universities demanded for tenure. Meaningful books for managers would not win tenure for junior faculty.

Skapinker goes on to argue, in a manner spearheaded by Hambrick (2007) and McGrath (2007), that few people pay attention to management research because it is irrelevant and does not engage with management practice. He also feels that the tenure argument is spurious. (Indeed, he asks what is to stop business school professors doing more relevant research once they have tenure.) He warns, in summary, that the challenge is there for business schools.

> The 'bull market' for business schools will not last forever and, therefore, they may have to look harder at the relevance of what they are doing.

The 'bull market' for business schools will not last forever and, therefore, they may have to look harder at the relevance of what they are doing.

- Paul Schoemaker (2008) stresses that the current paradigm and business school model (which Chris Grey, 2007, characterises as logical positivism) that emerged from the Ford and Carnegie Foundations-sponsored reports in the 1950s, with its strong focus on analytic models and reductionism, is not well suited to handle the ambiguity and high rate of change facing many industries today. Management problems are much more 'messy' and interdisciplinary in character.

Steven Watson (1993), a serial dean in the UK at Cambridge, Lancaster and Henley, asks what place universities have in management education given the resistance to management academics by academics from other, 'more legitimate' disciplines in universities. (A factor also noted by Lars Engwall, 2000, in his analysis of university education in Scandinavia and Germany.) In a later article Watson (2000) further asks why management academics are rarely asked for advice on the management of their own institutions.

There are many other contributions to the growing critical debate on the meaning, role and evolving purpose of business schools in the context of universities and the wider management and societal context. They lead inevitably to a series of questions examined in this chapter.

- What is the university world's view of the business school? Do business schools serve universities well? Are business schools integral to the functioning of the modern university? Are they tolerated as a necessary evil – a 'cash cow' – or welcomed as a legitimate academic discipline? Should business schools be 'spun off' and separated from universities? Has the university strayed too far from the liberal ideas of Newman (1852) and other philosophers?

What is the business world's view of the business school? Is it simply a source for well-trained business students? Why does it occupy such a precarious position attempting to achieve the twin goals of rigour and relevance in research? Is it linked well to the corporate world or is it simply seen as irrelevant for practice? Is management a discipline? What is the core body of knowledge in management? Should business schools be reframed and repositioned?

This chapter examines the difficult and tenuous relationship between universities and business schools by addressing the following issues.

- First, it discusses where the modern university and its critics now stand.
- Second, given the uneasy marriage between universities and business schools, the many criticisms of the modern business school are analysed.
- Third, given the current identity crisis, the re-evaluation and re-engineering of the business school model are discussed and some elements of the next generation school are identified.

THE UNIVERSITY AND ITS CRITICS

Kirp (2003), Angus (2009), Menaud (2010) and Cole (2010) argue that modern universities have abandoned their central concept of a liberal education and their positioning as havens and institutions of thinking and learning. Their viewpoint is that they have embraced increasing commercialisation and instrumental financial goals as guiding principles in their vision. These critics argue for clarity in the affirmation of the basic values of the modern university and of the role that professional schools such as business schools should play in their evolution.

Indeed, Readings (1996) describes the university as 'a ruined institution that has lost its historical *raison d'être* ... Henceforth, the question of the university is only the question of relative value for money, the question posed to a student who is situated entirely as a *consumer* [rather] than as someone who wants to think.'

In an insightful essay Rhodes (1998), in the words of Bowen and Shapiro (1998), asserts 'the importance of viewing scholarship as a public trust, taking seriously the university's obligation for service, and ensuring the characterisation of teaching as a moral vocation'.

In arriving at this judgement Rhodes (1998: 4) lists a series of common complaints and criticisms of research universities:

- unreasonably high tuition fees;
- neglect of undergraduate teaching in favour of inconsequential research;
- fragmented fields of study;
- garbled educational purposes;
- trivialised scholarship;
- improper accounting techniques, particularly with regard to federal research funds;
- falsification of experimental results;
- conflicts of interest;
- preaching of politics;
- imposition of political correctness.

More recently, in a column in *The Economist* magazine, Schumpeter (2010: 6) in a similarly critical vein asks whether America's universities will go the way of its car manufacturing. He notes that 'professors are not particularly interested in students' welfare. Promotion and tenure depend on published research not good teaching. Professors strike an implicit bargain with their students: we will give you light workloads and inflated grades so long as you leave us alone to do our research.'

> 'Professors strike an implicit bargain with their students: we will give you light workloads and inflated grades so long as you leave us alone to do our research.'

These complaints and criticisms are echoed by many other writers, who seek to remind educators of the core principles that should guide universities. They include the following.

- Michael Angus (2009) in an engaging book, *Love the Questions*, reminds us that the university is 'an institution of thinking' that has a larger social and public purpose of enlightenment. It should never lose its essential humanist tradition.
- Jonathan Cole (2010) offers a set of core values for a university ranging from favouring organised questioning and scepticism about anything that

resembles dogma to maintaining the intellectual vitality of the academic community by attracting the best minds.

- Cardinal Newman's idea of the university (1852) was that its sole purpose was to be a place in which liberal education could happen. He regarded it as a place for teaching universal knowledge.
- Delanty (2001) also points out, summarising many of Newman's and Von Humboldt's ideas, that the founding principles of the university include beliefs about the universality of knowledge, the quest for truth and the unity of culture.
- Bloom (1987) notes that 'in short there is no vision, nor is there a set of competing visions of what an educated human being is'.

Yet despite acknowledging the value of universities in developing transistors, new drugs and so on, the critics, notably Kirp (2003), stress that the universities are not businesses. They argue that the increasing commercialisation and marketisation of universities challenges their historical sense of identity and purpose.

Rhodes (1998: 6) points out that universities, in becoming more socially engaged, have changed significantly. This is probably most significant in terms of *inclusiveness* (more programmes of study and greater educational access and mobility); *professionalisation* (e.g. schools of law, medicine, management etc.) and the increasing trend towards professionalisation and a career focus in the creation of disciplines and sub-disciplines in the social sciences and humanities; and, finally, the growing ascendancy of *science and the model of scientific knowledge* in university thinking.

He goes on to assert that the moral influence of the great universities has diminished as they have established new partnerships with business and government. He has three urgent imperatives for universities – namely, recapturing the curriculum, rekindling the community and reinforcing our priorities.

There are many other reasons why academic institutions are not functioning as intended. Academic institutions have endured for 700 years and, next to the Catholic Church, they are probably our oldest institutions. Unsurprisingly, there is a lot of tradition involved and considerable inertia regarding change. And yet, over the past century and, above all, over the past decade or two, the number of academic institutions has increased dramatically. For such an ancient 'industry' it is also remarkably young.

IMPEDIMENTS TO CHANGE AND LIBERALISATION

There are a number of impediments, including governance and administrative structures, hindering the modern university in recapturing liberal traditions. The most common are as follows.

Inflexible academic structures

Academic departments and institutes are generally established initially in response to emerging academic disciplines or new needs for relevant coverage of research and/or teaching. The 'problem' is that, once established, it is usually difficult to demolish or, indeed, change these structures: departments or institutes tend to take on lives of their own. To close them down, merge or consolidate them in the face of diminished demand may be difficult.

Thus, universities may find themselves with significant resources tied up in activities that reflect the past and it may prove hard for them to find resources (funds, job positions, physical space) to adapt to future needs. The result is that many academic institutions become less well equipped than they should be to deal with new challenges facing today's people in today's societies. In turn, this can lead to inertia, denial of the need for change, arrogance, complacency and turf wars (see Sheth, 2008, for a similar argument in the context of business organisations).

The modern university is typically built up around an axiomatical structure

This is inspired by the seminal innovation of von Humboldt (1970) when he created a blueprint for the modern university in 1809 along disciplinary lines, with research and teaching following these. He implemented this at Berlin University.

Today, however, there is a greater need for eclectic teaching and research across increasingly narrow and focused disciplines. Modern research and teaching often require co-operation – cross-disciplinary teams – not professors in their own 'silos'. Today's networked working calls for a diverse 'we, we, we' culture, in contrast with the traditional hierarchical 'me, me, me' academic culture.

However, faculty favour retaining their current competencies and instead exhibit competitive myopia by rejecting or ignoring new ideas and methods of teaching, research and learning.

The missing balance between research and teaching

Research and teaching are two sides of the same coin – in order to teach the latest knowledge faculty must be active when it comes to research in their chosen field.

Faculty exhibit competitive myopia by rejecting or ignoring new ideas and methods of teaching, research and learning.

Over time, and especially recently, the research side seems to have become prioritised. Academic rewards, particularly academic prestige (and often financial bonuses), frequently depend on the publication of sole-authored refereed articles in high-quality academic journals. In the process, academics have become almost too busy to teach. (Teaching is then covered by lecturers and graduate students, who typically do not have the in-depth, research-based background. These are second-class citizens in the academic world.) The result is, of course, a diminution of academic value creation, and another manifestation of the hierarchical 'me, me, me' culture – perhaps even a strengthening of this structure.

Too many committees and red tape

Faculty-dominated governance, based on active involvement, consultation and collegiality is, of course, the backbone of strong academic value creation. Still, there is a danger of 'misguided involvement', which might manifest itself as committees to decide on almost every-thing – with much discussion but few decisions. An excessive involvement in committees for supervision and promotion is a typical sign of this. The result is relatively less time and energy being spent on academic research and teaching. In the end, there would be the clear risk of lessened academic quality and, potentially, an increasing number of turf wars about future academic pathways and directions.

Slow pedagogical progress; too little curriculum innovation

Each professor typically has a certain workload specified for him/her – typically a certain number of courses, each with a pre-specified number of sessions, and requirements as to readings, exams and so on. With this structure and the increasing focus on high-quality research there is little room for pedagogical innovation.

Why should a particular professor be interested in promoting new technology, say, to enhance faster learning and thereby cut down on his/her present teaching load, thus opening up 'slack' for new teaching assignments? These, in turn, might lead to more preparation, more work and a reduction in time available for research. Lack of innovation is further compounded by reliance on textbooks, which provide all the teaching aids a faculty member needs. And why should courses be modularised to reflect the modern world? And why should there be co-teaching? And, on top of the workload implications that would discourage most faculty members from embarking on such initiatives, there would typically be academic committees to be involved in, endorsing and approving any change. So, why would anyone want to go through this?

Too little top-down articulation of strategic direction

Many leaders of academic institutions are, of course, excellent. The challenge for them, above all, is to initiate and speed up portfolio changes. However, the bottom-up pressure from faculty to stick to what would add up to more-or-less the *status quo* can be real. Many academic leaders are elected by the faculty. And many have fixed, limited terms of appointment. This often implies that they will be relatively ineffective in counterbalancing bottom-up forces. Not only can this lead to a less effective portfolio-refocusing aimed at more future-oriented activities and disciplines but also to a less effective approach to academic cycles. This will often result in a push for more resources but with little room and reflection about the requirements for accelerations or decelerations in funding.

Explosion in student numbers

The number of students is rising quickly as more and more young people elect to study in universities as a way to 'invest' in their future and achieve sought-after social mobility. However, academic institutions generally follow a model of academic value creation that is not easily scalable. For example, there is considerable faculty and academic resistance to distance learning and, indeed, to preparatory learning in any other formats than the traditional ones. At the same time, there is an acute shortage of qualified faculty, especially at the entering PhD level. And the financial resources to service an increasing student population are not likely to be proportionally increased. The result, most likely, is another major threat to the quality of research and teaching in universities.

Therefore, radical innovations and fresh thinking are needed in universities to cope with their embedded institutional recipes and inertia. A radical rekindling of the liberal university tradition and the redesign of university structures and curricula are required across the spectrum of schools and faculties in the modern university.

As universities set their priorities and visions, it is even more important for the business school or, indeed, other professional schools to remember and reflect upon Newman's (1852) proposition that professional education should not belong in any university. Newman's principles of education, and his idea of the university, should be seen as guiding principles in examining the present, and future, positioning of management education.

Newman, who believed in both a moral authority and freedom of thought, argued that simply acquiring knowledge without simultaneously cultivating liberal, intellectual skills would result in a poor and inadequate education. The purpose of a liberal education is to develop those critically important intellectual skills of analysis, criticism and synthesis and to use them to leverage knowledge acquisition wisely and effectively. Consequently, Newman felt that the university context and the relentless pursuit of liberal education was probably not the place for training and learning professional knowledge. He advocated the separation of professional schools from universities (and included law and medicine as professional schools).

> Newman argued that simply acquiring knowledge without simultaneously cultivating liberal, intellectual skills would result in a poor and inadequate education.

Thorsten Veblen (1918) also argued against the presence of business schools in the university context, noting that they do not serve the needs of society relative to medical schools. He believed that business schools focused too heavily on teaching the methods and techniques for students to achieve personal, private gain (Gabor, 2002). It is coincidental that the Indian Institutes of Management (IIM) in India were set up by the federal government as autonomous stand-alone business schools, as were the Indian Institutes of Technology (IIT) too. Both have succeeded very well in developing business leaders in India. A similar successful model has been the formation of Singapore Management University (SMU) as a stand-alone management university.

The uneasy tension between universities and business schools has left many questioning whether business schools should exist inside modern universities at all. Dominant critics of current models of management education, notably Henry Mintzberg (2004), echo Newman's views by stressing the importance and value of a liberal general education for managers in such areas as creative and imaginative thinking and clear identification and articulation of managerial judgement. They feel that if intellectual change does not take place in management education it will become an increasingly weak element of the modern university.

Therefore, addressing the precarious locale of the business school in the modern university and the multiple criticisms of its legitimacy and identity is an important issue for the evolution of the business school and those who will take up leadership positions in those schools.

THE BUSINESS SCHOOL AND ITS CRITICS

The uneasy positioning of the business school in the modern university and the tension between school and university are evident in the following remarks.

Derek Bok, former President of Harvard University, notes that 'among the faculties none has a greater sense of purpose than the business school' (Bok, 2003: 6). Noorda (2011) amplifies this by saying 'Business Schools are fit for purpose because they serve the specific needs of the communities they relate to'.

On the other hand, Allan Bloom (1987) in his book *The Closing of the American Mind* charges the business schools with contributing to the excessive commercialisation of the university. He continues by stressing that 'the MBA [...] is not the mark of scholarly achievement [...] motivated by the love of the science of economics but by love of what it is concerned with – money'.

This uneasy tension and ambiguous positioning has been clear throughout the evolution and development of the business school. From the earliest origins of the concept, as noted in Chapter 1, there has been an endless jockeying about, and justification of, alternative business school models. It continues to the present day with the push towards a more inclusive and broader view of stakeholder capitalism.

The 'wasteland of vocationalism' allegedly characterised the early 'trade school' era (from the late nineteenth century to the middle of the twentieth century) until the Ford and Carnegie reports transitioned schools into the discipline-oriented, scientific rigour version.

This model largely dominated the landscape during the second half of the twentieth century. Yet criticism about the academic content and research quality of the business school has been constant in academia, while the professional management community has consistently complained about the research relevance and value of the business school.

Many university academics believe that business schools dilute the academic quality of universities and often strongly resist the development of business administration faculties. Further, it is notable that very few business school deans have ever been made presidents or even provosts of major research universities (Goodall, 2009).

What, then, is the appropriate positioning for the business school? What is, or should be, its *raison d'être* in the modern university?

Clearly, the advocates of business schools would argue that the role and purpose of the business school are to build and upgrade the quality of human capital in the management arena. And they would stress that by any standards, the business school has grown very rapidly and been a huge success. The 'business school' industry has indeed arrived (Pfeffer and Fong, 2004a, 2004b).

But there is no agreement on what constitutes the established body of management knowledge that should be taught in a business school or whether management constitutes a profession in its own right (Khurana and Nohria, 2008). Indeed, critical management theorists, such as Grey (2007: 112), argue that the business school is really no more than a finishing school.

There are indeed some parallels between the criticisms of universities, in general, outlined by Frank Rhodes and those that have been consistently voiced about business schools. None of this would surprise Allan Bloom (1987) and others discussed earlier who blame business schools for being the catalyst and stimulus for the increasing commercialisation, and de-liberalisation, of the modern university.

> There is no agreement on what constitutes the established body of management knowledge that should be taught in a business school or whether management constitutes a profession in its own right.

Current criticisms include the following.

The business school is a socialisation mechanism

As Grey (2007: 113) notes, 'The capacity of management education to socialize those subjected to it [...] is less the skills and knowledge it imparts and more its capacity to develop a certain kind of "person", deemed to be suitable for managerial work and enclutured into some vision of managerial values.' Van Maanen (1983) describes it further as 'anticipatory socialisation into the business community', whereas Whitley (1981) sees it as a way of perpetuating class differences and managerial elites (via the MBA). In short, a business school is a necessary rite of passage for senior management and more a 'finishing school' than an intellectual, liberal-thinking cauldron of activity.

> A business school is a necessary rite of passage for senior management and more a 'finishing school' than an intellectual, liberal-thinking cauldron of activity.

The business school emphasises shareholder capitalism

Khurana (2007) stresses how managers once had higher aims encompassing both personal profit and societal duty but this transitioned first to 'managerial capitalism', in which the managers are the owners' 'hired hands', and then to 'shareholder capitalism', which further reduces the scope of managerial authority. However, Hubbard (2006) argues that the appropriate pursuit of business is the relentless drive for entrepreneurial capitalism, in which a focus on the market and new business models becomes the business school's purpose. Absent from this analysis are models of stakeholder capitalism arguing that managers also need an ethical, moral and societal compass. Indeed, Locke and Spender (2011) confront the issue of the mystique of American managerialism, which they believe has had too much influence on business school design.

The business school does not provide a clear sense of purpose, morality and ethics with respect to its role in society

Ghoshal (2005) is most often quoted in relation to morality and purpose. He says, 'I suggest that by perpetuating ideologically inspired amoral theories, business schools have actively freed their students from any sense of moral responsibility.' Corporate scandals, often attributed to business school-trained CEOs, such as at World Com and Enron and more recently some financial institutions, merely add to the suspicion that the business school's ethical, moral and societal conscience can be summarised as 'greed is good'.

The business school focuses on analytics and does not develop wisdom, interpersonal and leadership/managerial skills

Mintzberg (2004) has been the most determined and resolute critic of schools teaching specialist, analytical skills and not managerial skills. Indeed, both Schoemaker (2008) and Bennis and O'Toole (2005) question whether schools' focus on analysis and discipline-oriented thinking has caused them to embrace scientific rigour at the expense of other forms of knowledge.

The business school produces ineffective, self-referential (but not useful) ideas and research; it is seen as irrelevant

Pfeffer and Fong (2002, 2004a, 2004b) argue that business schools have been ineffective in creating useful business ideas. And Beer (2001) believes that schools, with their unerring focus on so-called 'A-journal' research, produce research that is unimplementable

The business school embraces scientific rigour at the expense of other forms of knowledge

This criticism derives from the adoption of the analytic-oriented, scientifically rigorous research model advocated in the Ford and Carnegie reports. Indeed, Thomas and Wilson (2011) argue that 'physics envy' has been the legitimating force that has driven the growth of discipline-oriented business research.

The business school lacks academic respectability, legitimacy and professional identity

As noted already, the transformation of management education following Ford/Carnegie into a science-based model was ultimately a search for clear identity and academic respectability. Sadly, as Grey (2007) points out, the business school is an environment where logical positivism rather than qualitative or action learning research rules in a state potentially supporting scientific and academic identity but lacking relevance to the management community.

The business school has pandered to the business school rankings and has become too responsive to the consumer voice

Both Bok (2003) and Washburn (2005), among many others referred to earlier, have cautioned that the increasing and problematic influence of market forces commercialises university activities. Business schools have unfortunately accepted the market as the determinant of educational quality through their relatively unquestioned acceptance of rankings, league tables, student satisfaction surveys, and individual and corporate donations.

Khurana (2007) identifies the 'tyranny of the rankings', which can lead to dysfunctional managerial choices in business schools as they seek to manage rankings and league tables rather than educational processes such as investment in teaching and research excellence.

What is remarkable is that these current criticisms are essentially similar to those outlined over twenty years ago (Sheth, 1988) and in a noteworthy article on business schools by Professor Earl Cheit (1985) in the *California Management Review*. He framed his arguments by reflecting on J. Sterling Livingston's (1971) and Hayes and Abernathy's (1980) critiques of business school curricula. He argued that business schools may lead managers to a state of 'analysis-paralysis' in decision making, thus obscuring the value of experience over analysis. Further, he also noted that a focus on short-term investment criteria rather than longer-term productivity-oriented investments may lead organisations to economic decline.

Other Harvard Business School academics including Levitt (1978) also noted a bias for scholastic criteria over managerial common sense. All in all, their criticisms amounted to a belief that the business school agenda seemed too analytical and detached, too academic, too technical and far too narrow and specialised. Treatment of managerial skills had largely been 'crowded out'.

> The business school agenda seemed too analytical and detached, too academic, too technical and far too narrow and specialised.

Cheit (1985) points out, by way of introduction, Thorstein Veblen's (1918) argument that a college of commerce is 'incompatible with the collective cultural purpose of the university. It belongs in the corporation of learning no more than a department of athletics.' This criticism was probably generated by the extremely vocational nature of business schools in the early 1900s. However, not surprisingly, after the Ford and Carnegie reports, criticisms emerged by the 1980s that business schools were too academic and not producing high-quality managers for the world of business.

Cheit (1985: 50–1) noted in the 1980s that four main criticisms about business schools had emerged: namely, that they emphasise the wrong model, they ignore important work, they fail to meet society's needs and they foster undesirable attitudes. They substantially mirror present-day concerns and criticisms of business schools. We expand on each in turn.

(1) *They emphasise the wrong model.*
- The schools produce technical staff specialists rather than leaders.
- The schools are too quantitative, too theoretical, too removed from real problems.

(2) *They ignore important work.*

- The education ignores important human, organisational and communication skills.
- Inadequate attention is given to entrepreneurship, technology and productivity.
- The education neglects important international concerns.
- The schools fail to deal with managerial obsolescence – they are not providing sufficient continuing education.

(3) *They fail to meet society's needs.*

- The schools lag in affirmative action and thus American management remains unrepresentative.
- Business schools are unnecessary – Germany and Japan do well without them.
- Too many business schools are producing too many MBAs.
- The MBA is not worth the cost.
- MBA's salaries are too high.

(4) *They foster undesirable attitudes.*

- The schools foster a short-run, risk-averse attitude in their students.
- The schools encourage a variety of undesirable personal characteristics, including unrealistic expectations, job hopping, disloyalty.

As Cheit points out in his summary comments, there are two basic business school models: the *academic model* – which emphasises analytic rigour, path-breaking, theoretically focused research and is discipline-driven; and the *professional model* – which focuses on application, the functional fields of business and general management skills. It has an applied emphasis with research projects directed towards a business and management audience.

Cheit believed that schools meet the standards of the academic model but acknowledged criticisms that they fall short on teaching leadership, developing skill competencies and general management abilities. Consequently he recognised that changes should focus on three aspects of the criticisms made in the 1970s and 1980s: 'First, [...] the schools should increase emphasis on certain functional fields of business; second, [...] the international context of business deserves more attention; and finally, [. . .] the role of the manager should be more broadly defined' (Cheit, 1985).

What is abundantly clear is that the criticisms of the business school as being too academic, too analytically and scientifically focused, too divorced from (and irrelevant to) the real issues and problems of business and management and too market-driven and shallow (a 'high-class' finishing school) continue unabated to the present day. Further, recent financial crises and increasing concerns about sustainability and corporate social responsibility, have caused many critics to question whether the excessively commercial, market-driven focus of the business school is appropriate. They are concerned that business school graduates lack sufficient responsibility and appropriate sensitisation to ethics and social responsibility.

TENSIONS BETWEEN BUSINESS SCHOOLS AND TRADITIONAL UNIVERSITIES

Tensions between business schools, business school deans and the traditional university disciplines remain. We now discuss them, and their implications, particularly in examining issues of identity, academic acceptance and governance.

The rapid growth and marketisation of business schools has resulted in their alienation from the more traditional disciplines in the modern university. Tensions arise particularly in the areas of the very favourable administrative and governance options offered to business schools (e.g. autonomy and separate naming). As a result, their acceptance, identity and legitimacy are increasingly questioned by academics in other disciplines.

BUSINESS SCHOOL IDENTITY

As pointed out already, business school deans are sometimes characterised as being schizophrenic about how to handle the appropriate balance between academic rigour and practical relevance.

This leaves deans with the challenge of determining which path is going to best serve the needs of the school: the academic,

theoretical stance of the parent university, or the practical expectations and demands of leading the development of business and
industry? Funding is a major driver in how that decision is made.
The challenge is a difficult one. If we examine the detail of critiques
such as the increasing 'ivory tower' academic focus of business
schools (Bennis and O'Toole, 2005), the consequent relevance gap
between business research and business practice raises questions
about the ability of current MBA programmes to impart the kind of
lifelong learning skills that are particularly relevant to business
(Moldoveanu and Martin, 2008: 17).

> Business schools are turning to the same market techniques that major
> corporations adopt in order to differentiate themselves in a competitive
> marketplace.

Further, in order to attract high-quality candidates, business
schools are acting as businesses and commercialising their activities.
They are turning to the same market techniques that major corporations adopt in order to differentiate themselves in a competitive marketplace. This includes hiring public relations consultants, advertising
agencies and media training firms to shape their image. Business
schools the world over are working to rebrand, reposition or 're-image'
themselves, often on a grand scale (Bisoux, 2003: 26).

Branding will become one of the most prominent drivers of
value across the increasing number of business schools in the next
decade, according to Martin Roll of Venture Republic, a Singapore-
based strategy consulting firm specialising in branding. 'The branding
strategy and programme needs to go far beyond the product portfolio
and embrace the whole offering from the business school, including
products, people, price/value, and place,' he adds (Bisoux, 2003: 25).
Wynn Hartley of the Cox School of Business in the US has been
quoted as saying, 'We are a business and we realise that we need to
structure our spending on markets like a business [...] the market is
becoming more consumer oriented' (Bisoux, 2003: 26).

It is natural for those in academia such as Bok (2003) to regard this commoditisation and commercialisation of business education as a 'nail in the coffin' for the continued existence of the liberal traditions of higher education. Nevertheless, in order for individual business schools to get their message out, they are taking advantage of the same business tactics as the business sector itself: marketing and media differentiation and brand recognition.

Carolyn Woo of Mendoza College of Business at the University of Notre Dame in the US explains that 'everything we do has a branding implication'. And although more traditional faculty may at first reject this real-world notion, in the Mendoza example once they saw the success of branding, both faculty and staff developed a sense of pride in the specific positioning and identity of Mendoza College (Bisoux, 2003: 27).

BUSINESS ACCEPTANCE IN THE UNIVERSITY

The role of business schools within a university setting varies considerably in terms of image and acceptance from university to university. In more teaching-oriented universities, business schools are generally well accepted and integrated. These schools are not focused solely on MBAs but on robust undergraduate programmes. In research-oriented universities, on the other hand, business schools are perceived as important for their revenue-generating professional programmes rather than for their research; and in liberal arts and humanities/letters universities, they are looked upon with disdain and distrust.

Some institutions have not even allowed separate business schools to start. Princeton University is one example. Only recently have prestigious universities such as Yale and Johns Hopkins fully accepted and recognised their business schools. In these liberal arts universities there is an air of distrust between the liberal arts leadership (presidents, deans, provosts) and the business school faculty, who are aware that the liberal arts are not contributing to the financial bottom line. However, many liberal arts professors believe that liberal arts are still the knowledge bottom line and the underlying rationale for the existence of the modern university.

BUSINESS SCHOOL AUTONOMY

While business schools have in large part been given autonomy from their main universities, this may not bode well for either party. By not integrating the business school into the overall academic campus life, the parent university further lends itself to the appearance of mistrust between the business school and the university.

Some evidence of this separation is that business schools often have different names from their parent universities. Here are some leading American schools with their universities in brackets: Wharton (Pennsylvania), Sloan (MIT), Kellogg (Northwestern), McCombs (Texas). In fact, it is common for many MBA applicants to know the name of the school but not the name of the university. This practice accelerated in the 1970s and 1980s when endowment money was becoming scarcer due to the energy crisis and the resulting global recession. For example, if a donor offered $50 million or $60 million the school was willing to accept the funding in exchange for the autonomy and naming rights. So university presidents, in an attempt to balance their budgets, accepted such deals. It was, indeed, the university presidents themselves who by making these autonomous deals created the 'us versus them' environment. Cash flow and capital investment became an economic necessity to these administrators rather than purely educational pursuits. The most blatant examples were attempts in the 1980s to form separate schools of accounting funded by the then Big Eight accounting firms.

> It was the university presidents themselves who by making these autonomous deals created the 'us versus them' environment.

Today, the price tag for naming a business school is in excess of $100 million and the pressure to make deals with donors and corporations is as intense as ever.

As early as the 1960s, Columbia University Business School was setting the tone of business school autonomy by adopting a different calendar to the rest of the university. The business school operated in trimesters while the rest of the university was scheduled in semesters. This practice continues today with the business school operating to a different set of calendar sessions. But there were factors other than an assertion of autonomy influencing calendar changes. Business school calendars needed to correspond with a requirement for flexible scheduling for weekend and part-time business students and the rise of online and distance learning courses. Business schools took advantage of these non-traditional options well before other disciplines.

And the universities, wanting to maximise the use of the campus infrastructure, willingly worked with the business schools, scheduling summer semesters and special courses for senior executives or offering MBA degree programmes on location to large companies such as AT&T and IBM.

Therefore, at many private universities autonomy was granted by university administrators and tolerated over time because of the benefit to the financial bottom line. These autonomous schools were often allowed to have their own logos. As a consequence, they did not clearly fit in or belong to the university culture and this caused a sense of alienation from the parent university.

BUSINESS SCHOOL GOVERNANCE

The crisis over the value of business schools within university settings also often stems from the lack of university governance in the decision making of the school and a lack of understanding of how budgets, promotions and tenure are consistent with university mission and policy. Many academics in non-business disciplines contend that university administrators review the recommendations of business school deans differently from those of other university deans. As the economic viability of some universities has become dire, some university academics feel the pursuit of scholarship is being sacrificed to the exigencies of the marketplace.

The autonomy of business schools intensified in the 1970s as high school students, and their parents, decided they needed to go to college more for employment readiness than educational enlightenment. Liberal arts students began to shift their majors to business and accounting. This increase in demand also led to a rise in admission standards, often equal to or exceeding those in liberal arts and science. This change in market demand created even more resentment in the liberal arts colleges. The trend has continued unabated for the past forty years.

> High school students, and their parents, decided they needed to go to college more for employment readiness than educational enlightenment.

Business schools were able to take advantage of this increased demand and source of income to develop more flexible and non-traditional programmes, especially at the graduate level, such as evening and weekend MBA programmes. While the traditional university departments were offering continuing education and lifelong learning classes that did not lead to degree credits, the business schools were offering degree programmes on weekends and evenings for non-traditional students and working managers. These programmes met with resistance initially as university faculty and administrators questioned how the content and quality of material given in the traditional classroom setting could be maintained in evening and weekend pursuits where students would be spending only half their time in the classroom.

Business schools also decided not to abide by traditional standards of classroom instruction and research rules to accommodate or attract market demand, which also added to alienation. Business schools continued to diversify into evening and weekend MBAs and at the same time ramped up non-degree executive programmes.

The most dramatic examples are Duke Corporate Education of the Fuqua School of Business at Duke University, which became

one of the largest non-degree programmes, and the continuing prolife-
ration of executive programmes at Harvard and Wharton. These were
initially meant to be on-campus summer programmes to take advantage
of the school's dormitory infrastructure. Managers were brought in for
one-month programmes to get instruction along with the on-campus
experience of living in dorms. But students and companies wanted
something else and this developed into custom programmes for given
companies at their facilities instead of university programmes on
campus. This coincided with the rise of corporate universities.

Besides creating their own programmes or tailored programmes
for companies, business schools were allowed to bring in their own
non-tenured faculty to teach in these evening, weekend and off-campus
programmes. Practising managers were allowed to come in and teach
courses as long as they had at least a master's degree. A master's degree
was not an acceptable norm in other arts and sciences departments,
where having a PhD was the standard. The traditional university view
was you had to be a scholar to be a teacher; but in the business school,
teaching (pragmatic) and scholarship (theoretical) began to diverge.

Business schools also allowed a lot of courtesy appointments.
Therefore, if you were a retired CEO who wanted to be on campus,
you could be granted a courtesy appointment as 'professor'. This
rankled with other university department professors, especially at
well-known universities such as Harvard, Yale, Stanford, Berkeley,
Michigan and Illinois where academic reputation was so important.

This faculty flexibility/autonomy was much more contentious
at private universities compared to state universities. Private universities primarily offered graduate-level programmes and most of them
had no undergraduate business programmes. At state universities
where an undergraduate business degree was offered, there was at
least some prerequisite interaction with liberal arts courses. At the
undergraduate level, students and faculty from different disciplines
had a certain amount of interaction but once at the graduate level,
business students were no longer required to take courses outside
their core area of study.

Because at many universities business schools became income generators, they tended to increase their autonomy. University presidents allowed a volatile situation to fester and showed little or no leadership in encouraging business schools to become part of the overall university culture. Instead, they tolerated the stand-alone branding that was taking place.

Further, non-tenure-track faculty in the business schools were, and are, looked down on as second-class citizens. Tenure-track business faculty considered themselves as intellectuals and felt that they deserved academic privileges and incentives even though they did not generate significant income through their research contracts.

University presidents also lost the opportunity to promote scholarship in business schools as they do in liberal arts colleges and by the 1970s their major thrust was on fundraising and increasing endowments. Business schools, therefore, have become similar to athletics programmes, with their own stadiums where donors and alumni provide funding based on the success of the schools' teams rather than on the quality of the education. The 'boosters' phenomenon in sports and university athletics began to emerge in business schools with alumni exerting a much greater influence on a school's curriculum and culture.

BUSINESS SCHOOL ADMINISTRATION

Another aspect of business school autonomy has to do with the selection and recruitment of business school deans. This change has driven a wedge between business schools and other college disciplines within major universities. Formal recruiting of deans is a fairly new phenomenon. The traditional practice was to promote deans from the existing faculty with an informal process by the Chair of the Search Committee orchestrating the internal appointment. However, business schools began to adopt the practice of having external candidates brought in with a formal search process instead of a committee of scholars who required certain academic criteria to be met.

> Business schools have become similar to athletics programmes, with their own stadiums where donors and alumni provide funding based on the success of the schools' teams rather than on the quality of the education.

Academics wanted scholars to be deans while the university presidents began to rely on outside search firms to bring in candidates. The role of the dean began to shift from managing the internal curriculum and scholarship to a more external role of fundraising and managing external relationships such as alumni and potential donors. Their primary responsibility turned from scholarship to fundraising. These new deans, much like athletics directors, became fundraisers and promoters for big money and corporate sponsorship of the business school rather than developing research or scholarly pursuits.

This meant associate deans were often needed to run the internal operations of the school, much like a university president being the external representative of the university while the provost, as chief academic officer, focuses on scholarship. However, in order for associate deans to be promoted, they often had to abandon their scholarly pursuits. Business schools were often left in a no-win situation.

In addition, education budget cuts meant that state universities in the US had to depend less on state funding; business schools therefore began generating funds by building centres that were industry-oriented as opposed to discipline-oriented. As a result, centres for automobiles or semiconductors as opposed to engineering or economics as an overall study were put in place. In California, there are centres for entertainment or sports management or telecommunications, all of which have a management component, thus justifying an MBA programme. As a result, business schools became less discipline-oriented and more domain-oriented. This is not to say that other colleges do not have centres of study such as French Literature, Public Policy or an Institute for Advanced Studies in a number of policy areas. But these are almost all discipline-oriented with very well-known research scholars involved in policy research and advanced theory. University faculty see business institutes of study as merely centres of commerce, dictated by industry rather than scholarship.

Again, we must be critical of university presidents who have allowed this change in direction. By allowing outside deans from industry into the university environment an industry philosophy rather than an academic philosophy has been allowed to take hold. Even the aesthetics of the campus are impacted by this approach. The department generating the most funding gets to dictate the terms of engagement and even specific salary levels.

Business schools are viewed more like medical schools, driven by clinical practice, kept as autonomous and not expected to operate like the rest of the campus. In other words, integration with the rest of the university is neither desirable nor possible.

Arts and science faculty consider business schools in the same vein as law schools and medical schools, where instructors are practitioners rather than PhDs. They do not consider the courses taught as intellectual, even though business incorporates many disciplines of behavioural and social sciences including economics. Consequently, business disciplines are perceived as applied and not fundamental. Unless business schools generate their own frameworks and theories, which other more respected disciplines apply and use, this image will persist.

> Business schools are viewed more like medical schools, driven by clinical practice, kept as autonomous and not expected to operate like the rest of the campus. In other words, integration with the rest of the university is neither desirable nor possible.

A further division has taken place between undergraduate versus graduate faculty within business schools. In science and humanities, faculty not only do basic research, they also teach large undergraduate classes. However, too often in graduate business schools, graduate faculty look down on undergraduate courses. The first question we are often asked is 'Do you teach graduate or under-graduate classes?' There is also a class-size disparity between graduate and undergraduate classes. Too often, business school faculty get away with teaching small graduate classes, especially in state universities where there is a large undergraduate programme.

The underlying conflict between business school deans and liberal arts school deans is in terms of budget. The competition for funding encourages competitive biases and significant differences in treatment between departments. Faculty disparity in pay and in staffing is exacerbated. Business school faculty often earn extra income by consulting but liberal arts faculty are limited in the amount of outside consulting they are allowed to do.

The resulting problem is not with business school deans but with the university presidents who condone these tensions. The only place where this happens to a lesser extent is where the university grew out of the business school – for example, a commerce college that became a university. An example of this might be the University of St Gallen in Switzerland.

Most universities do not trust business school deans to become presidents or provosts just as they would not trust the head of the athletics department to be at the helm, mostly because of reasons of reputation or prestige. However, the universities still depend on the business school to generate income. The cynics see the business school as a commerce trader and 'cash cow'; it may be powerful but the money generated is still considered to be a 'sell-out' to finan-cial interests.

Business is not respected in universities. We believe that uni-versity presidents must work to integrate schools and make them cross-disciplinary and not just income generators.

These continuing tensions between business schools and universities have shortened the administrative life cycle of many business school deans, who have increasingly become frustrated with championing reform at entrenched institutions. The average tenure for a business school dean is three years and two months (according to

AACSB data); most do not survive the standard five-year contracts. Even world-class business leaders who want to contribute to effective change in business schools are often demonised by trying to apply corporate business models to universities, not realising that autocratic models do not work in academia.

In order for both the business school and university to thrive, the goal of co-existence instead of integration is often the choice. This is the model used by engineering schools and medical schools at, for example, Carnegie Mellon and MIT. In these situations the co-existence is amicable and the main university tolerates the school although it does not necessarily feel a connection with it.

Corporations and governments all over the world, and particularly in emerging markets, are expressing a need for high-quality managers. This demand is being met by various programmes but university business schools have the most to gain by structuring programmes, curricula and departments in such a way that benefits universities, students, faculty and researchers and meets the needs of the global economy.

RE-IMAGINING, RE-EVALUATING AND RETHINKING THE MODERN BUSINESS SCHOOL

Clearly, the challenge for business school educators is to arrive at a new framework or concept of the business school, and its curriculum, with respect to positioning, knowledge creation and knowledge dissemination.

Peters and Thomas (2011) note:

> [A]t the core of each business school, a dialectic takes place between two distinct purposes – the goal to produce knowledge and the goal to educate students. Individual institutions have different views. At one end of the spectrum there are research intensive institutions while at the other there are even teaching-led or research-less schools. Most schools are somewhere in between leaving them with a dual system of purposes and corresponding metrics, which are all too often contradictory rather than cohesive.

> The challenge for business school educators is to arrive at a new framework of the business school with respect to positioning, knowledge creation and knowledge dissemination.

The choices that individual institutions make are very often anchored around the dominant models of management education, which are probably unsustainable in the long term and are typically focused on analytical models and the view of management as a science not an art. Indeed, critics such as Starkey and Tiratsoo (2007) and Ghoshal (2005) contend that the existing models fuelled the greed and corporate scandals stretching from Enron to the global financial crisis. Some guiding principles, and opinions about these innovative strategic choices and new business school paradigms, are now much more evident in current dialogues and debates. For example, Schoemaker (2008) offers clear and useful opinions and guiding principles as follows (see also Tables 2.1 and 2.2).

In discussing how managers must learn to live with ambiguity and paradox Schoemaker (2008: 126) stresses that 'excessive reductionism or functional specialisation are unlikely to offer satisfying solutions. Holistic thinking, balancing analysis and intuition, living with ambiguity, and practising strategic flexibility are increasingly important, as are some of the other skills shown in [Table 2.1].'

He then uses these imperatives to draw implications for business schools (see Table 2.2).

Without specifying which way the organisational models of business schools will go in the future, he nevertheless believes that business schools will be defined more clearly by networks, intellectual property and deep relationships with key stakeholders. Further, the business school's perspective and image must change so that the pursuit of market-based enterprise in global and stakeholder environments is perceived as a force for good not an apostle of corporate greed and excess.

Similar themes are evident in the work of the 50+20 Management Education for the World project. In an interim report they demand that business schools in the future should focus on

Table 2.1 *Some imperatives for a new business model*

- View planning as learning and reinvention rather than as prediction and control.
- Always frame complex business problems through multiple disciplinary lenses.
- Recognize the importance of intuition and seasoned judgment while also understanding its heuristic and often unreliable nature.
- Master the art of constructive dialogue with diverse global constituents representing perhaps conflicting ideologies and value systems.
- Cultivate the human side of leadership especially in entrepreneurial and creative ventures.
- Appreciate the counter-intuitive nature of complex systems, especially when non-linear.
- Learn how to manage uncertainty rather than try to predict, control or subjugate it.
- Properly balance descriptive and normative models to arrive at truly practical solutions.
- Move from a firm-centric view of business toward network and ecological perspectives.
- Practice the art of self-renewal, individually, in teams and organisationally.
- Reinsert ethics and morality in the training and development of tomorrow's leaders.

Source: Schoemaker (2008: 127)

developing leaders who will drive global problem solving together with all stakeholders and make business more socially responsible and sustainable.[1]

Others, including Starkey and Tiratsoo (2007), Lorange (2008), and Durand and Dameron (2008), offer a range of business school futures and scenarios. Starkey and Tiratsoo specify a number of variations on Cheit's categorisation into *academic* and *professional* models.

---

[1] Muff, K. (2012). Management education for the world: providing responsible leadership for a sustainable world. Paper presented at ESMT, EFMD Conference on the 'Future of Management Education'. Berlin, 1–2 March 2012.

Table 2.2 *Implications for business schools*

Teaching

- Improve the blending of clinical and research-based faculty and topics.
- Adopt a problem-centred teaching approach using real-world challenges.
- Encourage cross-disciplinary instructor teams who co-teach all classes.
- Bring in speakers from industry and government to add richness and context.
- Make students co-creators of the educational content and the learning experience.
- Foster student teamwork on real cases; reward student leadership and creativity.

Research

- Tackle big, relevant problems requiring a long-term commitment.
- Encourage more teamwork across multiple academic disciplines.
- Partner with thought leaders in industry, government, and consulting.
- Stimulate and fund field research – get researchers out in the real world.
- Validate and challenge guru advice and popular books – set the agenda.
- Participate in key industrial, national and global dialogues about business.

Institutional

- Organise around clinical domains rather than purely academic disciplines.
- Rethink the cost and benefit of tenure; create other respectable academic career paths.
- Assess scholarship in terms of its broader impact beyond a narrow specialty.
- View the business school not as a place but as a set of complex stakeholder relationships.
- Reward extended academic sabbaticals outside of academia in business or government.
- Orchestrate deep, lifelong relationships with students, faculty, alumni and donors.
- Encourage deep alliances beyond the ivory tower; while preserving core values.

Source: Schoemaker (2008: 128)

For the academic model Starkey and Tiratsoo offer the following: the social science model (the Booth School at the University of Chicago is a strong example), the humanities agenda (e.g. Drucker, 1974; Mintzberg, 2004), which views management as a liberal art, and the knowledge economy agenda, focusing on growing technology and entrepreneurship based on growth (e.g. University of California, San Diego, among others).

For the professional model, they advocate the development of professional credentials, action-based learning and the formation of academic/practitioner networks. These forums and debates would then enable research in business practice and hence develop useful networks for innovation.

Starkey and Tiratsoo, Lorange, and Durand and Dameron believe that 'cash cow' and 'muddling through' scenarios are both unsustainable and unacceptable in the medium term. They favour scenarios and new paradigms encompassing globalisation, theoretical pluralism and multiple stakeholders. Their work offers much food for thought as business educators contemplate alternative model configurations, some of which will be discussed in Chapters 3 and 4.

CONCLUSION

The initial discussion here about future directions and scenarios leads naturally to the in-depth discussion of business school legitimacy and what management education is, or should be, about. Chapter 3 therefore addresses questions such as what skills and knowledge bases are required and what should the new paradigms and business models be?

REFERENCES

Angus, I. H. (2009). *Love the Questions: University Education and Enlightenment.* Winnipeg: Arbeiter Ring.

Beer, M. (2001). Why management research findings are unimplementable: an action science perspective. *Reflections,* **2**(3): 58–65.

Bennis, W. G. and O'Toole, J. (2005). How business schools lost their way. *Harvard Business Review,* **83**(5): 96–104.

Bisoux, T. (2003). The Zen of B-school branding. *BizEd*, November/December: 24–9.

Bloom, A. D. (1987). *The Closing of the American Mind: How Higher Education Has Failed Democracy and Impoverished the Souls of Today's Students*. New York: Simon & Schuster.

Bok, D. (2003). *Universities in the Marketplace: The Commercialization of Higher Education*. Princeton University Press.

Bowen, W. and Shapiro, H. (1998). *Universities and Their Leadership*. Princeton University Press.

Cheit, E. F. (1985). Business schools and their critics. *California Management Review*, **27**: 43–62.

Cole, J. (2010). *The Great American University*. New York: Public Affairs Perseus Books.

Delanty, G. (2001). *Challenging Knowledge: The University in the Knowledge Society*. Buckingham: Open University Press.

Drucker P. (1974). *Management: Tasks, Responsibilities and Practices*. New York: Harper & Row.

Durand, T. and Dameron, S. (2008). *The Future of Business Schools*. Houndmills: Palgrave Macmillan.

Engwall, L. (2000). Foreign role models and standardization in Nordic business education. *Scandinavian Journal of Management*, **16**: 1–24.

Gabor, A. (2002). *The Capitalist Philosophers: The Geniuses of Modern Business – Their Lives, Times and Ideas*. New York: Three Rivers Press.

Ghoshal, S. (2005). Bad management theories are destroying good management practices. *Academy of Management Learning and Education*, **4**: 75–91.

Gladwell, M. (2002). *The Tipping Point: How Little Things Can Make a Big Difference*. Boston: Little, Brown.

Goodall, A. H. (2009). *Socrates in the Boardroom: Why Research Universities Should be Led by Top Scholars*. Princeton University Press.

Grey, C. (2007). Possibilities for critical management education and studies. *Scandinavian Journal of Management*, **23**: 463–71.

Hambrick, D. C. (2007). The field of management's devotion to theory: too much of a good thing? *Academy of Management Journal*, **50** (6): 1346–52.

Hayes, R. H. and Abernathy, W. J. (1980). Managing our way to economic decline. *Harvard Business Review*, July/August: 138–49.

Hubbard, G. (2006). Business, knowledge and global growth. *Capitalism and Society*, **1**(3): 1–10.

Khurana, R. (2007). *From Higher Aims to Hired Hands: The Social Transformation of American Business Schools and the Unfulfilled Promise of Management as Profession*. Princeton University Press.

Khurana, R. and Nohria, N. (2008). It's time to make management a true profession. *Harvard Business Review*, **86**(10): 70–7.

Kirp, D. (2003). *Shakespeare, Einstein, and the Bottom Line: The Marketing of Higher Education*. Cambridge, MA: Harvard University Press.

Levitt, T. (1978, 18 December). A heretical view of management science. *Fortune*, 50–2.

Livingston, J. S. (1971). Myth of the well-educated manager. *Harvard Business Review*, **49**(1): 79–89.

Locke E. R. and Spender, J. C. (2011). *Confronting Manageralism*. London: Zed Books.

Lorange, P. (2008). *Thought Leadership Means Business: How Business Schools Can Become More Successful*. Cambridge University Press.

McGrath, R. (2007). No longer a stepchild: how the management field can come into its own. *Academy of Management Journal*, **50**: 1365–78.

Menaud, L. (2010). *The Marketplace of Ideas. Reform and Resistance in the American University*. New York: W. W. Norton.

Mintzberg, H. (2004). *Managers, Not MBAs: A Hard Look at the Soft Practice of Managing and Management Development*. San Francisco: Berrett-Koehler Publishers.

Moldoveanu, M. C. and Martin, R. L. (2008). *The Future of the MBA: Designing the Thinker of the Future*. Oxford University Press.

Newman, J. H. (1852). *The Idea of a University*. London: Longmans Green.

Noorda S. (2011). Future business schools. *Journal of Management Development*, **30**(5): 519–25.

Nussbaum, M. C. (1997). *Cultivating Humanity: A Classical Defense of Reform in Liberal Education*. Cambridge, MA: Harvard University Press.

Peters, K. and Thomas, H. (2011). A sustainable model for business schools. *Global Focus: The EFMD Business Magazine*, **5**(2): 24–7.

Pfeffer, J. (2007). *What Were They Thinking? Unconventional Wisdom about Management*. Boston: Harvard Business School Press.

Pfeffer, J. and Fong, C. (2002). The end of business schools? Less success than meets the eye. *Academy of Management Learning and Education*, **1**(1): 78–95.

(2004a). The business school 'business': some lessons from the US experience. *Journal of Management Studies*, **41**: 1501–20.

(2004b, 22 May). But can you teach it? *The Economist*: 61–3.

Podolny, J. M. (2009). The buck stops (and starts) at business school. *Harvard Business Review*, **87**: 62–7.

Readings, B. (1996). *The University in Ruins*. Cambridge, MA: Harvard University Press.

Rhodes, F. (1998). The university and its critics, in W. Bowen and H. Shapiro (eds.), *Universities and Their Leadership*: 3–15. Princeton University Press.

Schoemaker, P. J. (2008). The future challenges of business: rethinking management education. *California Management Review*, **50**(3): 119–39.

Schumpeter (2010, 2 September). Declining by degree. *The Economist*.

Sheth, J. N. (1988). Changing demographics and the future of graduate management education. *Selections*, Spring: 22–7.

(2008). *The Self Destructive Habits of Good Companies ... and How to Break Them*. Upper Saddle River, NJ: Wharton School Publishing.

Skapinker, M. (2011, 24 January). Why business still ignores business schools. *Financial Times*.

Starkey, K. and Tempest, S. (2008). A clear sense of purpose? The evolving role of the business school. *Journal of Management Development*, **27**(4): 379–90, Special Issue on 'Challenging the Purpose of Business Schools', ed. H. Thomas.

Starkey, K. and Tiratsoo, N. (2007). *The Business School and the Bottom Line*. Cambridge University Press.

Thomas, H. and Wilson, A. D. (2011). 'Physics envy', cognitive legitimacy or practical relevance: dilemmas in the evolution of management research in the UK. *British Journal of Management*, **22**: 443–56.

Van Maanen, J. (1983). *Qualitative Methodology*. London: Sage.

Veblen, T. (1918). Business and the higher learning, in *The Higher Learning in America. A Memorandum on the Conduct of Universities by Business Men*. New York: B. W. Huebsch.

von Humboldt, W. (1970). University reform in Germany: reports and documents. *Minerva*, **8**: 242–50.

Washburn, J. (2005). *University Inc: The Corporate Corruption of American Higher Education*. New York: Basic Books.

Watson, S. R. (1993). The place for universities in management education. *Journal of General Management*, **19** (Winter): 14–42.

(2000). Why is it that management academics rarely advise on the management of their own institutions? *Human Resource Development International*, **3**(1): 89–100.

Whitley, R. (1981). Women, business schools and the social reproduction of business elites: Britain and France, in C. F. Epstein and R. L. Coser (eds.), *Access to Power: Cross National Studies of Women and Elites*: 185–92. London: George Allen & Unwin.

3 Rethinking management education and its models: a critical examination of management and management education

The previous chapter outlined the continuing tensions between business schools and universities regarding legitimacy, identity and relevance of research and curricula. It pointed out the consequent need to reframe and re-examine business and management education through the lenses of new paradigms and models.

In this chapter, we take up the challenge of rethinking management education and its potential alternative approaches and models. We take a critical view of management education and ask, alongside other critics, whether we really know what management education is, or should be, about. Our position is that we need to rethink the meaning and concept of the 'business school' and our current philosophies of management education. Consequently, we pose the following questions:

(1) What is management about? Is it an Art or a Science?
(2) Do we have a theory of managing?
(3) What is the proper content of management education?
(4) What are the core management skills?
(5) Is there a new, more radical management education model that can focus our thinking and hence provide insights into the logic of the range of alternative models that are currently being proposed?

Let us start with a discussion about the nature of management and the content of management education. How should educators react to the many criticisms of existing models, which are seen as too narrow, too technical, too analytical and not managerial? Let us also examine the key forces driving change in management education arising from both internal and external forces. Then, let us advocate the creation of new management education models using the new radical model underlying the Lorange Institute of Business in Zurich, Switzerland, as a vehicle for dialogue and debate about design options for new models and paradigms.

Conclusions are drawn from this discussion to provide insights and guidelines for the critical examination of other new, innovative models of management education, presented in Chapters 4 and 5.

WHAT IS MANAGEMENT AND WHAT SHOULD BE THE CONTENT OF MANAGEMENT EDUCATION?

For many years the most strident, and important, critic of management education has been Professor Henry Mintzberg. In his book *Managers, Not MBAs* (Mintzberg, 2004), which summarises and synthesises much of his thinking, he states in his preface: 'I was simply finding too much of a disconnect between the practice of management that was becoming clearer to me and what went on in classrooms, my own included, intended to develop managers.' More importantly, he argues that management is not a science: 'Management certainly applies science: managers have to use all the knowledge they can get, from the sciences and elsewhere. But management is more art, based on "insight," "vision," "intuition"' (10).

In essence, agreeing with Drucker (1989), he summarises the practical role of the manager as follows: 'Put together a good deal of craft with a certain amount of art and some science, and you end up with a job that is above all a practice' (Mintzberg, 2004; 10).

Focusing more on the content of management education, Livingston (1971), in his article on the 'Myth of the Well-Educated Manager', wrote the following comments, also quoted in Mintzberg (2004: 38): 'Formal management education programmes typically emphasise the development of problem-solving and decision-making skills ... but give little attention to the development of skills required to find the problems that need to be solved, to plan for the attainment of desired results, or to carry out operating plans once they are made.'

> The field of management education should be broad, including careful examination of managerial skills of problem search and framing, strategising and implementing change.

Above all else, the proposition is that the field of management education should be broad, including careful examination of managerial skills of problem search and framing, strategising and implementing change. It should not be beset by narrow functional specialisation. It is clearly characterised by paradox and ambiguity (Schoemaker, 2008) and, hence, requires holistic thinking and important skills of synthesis as well as insights into analysis and analytic thinking.

WHAT IS THE CONTENT OF MANAGEMENT EDUCATION?

Watson (1993) – an experienced dean who has held the position at three schools in the UK (Cambridge, Henley and Lancaster) – focuses very clearly on the proper content, and positioning, of management education. Many of the themes he stresses draw on Mintzberg's descriptions of managerial work and management practice though he also advances Cardinal Newman's (1852) ideas on liberal education and Hirsch's (1987) work on cultural literacy as important influences on well-designed curricula of management education.

He uses Mintzberg's (1973) seminal analysis of managerial work – in essence Mintzberg's doctoral thesis research – to throw light on the skills and key roles of the manager. As noted by Watson (1993: 16), Mintzberg identifies ten roles that managers fulfil. Three are seen as *interpersonal*, involving personal and organisational skills; three are seen as *informational*, requiring monitoring and dissemination of appropriate information; and four are viewed as *decisional*, including resource allocation, negotiation and entrepreneurial skills.

Watson (1993: 17) then translates the necessary managerial skills and qualities that should be possessed by good managers:

- *Peer skills*: the ability to enter into and maintain peer relationships;
- *Leadership skills*: the ability to motivate and train subordinates, to provide help and to deal with problems of authority and dependence;
- *Conflict resolution skills*: the skills of mediating between conflicting individuals and handling disturbances;
- *Information-processing skills*: the abilities to discover relevant information and to present it to others both orally and in writing;
- *Skills in decision making under ambiguity*: how to realise that a decision has to be made and then how to make that decision;
- *Resource-allocation skills*: the skill of choosing between competing resource demands;
- *Entrepreneurial skills*: the ability to search for problems and opportunities and to implement change in organisations;
- *Skills of introspection:* managers need to understand themselves and to learn how to learn.

Mintzberg's (2004) view is that at least one-third of all management education programmes should be devoted to addressing this managerial skill base.

However, it is doubtful whether few, or indeed any, programmes other perhaps than Mintzberg's own IMPM programme (2004 and discussed in Chapters 4 and 5) satisfy, or even come close to this criterion, despite the many wide-ranging criticisms of management education programmes.

If one-third of an ideal programme should encompass training in Mintzberg-type managerial skills, what should constitute the other two-thirds?

Watson (1993) argues that the remaining elements of management should include both the traditions of liberal education as exemplified by Newman (1852) and also detailed exposition of the underlying knowledge base of the competitive, economic, social and technological environment faced by the manager.

Adopting Newman's principles of liberal education into the management curriculum would involve the development of the extremely important intellectual skills of *analysis, criticism* and *synthesis*. For Newman these skills were fundamental and their objective was clear.

They allowed the individual to become introspective, open-minded, insightful and possess the ability to absorb knowledge critically in framing problems and making decisions. Such liberal education courses are currently not common in existing business school curricula.

In addition, the domain of management knowledge and knowledge about the structure and functioning of organisations is usually the dominant core component of most existing management programmes. Most curricula typically focus on the following elements: the social and organisational environment (the domain of social scientists); the economic and financial environment (the domain of economists, business cycles, lawyers and accountants); and the strategic and quantitative elements of marketing, operations, logistics and public/corporate policy (the domain of managing growth and organisational direction).

Overall, this domain knowledge encompasses the roles and activities of the manager and the organisation. Careful articulation of this domain knowledge, therefore, produces a sound competence level for the managerial knowledge base.

However, most current programmes over-emphasise domain knowledge and underemphasise the multi-disciplinary nature of the management task. Without proper grounding in Newman's intellectual and synthetic skills, Mintzberg's panoply of interpersonal skills and – given the global environment – Hirsch's (1987) skills of cultural literacy and sensitivity, thorough grounding in domain knowledge is clearly insufficient. And the urgent challenges of change in management processes and the global business environment will force a redesign of many existing curricula.

We now examine the influence of the many challenges and forces driving change in the management environment as a prelude to synthesising the key elements of the current debates about new models and paradigms in management education.

> Most current programmes over-emphasise domain knowledge and underemphasise the multi-disciplinary nature of the management task.

WHAT ARE THE CHALLENGES AND KEY FORCES DRIVING CHANGE IN MANAGEMENT EDUCATION?

Some immediate observations can be made about the current academic environment and its implications for the conduct of management education.

- The funding of higher education (see, for example, the original introduction of so-called 'top up' fees in UK higher education, in *The Economist* (2005), and the subsequent escalation of such fees to current levels of £9000 per annum) is a critical issue across the world. The consequences of continued alleged under-funding of universities have been the increasing use of part-time faculty, the relative unattractiveness of academic careers and mounting evidence of financial failure. Further, pressure from governments and regulatory bodies such as Britain's QAA (Quality Assurance Agency), with its focus on teaching quality, and the RAE/REF (Research Excellence Framework), with its focus on research quality, will require business schools to balance quality education against criteria of cost efficiency and organisational effectiveness.

- The growth of the global economy and the recent significant shift of economic power from the West to the East create new opportunities and challenges for business schools. In parallel with the rapid development of quality business schools in Europe and Asia (see, for example, the current listing of Global MBA programmes in the *Financial Times* (FT) annual ranking of global business schools), successful competition with foreign schools will require a balanced global view of business education and increased recognition of cultural diversity through multinational and ethnic diversity in teaching methods, teaching materials and case studies.

- Student-demand patterns, particularly in large growing economies such as China and India, and the emergence of new learning technologies will require schools to pay increasing attention to the potential of educational models based on flexible just-in-time learning and the blend between face-to-face campus-style learning and interactive e-learning technologies.

- Social factors including population ageing, two-income families and increased life expectancy will probably result in increased demand for innovative forms of lifelong learning in many countries.

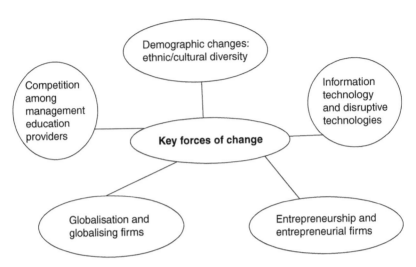

FIGURE 3.1 Impacts and implications of key driving forces

A more detailed evaluation of the pressure of environmental forces and drivers of change in management and management education follows.

Successful competition with foreign schools will require a balanced global view of business education and increased recognition of cultural diversity through multinational and ethnic diversity in teaching methods, teaching materials and case studies.

Key forces driving management education

The key forces and drivers of change in the management education environment are illustrated in the change model (Figure 3.1).

IMPACTS AND IMPLICATIONS OF DEMOGRAPHY AND DEMOGRAPHIC CHANGE

Hoare (2006) points out that 'business schools say that numbers of "grey MBAs" are rising and some schools are actively recruiting in the older age bracket as applications from younger students fall away'. For example, the average age for MBA students at Ashridge Management College and Lancaster Management School in the UK is reported as being in the mid-thirties. Reasons for the 'greying' of the MBA market are not difficult to discover. They include, *inter alia*, the following.

- People now have an increasing life-span as a result of health advances and an emphasis on an appropriate balance between work and family life. Consequently, education increasingly becomes a lifelong commodity rather than one consumed at an early age.
- With the advent of increasing employee life-spans, employers are beginning to recognise the need to invest in developing key individuals among their 40- and 50-year-olds, particularly since the retention of excellent employees becomes critical with both a less loyal, more flexible workforce and, in some Western countries, a declining birth rate potentially reducing the number and quality of new entrants to the workforce.
- The impacts of legislation and adequate pension provision are changing employment patterns, leading to a rise in retirement age. For example, European anti-age discrimination legislation is forcing employers to recognise and adapt to the age distribution of their employees. And, in the political debates about pension provision, there is a clear view that adequate pensions can only be paid if both employee contributions increase and the retirement age rises.
- There is a growing recognition that older employees have retraining needs but possess considerable experience, well-developed individual qualities and a commitment to the workplace. Such retraining may, in turn, require the development of more flexible and customised business school approaches. *The Economist* (2006) notes, for example, that 50 per cent of the employees in B&Q, a British do-it-yourself chain, are over 50 years of age and one is 91 years old.

> In the political debates about pension provision, there is a clear view that adequate pensions can only be paid if both employee contributions increase and the retirement age rises.

The impacts of demographic change for business schools therefore include the need for more flexible curricula, a greater emphasis on lifelong learning and recognition of the changing characteristics and skills required from business school graduates.

For example, an article in *The Economist* (2006) stresses the need to address the talent and skill shortage, which has been labelled and described as 'the war for talent' or 'the battle for brainpower'. It points out that with the current generation of 'baby boomers' retiring there will be a growing gap in employees aged 15 to 64 – most dramatically in Europe and Japan – with projections about the decline of people in that age range estimated at around 10 per cent.

It questions whether there will be enough qualified employees to satisfy the demands of growth markets in technology and other areas, particularly professional service firms. It quotes a recent Corporate Executives Board survey indicating disquiet about the quality of recruits and the time taken to find suitable job candidates. Similar disquiet is being expressed by critics of business schools following the global financial crisis. They are concerned about issues such as the ethical, moral and human compass of business school graduates and their narrowness and analytic focus.

The problem for business schools and the resulting challenge for curricula development is that recruiters increasingly require higher-level candidates who possess complex interactive and people skills (e.g. the ability to link things together and frame complex problems) involving an enhanced judgemental mindset.

An important and more recent study of demographic trends by an influential professor of demography (Lutz, 2011) identifies the main demographic shifts that are likely to occur over time. They include the following. First, the size of the world population will stop growing in the second half of the twenty-first century and possibly enter a lasting decline due to lower birth rates (already evident in Japan and Europe). Second, population ageing in Western countries is accelerating due to increased life expectancy. Third, these trends of lower population growth and increasing population ageing mean a shift from quantity to quality of human capital. In other words, the skill base of the workforce becomes a critical issue and investments in better education, well-being and international competitiveness will come to dominate government policies.

The implications for business schools may be that faculty members will have to work longer. Age management of faculty by deans will require careful balancing of continued employment for older faculty while maintaining good career progress for younger faculty. In addition, the challenges of demographic change will need to filter into curricula in areas such as marketing and human resource management.

> Age management of faculty by deans will require careful balancing of continued employment for older faculty while maintaining good career progress for younger faculty.

In summary, the challenges of demographic change for management education include the following.

- A greater number of older, more experienced students will require relevant professional education.
- Project- and team-based content and experiential learning will be emphasised.
- An increasing challenge is the development of culturally based teaching materials.
- Continuous, lifelong learning becomes a core business.
- Degree programmes will become shorter.
- Affordability of management education will be a critical issue and will encourage the development of e-learning educational models.
- The management of business schools may become the trendsetter in age management as faculty shortages shrink the available supply of high-quality faculty.

IMPACTS AND IMPLICATIONS OF TECHNOLOGY

McCann (2006) questions whether we are preparing students for the 'next economy', which is not driven by a manufacturing or service orientation but by a science- and knowledge-based perspective. He believes that new industries are being built that 'revolve around the convergence of technologies such as computing, communication and engineering, and the growing importance of the life sciences such as physics, biology and chemistry'. As a consequence, linkages between business schools and science faculties will become increasingly important. Curricula must embrace a clear understanding of how radical technological innovations and competence-destroying innovations (McGee et al., 2010) change the nature of the competitive marketplace and require the development of new competencies, skills and capabilities.

Understanding of technology and technological change should thus go far beyond the possession of computer skills and require an appreciation of general engineering and scientific principles and advances. This has traditionally been the domain of specialised technology management programmes such as those offered by MIT (Massachusetts Institute of Technology), RIT (Rochester Institute of Technology) and Carnegie Mellon Universities in the US. However, the implication is that these issues should probably be brought into the mainstream of all curricula offerings in business schools.

An example of a disruptive technology (Christensen, 1997) for management education is the advent of electronic markets for learning, resulting from the growth of information and communication technologies (ICT) associated with e-learning. Hawawini (2005) indicates a growing client demand for 'blended' programmes that combine 'on-campus' instruction with learning in the workplace facilitated by ICT, particularly in the areas of lifelong learning and executive education. The growth of ICT has, in turn, prompted the search for new forms of learning in business schools as they transform from 'brick and mortar', conventional, campus-driven institutions faced with an increasing cost structure to 'click and mortar' schools that embrace e-learning alongside their traditional 'face-to-face' campus offerings in the physical world.

In a special supplement of the *Financial Times* (2006) devoted to e-learning, the growth of the technology in management education was reviewed. It concluded that it has acted as a catalyst for the creation of electronic markets for management education (Hamalainen et al., 1996) through the convergence of digital technologies and the growth of the internet. This, in turn, has enabled the parallel development of digital libraries, just-in-time on-the-job training, lifelong learning and purely virtual 'click' universities. This 'new technology' has allowed schools to take the distance out of distance learning and has changed the nature of distance learning for students. It has opened up tremendous opportunities for building global learning networks. Indeed, the flexibility of ICT now available allows for such innovative elements as asynchronous and synchronous video, video streaming, and instant messaging to enrich 'distance' and 'blended learning' programmes. This, together with the evolution of extra bandwidth, which improves both course content and interactive delivery, has stimulated business school educators to increasingly use their imagination and creativity in designing programmes.

In future, the strategic question for business school deans may be in finding the optimum balance between 'brick and mortar' and 'click and mortar'. Already we see, following the emergence of the iPad, the ability to provide students with teaching and learning materials on a tablet. And Apple has recently announced tie-ups with major publishers such as McGraw-Hill to offer academic textbooks as e-books on the iPad (Thomas and Thomas, 2012).

> In future, the strategic question for business school deans may be in finding the optimum balance between 'brick and mortar' and 'click and mortar' activities.

In a very important discussion of blended learning and learning communities, James Fleck (2012), the retiring dean of the Open University Business School in the UK and a pioneer in e-learning in education, offers a series of opportunities for future blended learning programmes as follows.

Despite these serious challenges and barriers, the opportunities for different forms of blended learning are also very clear. These opportunities include:

There is potential for using blended learning to improve the effectiveness of teaching and learning, on account of the surfacing of basic pedagogic principles necessitated by the explicit design of the learning experience.

There is clear potential as well as many already well-attested examples where technology has enabled greater flexibility in the provision of education [. . .]

Suitable configurations of blended learning can provide wider access to learning for the learners and to new markets for the providers.

Certain forms of blended learning that include practice-based elements offer great scope for far more immediate and directed relevance of what is learned.

The harnessing of learning communities through appropriate forms of blended learning provides scope for 'co-production' of effective knowledge, by enabling practitioners, academic analysts and observers to work together in forging a more powerful, as well as theoretically and pragmatically integrated, body of management and business knowledge.

Finally, the design of suitable blended learning operations could provide further scope for the more systematic integration of diverse geographic, cultural, economic and political perspectives, thereby giving a direct voice to different, and often overlooked, viewpoints through learning community processes, in contrast to the monolithic promulgation of the current dominant Anglo-American paradigm for management.

(Fleck, 2012)

In summary, the implications of ICT for management education include:

- growth of real-time, internet-based interactive education particularly in emerging markets;
- a significant rise in self-study programmes;
- impacts on information-gathering and research – the rapid growth of electronic libraries and databases;

- a changing role of faculty as video-professors; and the creation of active learning communities;
- changes in distribution channels – distributed delivery;
- value-chain thinking making obsolete conventional economic concepts such as scale economies, vertical integration and so on in the context of management education;
- developments in practice-based, blended learning programmes (see also Iniguez, 2011);
- increasing roles, and uses, of iPads and other tablets in revolutionising the teaching and learning process.

IMPACT AND IMPLICATIONS OF GLOBALISATION

Cabrera and Bowen (2005) quote World Trade Organisation (WTO) data to show that global trade grew from 20 per cent of world GDP in 1990 to more than 30 per cent in 2003. And, over the same period, foreign direct investment grew from 4 per cent to 11 per cent. Consequently, globalisation is an established fact of life neatly encapsulated in the popular title *The World is Flat* by Thomas Friedman (2005) and in the writings of Porter (1990) and Bartlett and Ghoshal (1989) and, most importantly, in the recent extensive report on the globalisation of management education by AACSB (2011).

As a result of globalisation, economic power is now spread across the world. The growth of trading blocs (Ohmae, 1985), such as the EU in Europe, ASEAN in Asia and NAFTA in the Americas, and the growing power of China and India in Asia, point to a rapidly changing geopolitical order with a shift in power from 'West to East'. As McCann (2006) says, 'global competence is a core competence; knowing how to confidently and competently work across cultures is essential in a global economy'.

World Trade Organisation data show that global trade grew from 20 per cent of world GDP in 1990 to more than 30 per cent in 2003.

What are some of these global competencies and skills? Laura Tyson, a former dean of London Business School (LBS), together with colleagues at LBS, recently carried out a survey of global business capabilities based on interviews with around 100 global business executives. She concludes (Hoare, 2006), echoing the writings of Hirsch (1987), that from a list of about forty capabilities the skills of 'flexibility, cultural sensitivity and integrity' topped the preferred list of managerial attributes. Cabrera and Bowen (2005) further believe that, in addition to Tyson's key capabilities, a global manager is a citizen of the world possessing a global mindset as the unique, value-added competence. This global mindset requires fusion of global business, international studies and cross-cultural proficiency enhanced by a set of core ethical values and professional conduct norms.

From a strategic perspective, the issue for a school is how to build knowledge of internationalisation and global capabilities into the curriculum. Indeed, surveys suggest that less emphasis is often paid to the teaching of international business and globalising business in many schools. Ghemawat (2008) notes that although some significant commitments to globalising curricula have been made, 'rhetoric has outpaced reality'. As Hawawini (2005) points out, the typical internationalisation strategies are the import model of internationalisation ('bringing the world to the school' through attracting global students and faculty); the export model of internationalisation ('sending abroad faculty as students' either through faculty sometimes delivering courses off campus in selected locations or by students attending foreign alliance schools); or the network model of internationalisation involving the creation of a multiple-site institution with fully fledged campuses across the world (a more pure 'brick and mortar' strategy).

Hawawini clearly favours the network model as the model of a truly global school – one with complementary and interconnected campuses across the major economic regions of the world (i.e. the Americas, Asia, Europe and the Middle East). This is evident, for example, in the development of INSEAD campuses in Singapore and Abu Dhabi and the parallel strategic alliance between INSEAD and Wharton. The strategic question here surrounds the degree to which the globalisation of business education will favour the adoption of a mixed, 'click, brick and mortar' approach rather than a network model in creating the future global business school.

In summary, the implications of globalisation for management education include:

- the growth of multinational student diversity;
- the need to understand global competitive rules and regulations (e.g. NAFTA, EU, ASEAN, etc.);
- cross-cultural content becoming critical in teaching;
- the growth in customised executive education programmes for multinational corporation clients;
- the requirement to form cross-functional teams to manage global accounts;
- business education operating in a 'think global – act local' mode;
- distance, e-learning as an appropriate educational model;
- business education offered on a global basis recognising the fast growth of management education in emerging markets;
- strategic alliance partners becoming important and critical.

Arnoud De Meyer (2012), President of Singapore Management University, provides further counsel about the implementation process in addressing globalisation in management education. While globalisation initiatives are easy to announce, the details of implementation, with respect to the leadership team, the business model, the deployment of technology and the brand-building exercise, will require careful and important strategic investments.

A particularly important strategic context, certainly in the Asian region and Singapore, is how globalisation will affect emerging markets. Because of its importance the next section focuses in detail on the potential implications of globalisation on the growth of management education in emerging markets. One clear difference in emerging markets is the extremely fast-paced economic growth relative to mature Western economies.

GLOBALISATION, EMERGING MARKETS AND THE GROWTH
OF MANAGEMENT EDUCATION

In the second half of the twentieth century, the world was categorised as developed, developing or third world. Now, well into the second decade of the twenty-first century, advanced countries such as the US, Japan and Germany are being eclipsed economically by emerging markets, most notably those referred to as BRIC nations (Brazil, Russia, India and China). The continued growth of these emerging economies will be the driving force in the global economy and will have long-term implications not only for business but also for business schools (Sheth, 2008; Sheth and Sisodia, 2004).

It has been forecast that by 2020 China will have the world's largest single economy, which will eventually be surpassed by India by 2050. Table 3.1 is a forecast by the International Monetary Fund (IMF) predicting that, based on purchasing power parity GDP, the three largest economies in 2015 will be US, China and India.

The forces driving this new world economic order include the following.

Ageing population in advanced countries

Recent statistics show that in the US 10,000 people reach retirement age every day. This rate will probably continue for more than a decade. Further, the birth rates in these markets are decreasing as the population ages, thus magnifying the influence of an ageing population. In 1999, Peter Drucker also identified the worldwide decline in birth rates as the number one issue that society faces today (Sheth and Sisodia, 2004: 11).

In addition, immigration has been stymied in the post-9/11 world. In terms of the current US dominance in management education, American business schools can no longer depend on foreign students to travel overseas, which will also have a strong financial impact. The first truly global generation is now coming from business schools across the world (Datar et al., 2010: 85). Evidence from global

Table 3.1 *Forecast of the largest global economies in 2015*

1 US	$18 trillion
2 China	$17 trillion
3 India	$6.0 trillion
4 Japan	$5.0 trillion
5 Germany	$3.4 trillion
6 Russia	$2.9 trillion
7 Brazil	$2.8 trillion
8 UK	$2.7 trillion
9 France	$2.6 trillion
10 Italy	$2.0 trillion

Source: International Monetary Fund

business school rankings, such as the *FT*, shows clearly that there has been a rapid growth of high-quality competitive schools in Asia and Europe over the past decade and an increasing demand for management education in emerging markets.

Local educational options and non-traditional competition

Business schools have been established in emerging markets. India already has more than 3,000 private management schools and will be the largest granter of PGDM/PGPM business certification (equivalent to the MBA degree) in the world by 2020. While institutions founded centuries ago may question the legitimacy of these newer degrees, the admission standards in these programmes are very high. In addition, a relatively new private business school, the Indian School of Business (ISB), now has more than 500 one-year MBA students each year with one of the highest average GMAT entry scores (more than 700) of students relative to any other business school in the world. Also, it is now ranked among the top twenty business schools in the world by the *FT* and has built another campus in North India (it is already in Hyderabad), which will double its annual intake of students.

The Indian government, like most other governments, subsidises top-tier universities. All applicants are required to pass rigorous tests (the Common Admissions Test or CAT) for admission. Student standards (with many thousands of applicants) exceed those required by the GMAT (Graduate Management Admissions Test). These government-run prestigious institutions, known collectively as the Indian Institute of Management (IIM), are very much on a par in quality terms with Harvard and MIT. The government has now invested in several new IIM campuses to allow more students to be admitted to the PGDM (MBA) programmes and Executive MBA programmes.

> The Indian School of Business (ISB) now has more than 500 one-year MBA students each year with one of the highest average GMAT entry scores relative to any other business school in the world.

China, too, has established a range of top-tier MBA programmes such as those at Fudan University and Peking University in addition to well-established functional certifications. The top-tier programmes aspire to be as well renowned as their research-driven counterparts in the US.

The Chinese government has also invested heavily in high school education. Reading and technical skills are paramount in such government-run school systems. However, this learning tends to neglect the development of problem-solving skills, much needed in volatile business settings, in favour of rote learning.

Even so, China is creating large numbers of literate, educated people who want to advance in their careers by attending universities and MBA programmes in the expanding Chinese economy. Similarly, hundreds of thousands of students from India see the accomplishment of an MBA as a path towards social and economic betterment.

Therefore, when China opted to become somewhat more capitalistic in orientation, government enterprises quickly understood that they would need to operate and be managed in the same manner as private corporations. Consequently, in 1991 they created a programme of training Chinese bureaucrats in MBA-style programmes in nine local universities; a decade later there were almost 250 pro-grammes, graduating more than 20,000 business professionals (Scri-menti, 2010).

This means that Chinese business professionals have other options besides studying abroad. And the government benefits because its best and brightest remain at home. This means China is avoiding what used to be termed the 'brain drain'. The presence of multinational corporations throughout China reinforces the demand for well-trained professionals who speak English or at least one other European language.

According to Scrimenti (2010), the China Europe International Business School (CEIBS) and Tsinghua University recently ranked behind Kellogg and Sloan as the best business schools to attend in the next ten years. Faculty from major universities all over the world are also accepting invitations to teach in China. Many more Chinese universities are forming joint ventures with American universities. University hubs are being set up throughout China, and not just in major cities such as Hong Kong, Shanghai and Beijing. As the Asian market continues to expand, there will continue to be greater demand for business expertise.

India, like China, is an expanding economic market. The invest-ment in education is not as government-driven as in China but a range of private entities are investing in India's corporate infrastructure. Regional expansion of educational institutions is another indicator of India's emergence. For example, the privately funded SP Jain Institute of Management and Research founded in Mumbai in 1981 is now recognised as a very competitive global business school with campuses in Singapore, Dubai and Sydney. It offers a one-year MBA programme taught by an international faculty though the students are almost all from India. In order to maintain academic freedom and flexibility, SP Jain is completely autonomous from Bombay University.

The Indian School of Business, with its strong global reputation and links to such US schools as Kellogg and Wharton, provides a platform for ISB students to be hired, for example, by management consulting companies for global assignments. As a result, India's best and brightest are more willing to stay within their home country, particularly with education and job opportunities on the rise, eliminating another reason for students to travel abroad.

Other growing for-profit universities in Asia are modelled on the University of Phoenix (Apollo Group) in the US. For example, India's Manipal University (formerly the Manipal School of Higher Education) was primarily a health science medical school that added engineering to its curriculum. It recently added business management to its course offerings and is also establishing itself internationally.

These for-profit schools are private institutions with private equity and have access to capital and are not subject to boards or regents or endowments for funding as with private and state universities in the US. Furthermore, as corporations they are now increasingly listed on stock exchanges, which allows for public equity capital. Other examples in India include EduComp and Everonn.

Corporate universities are yet another alternative. The MBA has become a generic degree (as opposed to a CPA or law degree, which requires testing and certification) and corporations prefer customised internal MBA programmes because they feel that while external offerings may have certain attractions there is no outside programme that addresses their needs or has the specific expertise their company requires. Another advantage is that internal MBA candidates do not need to leave the employer to further their education and may be able to continue their job duties in conjunction with their course work. Corporate universities have been on the rise since the 1980s. The most visible has been General Electric's Workout Program (Crotonville, NY).

In India, Infosys Technologies has the largest corporate education centre in the world in Mysore. It can accommodate 14,000 candidates at a time.

In India, Infosys Technologies has the largest corporate education centre in the world in Mysore. It can accommodate 14,000 candidates at a time. Infosys recruits 30,000–40,000 employees every year, most of them directly from undergraduate school. The group has built its own modern campus that no traditional university could replicate. Internal candidates attend eight to nine months of internal company training. At the end, they must pass an internal examination that is tougher than most private institutions' certification tests.

Infosys is making such a large investment in employees because it believes the best students will remain loyal and productive to the corporation. Society benefits because even those students who are not retained have acquired a skill set that they can use elsewhere. While this programme is focused on software workers, it is not difficult to duplicate for business education needs.

While most corporations view each other as competitors, there still remains a shared interest in having a well-trained workforce. Therefore, some organisations are collaborating to offer combined training courses, with each company responsible for one course rather than the entire curriculum. This system makes education programmes more affordable. For example, Wipro, Genpact, Mahindra & Mahindra, Colgate, Aditya Birla Group, Dr Reddy's and HDFC Bank in India have a shared leadership programme co-designed by them and delivered on their own campuses.

Education 'cities' and global knowledge hubs, which group educational institutions and even companies on the same site, are becoming more common in emerging markets.

For example, INSEAD prides itself on being an international business school with campuses in Singapore, Abu Dhabi and a research centre in Israel. It also partners with Wharton in the US, Tsinghua University in China and Fundação Dom Cabral in Brazil. In this way it can live up to its charter of providing graduates with a global perspective and cultural diversity (in its own words 'the business school for the world'). Although INSEAD's association with Wharton is privately funded, the governments of Singapore and the UAE invested heavily to have INSEAD on-site in their countries.

Other examples include Dubai, which hosts several top-tier universities including Boston University and Harvard University, London Business School, and the Rochester Institute of Technology. Qatar hosts Carnegie Mellon University, Georgetown University, Northwestern University, Texas A&M University, Virginia Commonwealth University, Weill Cornell Medical College; Incheon, in South Korea, has attracted SUNY at Stonybrook and North Carolina State University; while Kuala Lumpur, hosts Royal Holloway, a college of the University of London.

In summary, the demand for managers is being distributed globally and the desire of foreign students to go to American universities will continue to wane as more opportunities present themselves in the local context to students from India, China, Eastern Europe, the Middle East and Latin America.

Inclusive distance learning education

Many emerging economies have decided that it is as important to educate the base of their population (often below the poverty level of $2/day income households) as it is to provide opportunity to the literate elite of their societies. They realise the benefit of having a literate population and increasing educational opportunities from basic primary and secondary studies on through higher education.

The advent of new technologies is allowing many governments to develop affordable models using distance learning, web learning and open universities without formal admission standards. An example is the Indira Gandhi National Open University (IGNOU) in India. This has been modelled around the pioneering efforts of the Open University in the UK. And the affordable university model is also now becoming mainstream. Many state colleges and community colleges in the US are now offering undergraduate programmes through open enrolment, and online taught classes.

> Governments are coming to see innovative and affordable models as the best way of providing quality education to their citizens.

Other governments, which are the main providers of education funding, are coming to see innovative and affordable models as the best way of providing quality education to their citizens at much lower cost than brick and mortar schools. The 'open university' is not a new concept. The Open University in the UK, for example, began offering courses in the 1960s. Since its establishment, IGNOU has contributed significantly to the development of higher education in India through the Open and Distance Learning (ODL) mode.

Known as the 'People's University', IGNOU's curriculum follows a learner-centric approach and has successfully adopted a policy of openness and flexibility in entry qualifications, time taken for completion of a programme and place of study. The university at present offers 338 study programmes through over 3,500 courses in every state in India, giving accessibility and affordability to over 3 million students.

The Thunderbird School of Global Management, based in Glendale, Arizona, in the US, is a stand-alone business university that also offers a variety of full-time and part-time degrees and certification programmes throughout Latin America in Spanish using a distance learning model.

Higher education is no longer reserved for the elite. The accessibility and affordability of knowledge in emerging countries is not the result of traditional non-profit universities but of the initiative of local governments investing in alternative programmes. Just as societies are realising the importance of alternative sources of energy and medicine, so too are they understanding the value of alternative forms of education.

Distance learning is no longer on the fringe but is part of the mainstream and democratises the learning process in many emerging countries. What was once offered simply as continuing education has flourished into a variety of courses and curricula allowing people of all ages and situations to earn undergraduate and graduate degrees.

Students in emerging markets, therefore, can now choose to earn an MBA in a traditional brick and mortar, full-time programme, through weekend or limited residency programmes, through distance learning and in a variety of hybrid programmes being offered by traditional non-profit institutions, for-profit colleges and in-house corporate universities.

SUMMARY

As recently as the 1990s, middle managers and college graduates from Latin America and Asia were most likely to attend a business school in the US or the UK if they wanted to gain an MBA. Many secured jobs in multinational companies and quite often stayed in the West. Now, as commerce becomes more global, graduate education is becoming more local, exemplified by the expansion of both business programmes and graduates in China. In 1991 there were nine graduate business schools in China. At the time of writing, there are around 250 programmes and over 30,000 MBA graduates per year.

While most of these programmes do not represent the calibre of Harvard, Kellogg, Wharton, Sloan, Chicago, INSEAD, LBS, ESADE or IMD or a host of other prestigious MBA institutions, the influx of visiting professors from leading American business schools and the partnering of US/China programmes, such as Fordham and Peking University and the Sloan Center and Lingnan University, are welcome developments. Further, the progress of HKUST and CEIBS in China and ISB in India as highly rated business schools in the *FT* global rankings shows the rapid growth and competitive success of Asian and Indian business schools.

And as middle-class populations in China and India continue to grow, the demand for these programmes can only increase. All involved in providing higher education in management are in search of new resources. This search tends to both blur and revive the traditional distinctions made between public and private spheres of education (Durand and Dameron, 2008: 50). Nonetheless, as demand continues to grow in diverse populations those universities that avoid stagnation and the *status quo* will continue to develop relevant programmes.

It is estimated that within China alone over the next decade an additional 75,000 MBAs (who speak English) will be needed to satisfy Chinese business interests (Scrimenti, 2010: 7). Another interesting trend is that just as foreign students sought entry into American business schools for much of the latter part of the twentieth century, some Western students are now applying to Chinese, Asian and Indian business schools.

India's burgeoning economy, fuelled by a growing middle class, has made the MBA a more valuable degree than ever before. The rise of top-tier management schools such as the IIMs and ISBs is making it more appealing than ever for Indians to go to business school in their home country rather than pay for a brand-name American degree (Damast, 2008: 3).

> India's burgeoning economy, fuelled by a growing middle class, has made the MBA a more valuable degree than ever before.

The rapid growth of emerging markets is generating an unprecedented demand for educated and certified business professionals and leaders. This, coupled with more advanced and accessible technology, has given rise to a hybrid of university-based and corporate-based bachelors' and MBA programmes. Online and distance learning MBAs are one of the fastest-growing segments in education – gaining respect, influence and a niche of professional students thirsty for a degree that allows them to stay within their region of the world (Hochberg, 2006: 7).

Universities and business schools must seize this opportunity to educate a growing crop of business leaders in emerging markets. No matter how large or prestigious a university is currently, it will not continue to retain its size, scale, budget reserves or influence if it is not willing to change and adapt to the current status of the world. Stagnation is the greatest threat to educational institutions, especially since the life cycle of knowledge (i.e. software, social media, supply chain and energy) is decreasing. Much of what is known in the business arena is obsolete in eighteen months or less.

As once-isolated cultures join the global marketplace thanks to emerging technologies and the investment in infrastructure (e.g. fibre optics and satellite) by their governments, more and more working professionals are demanding MBA programmes that offer expertise, connectivity and flexibility.

Schools must give business managers and leaders the ability to compete in the global marketplace. This preparation includes addressing the business and social issues around energy, transportation, food and water, technology, healthcare and the environment. Social consciousness and stakeholder awareness will also prove to be very significant considerations in the marketplace. Just as MBA programmes need to adapt to global demands so too must business professionals not be content with obtaining a single degree or certification. They must participate in lifelong learning, which provides endless opportunities for universities to develop more programmes.

IMPACTS AND IMPLICATIONS OF ENTREPRENEURIAL ENTERPRISE

There has been a profound change in recent business school thinking. It has moved away from a concentration on big business and the rise of the multi-divisional firm towards a greater focus on the entrepreneur and entrepreneurship as legitimate areas of study. The growth and speed of technological change has created many new small businesses and many self-made billionaires, including the founders of Amazon. com (Jeff Bezos), Google (Larry Page) and Facebook (Mark Zuckerberg). Further, many entrepreneurial role models exist on both sides of the Atlantic, from Phil Knight at Nike, Frederick Smith at Federal Express, the late Steve Jobs at Apple and Bill Gates at Microsoft in the US to Alan Sugar at Amstrad, Richard Branson at Virgin and Philip Green at British Home Stores in the UK. In Asia we can point to Tony Fernandes, who modelled Air Asia on Ryanair and Southwest Airlines.

Their success has led many recent graduates to harbour entrepreneurial ambitions and set up their own businesses rather than settling for more conventional careers as corporate 'civil servants'.

Vesper and Gartner (1997) measured the progress in entrepreneurship education through the 1990s and reported that 311 business schools (about a third of the overall population of schools at that time) had some form of entrepreneurship programme – 233 of them were US schools, 16 were Canadian schools and 62 were schools in other countries. The top-rated US school was Babson in Wellesley, MA, which has developed entrepreneurship as a 'niche' area of strength. Harvard Business School and the Wharton School at the University of Pennsylvania closely followed it. In addition, guides to business schools such as those published by *US News and World Report*, *Businessweek* and *The Economist* also more recently reported that a majority of MBA programmes now offer entrepreneurship concentrations and elective courses for potential entrepreneurs. They are also adopting a range of innovations such as endowed entrepreneurial research centres, venture-capital funded prizes for the best entrepreneurial business plans and seed capital financing for students with innovative ideas and promising business plans.

> A majority of MBA programmes now offer entrepreneurship concentrations and elective courses for potential entrepreneurs.

Entrepreneurship, however, is not just the preserve of Western developed economies. For example, Infosys Technologies, set up in 1981 by seven young Indian entrepreneurs, is now a multi-billion dollar software company with 58,000 employees and a campus on the outskirts of Bangalore (*The Economist*, 2006: 9). Further, ethnic and minority business owners have grown many successful businesses in the UK, particularly in the food and hotel industries. Consequently, the study of family business has become important to business schools in the UK in cities such as Bradford, Leicester and Nottingham, which have strong minority interests and a range of successful businesses reflecting their ethnicity, cultural heritage and characteristics. Family businesses are also very important engines for growth in several Asian and Western countries.

Business schools must therefore recognise that demographic factors such as age and cultural/ethnic background are interacting with the growth of entrepreneurial activity to create a much stronger focus on the role of the small and medium-sized enterprise in business and economic growth. The recent global financial crisis has also stimulated many business school students to develop entrepreneurial ventures. With the increasing pace of technological change they may also need to provide entrepreneurship training for graduates from strong technical and scientific backgrounds whose ideas, if properly implemented, may themselves generate significant technological innovation and change.

In summary, the implications of entrepreneurial enterprise for management education include the following.

- Small businesses (new ideas, disruptive technologies) will become increasingly important as engines for economic growth.
- Family businesses, and their growth opportunities, will be an increasing focus in emerging markets.
- There will be a new focus on linkages between technology (IT, engineering, etc.) and management.
- There will be enhanced teaching of entrepreneurial and emerging business skills.
- New business start-ups and ideas will be made the focus for real-time projects in entrepreneurship education linking incubators and university start-ups to business schools.

COMPETITIVE FORCES AND DYNAMICS FOR BUSINESS SCHOOLS

The main elements in the competitive environment are illustrated in Figure 3.2, which maps the competitive forces influencing business school rivalry.

The competitive landscape in management education is clearly changing with the advent of increasing competition from quality schools in Europe, the Americas and Asia and with engineering- and science-based management programmes offering substitutes (e.g. Sciences Po, Paris, or Imperial in the UK) for conventional business

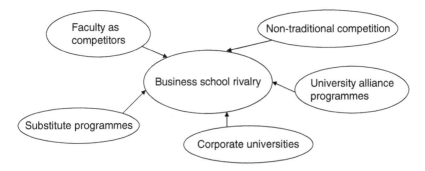

FIGURE 3.2 Competitive forces and dynamics for business schools

school programmes. As Hawawini (2005) notes 'top business schools will either transfer themselves to meet the demands (of a more complex environment) or cede some of the terrain to alternative providers of business education'. Some of those providers are illustrated in Figure 3.2 and include the types discussed below.

CORPORATE UNIVERSITIES

The best-known example of a corporate university is General Electric's Crotonville campus, often dubbed Harvard-on-the-Hudson. According to *The Economist* (2006), Jack Welch, the former CEO, spent half of his time on 'people development' and visited Crotonville every two weeks. Crotonville was seen as the engine for developing and strengthening GE's corporate talent. Other companies such as Goldman Sachs and EON in Europe, Infosys in India, and Apple and Motorola (Reynes, 1998) in the US have also developed their version of corporate universities. Such 'universities' compete, but sometimes also collaborate, with the customised executive education programmes developed for corporations by leading business schools worldwide (Meister, 1998).

FACULTY AS COMPETITORS

Leading academic gurus such as Michael Porter at Harvard, Henry Mintzberg at McGill and Gary Hamel at LBS have become quasi-competitors and almost industries in themselves. For example,

Porter is one of the founders of the Monitor Consulting Company while Hamel is similarly one of the founders of Strategos Consulting. Often companies view such faculty gurus and stars as key strategic resources and approach them to provide training, consulting and coaching services that might otherwise be provided through executive training from leading business schools. Perhaps the most innovative faculty-based consulting company was Management Analysis Center (MAC), which encompassed more than 100 faculty members from all over the world. They were backed up by professional consultants who handled the operational logistics. Academics who brought projects into the firm were then given attribution by the firm and ideally encouraged to lead the follow-through to project implementation.

UNIVERSITY ALLIANCE PROGRAMMES

Any issue of *The Economist* magazine offers examples of alliance programmes in its classified advertisement section. Examples include the TRIUM Global Executive MBA, which offers a collaborative programme using faculty drawn from New York University (NYU) in the US, Hautes Ecoles Commerciales (HEC) in Paris and London School of Economics (LSE) in London to produce an MBA degree with an international flavour. Other programmes such as the the HKUST–Northwestern EMBA offer the best of two MBA programmes and thus attempt to enhance the career prospects of students. The aims are typically to enhance the perceived reputation and brand image of each school in the alliance and to strengthen its competitive positioning. Further objectives are often to build global identity and strength for each partner at the expense of other rivals but also to enable Executive MBA students to build global expertise and enhance their cultural intelligence and sensitivity.

NON-TRADITIONAL COMPETITION

The earlier discussion on emerging markets shows clearly that an increasing number of universities, but also for-profit providers, are offering distance learning education programmes off campus generally using online resources. The largest of these, the Apollo Group (traded on NASDAQ), which owns the University of Phoenix, caters for over 40,000 MBA students according to the *FT* survey of distance learning education (*Financial Times*, 2006).

Existing university providers in the UK including Henley, the Open University and Warwick Business School (WBS) cater for much smaller numbers – around 5,000, 4,000 and 1,750 students respectively. These schools and a range of other university-based schools are at a competitive disadvantage relative to the University of Phoenix, which has lower costs, access to flexible resources, the ability to move rapidly to change content and a very competitive pricing strategy. However, the relative strength of the top universities is their ability to tap research and devise 'leading-edge' educational content.

As Lorange (2005: 785) notes, 'a new competitive landscape for today's business schools is emerging'. Innovation is clearly needed to overcome the strong and overly disciplinary focus of undergraduate business education and change MBA offerings to develop managers and not conventional MBAs graduates (Mintzberg, 2004), perhaps with modified forms of project-based action learning. Executive and non-traditional forms of MBAs will grow in importance as flexible, on-the-job training becomes the norm.

> Executive and non-traditional forms of MBAs will grow in importance as flexible, on-the-job training becomes the norm.

In summary, the implications of competition and competitive dynamics for management education include:

- a future shake-down of business school programmes;
- a consolidation of departments and programmes;
- a constant search for productivity improvements because of competitive pricing and creative segmentation;
- continuing growth of alliances, inter-university consortia programmes;
- a renewed focus on business school core competencies and viable niches (e.g. location, entrepreneurship);

- regular refocusing of the core disciplines;
- an examination of multi-disciplinary perspectives;
- a search for new business school models and paradigms;
- a greater stakeholder orientation.

RETHINKING THE BUSINESS SCHOOL MODEL

The many criticisms examined so far make the case for a reconfigured business school playing a central role in the context of the new global economy and knowledge society. Such a school would develop new thinking and knowledge and provide a reflective and reflexive site for inquiry into business management. This knowledge-based business school is an alternative to more 'business-as-usual' scenarios. These involve variations of the existing US model including takeover by management consultants/alternative providers leading to 'dumbing down' and commoditisation of programmes. Other, more academic approaches focus on either a professional school (i.e. practically relevant agenda) model or a more rigorous intellectual agenda grounded either in the social sciences or a liberal arts agenda (see also Ivory et al., 2006).

UK and European business schools provide evidence of the existence of alternative business school models. For example, LBS and INSEAD focus very closely on peer US schools such as Wharton, Harvard and Northwestern and adopt a variation of the US-style business school model. Ashridge, Henley and Cranfield and probably Instituto de Empresa in Madrid have an agenda of practical relevance (e.g. Cranfield's recent advertisements stress that over 90 per cent of their faculty have real business experience) and exemplify professional schools. Lancaster and WBS build their programmes on strong social science-based research. On the other hand, the model of a critical school of management is perhaps closer to the humanities and liberal arts rather than the social sciences.

However, the strategic choice among alternative and new business school models is very significant as school deans and senior managers increasingly grapple with the pressing issue of how to rethink and reconfigure the business school model in a very challenging and critical environment.

An interesting but very radical new model has been put forward by Peter Lorange as an innovative business school approach and we present this here simply as a vehicle for dialogue and debate which should illuminate the process of critical and thorough evaluation of several further new approaches examined in Chapters 4 and 5.

Lorange has a unique experiential background that might give credence to his way of thinking. Not only does he have a long experience from leading academic institutions – as a professor at Sloan (MIT) and Wharton and as President of the Norwegian Business School (BI) and IMD (for fifteen years). He also built, and solely owned, a substantial shipping company. Thus, his experience stems from both camps: academia and practice.

THE LORANGE INSTITUTE OF BUSINESS MODEL FOR MANAGEMENT EDUCATION

We would state at the outset that this description of the Lorange model is summarised from earlier articles and robust discussions with Peter Lorange. Consequently, we have used the first-person singular at times in the exposition to reflect the strength of his commitment to these issues (see Lorange, 2010, 2012).

Introduction

Several prominent voices have criticised business schools and the traditional full-time MBA. They argue that the classical business curriculum helped develop business leaders who contributed to today's global economic crisis. There are several good reasons why their criticism, at least in part, is valid.

> Students do not learn to recognise critical turning points or understand the factors that make the difference between success and failure.

First, most business schools teach *linear thinking*. Too often, students learn to make decisions in an 'either/or' or 'positive/negative' fashion. They often do not work actively with the constant up–down, in–out, long–short movements of business cycles. They do not learn to recognise critical turning points or understand the factors that make the difference between success and failure. Those students then become real-world leaders, whose lack of understanding can lead to decisions and strategies that make the peaks and valleys of business cycles much more severe.

Perhaps such a fallacy of linear thinking might most readily be seen in the ocean shipping business, where timing is all. But it is also true for other capital-intensive businesses such as cement and pulp paper. Indeed, it is relevant to all industries since they seem to be exposed to cycles to some degree.

Second, business schools often teach students to focus on *short-term bottom-line results* even though long-term growth is equally important. They often fail to remind students that a company's customers are just as important to its financial success as its shareholders.

Third, while business schools have made changes to their curricula to eliminate 'silos' and teach across disciplines, they still are hampered by outdated approaches that keep the silo mentality firmly entrenched.

Finally, in general, today's business schools seem to be heavily committed to *full-time education*, particularly the full-time MBA. But that does not reflect the rapid pace of business, where leaders need lessons they can use in the workplace today, not one or two years from now. Part-time educational formats are more important than ever because they allow students to continue to work during their courses and offer them opportunities to apply immediately what they learn. Equally importantly, part-time programmes allow students to bring to the classroom the practical insights they gain on the job. And, speed is key here – what matters is to be able to develop the relevant knowledge in business *today*. The implication is that the bureaucratic discussion so typically associated with many business schools may become more of an impediment than ever before.

Executive education deserves a more prominent role in a business school's mission statement. To use language from marketing, many business schools might need to change the 'mix' of their offerings to better reflect the needs of twenty-first-century business.

Moving from 'me' to 'we'

Some business schools have recognised that teaching in silos is a dysfunctional way to teach management – and that is a good thing. These schools have devised new, more integrative curricula. They are assigning more project work and encouraging faculty from different disciplines to work as teams to teach the same courses. These efforts are all admirable – however, they might not be enough.

Why? Because while business schools might be changing how they teach, they are not necessarily changing how their faculty thinks. Even with business schools' efforts to integrate curricula, too many faculty members still work in disciplinary isolation. They may still work in separate departments, garner titles based on academic speciality and seek tenure in their disciplines. They may pursue scientific research and publish predominantly in leading journals. The business curriculum might be integrated; but business faculty, most often, may not be.

That reality encourages a 'me, me, me' attitude among faculty members, which keeps them separate from their colleagues in other disciplines. As long as this is the case, the silo mentality will stay strong.

But eliminating departments might not necessarily eliminate disciplinary silos. For example, at IMD in Lausanne, Switzerland, there were no titles, no departments and no tenure. Still, the bulk of IMD's professors stayed with the school for a long time, settling into their specialities. As a result, even at IMD, we had silo elements. Even there we could not break free into a truly integrated way of thinking.

However, in today's world it seems evident that academics must work across boundaries to create learning, teaching and research environments that embrace a 'we, we, we' spirit. Today – more than ever – we need an environment with no silos, where business is seen as a whole, not as a series of parts.

The right direction

I have not seen a business school today that completely fits my vision of what management education should be. But several schools seem to be heading in the right direction.

IMD heavily emphasises executive education and the Executive MBA, which allows participants to transfer knowledge into their companies and encourages them to consider how what they learn in class will work in practice. The Scandinavian International Management Institute in Copenhagen, Denmark, relies on part-time faculty and so does IEDC-Bled Business School in Slovenia. This might lead to fewer silos by design.

Duke Corporate Education – the customised executive education arm of Duke University's Fuqua School of Business in Durham, North Carolina, in the US – has done a particularly good job in dissolving silos. With its partners, the LSE in the UK and the Indian Institute of Management Ahmedabad, Duke CE uses part-time faculty almost exclusively and allows clients to have a say in the design of their programmes and the choice of faculty. Still, the faculty who teach this programme have completed their research at their primary academic institutions, where they have been largely isolated by discipline.

A new paradigm

How can we develop a new paradigm of management education, one that links the classroom, the real world and business disciplines in a fluid fashion? In August 2009 I purchased the Graduate School of Business Administration (GSBA) Zurich – which has now been renamed the Lorange Institute of Business Zurich – where we can put this model into practice.

I chose GSBA Zurich for several reasons. With its network of forty part-time professors and a student body of approximately 900 students, GSBA is a relatively small school, one that I could better 'get my hands around' to create a new environment for students and faculty. In addition, its infrastructure is not as driven by bureaucracy as other, larger schools. The physical campus facilities are excellent for executive learning in a great location on Lake Zurich. Finally, the 40-year-old institution offered the advantages of an established network of students and alumni and a location in a business centre only thirty minutes from Zurich airport.

The programmes will be completely part-time, there are no permanent faculty and there will always be fresh perspectives coming through the doors. Because our students continue to work and our faculty come from a variety of institutional and research backgrounds, we will maintain a continuous connection to the changing business world.

> The aim of the Lorange Institute is to develop an alternative 'blueprint' for how a top business school will look in the future.

The brand

The Lorange Institute of Business Zurich stands for visionary thinking, with high quality and credibility for all its activities.

Faculty

There are three types of faculty – senior faculty, junior faculty and practitioners. Senior faculty are called upon as needed through a student-/user-/customer-driven way of activating faculty inputs. The aim is to find the best professors worldwide to become involved in any programme that the school offers. To ensure a stable senior faculty network, relationships are developed both with the faculty member and with the school where he or she has his/her primary appointment. Full transparency is sought for faculty members' involvement.

It is key that each senior faculty member sees himself/herself as both a member of his/her host academic institution and as a member of the Lorange Institute. This relationship requires a deeper commitment than occurs when someone 'moonlights' at another institution. Commitment is central to any meaningful learning process. The senior faculty member's temporary residence in Zurich ensures informal interaction with students and other stakeholders on campus and during meals, field trips and other curricula and activities. The faculty thus represents a stable – almost permanent – group of part-time lead individuals.

> It is key that each senior faculty member sees himself/herself as both a member of his/her host academic institution and as a member of the Lorange Institute.

The institute works with each senior faculty member on a regular basis regarding his/her research, pedagogical approaches and curricular developments as well as maintaining an active relationship with the faculty member's primary school.

In addition, it involves senior faculty extensively in the governing processes. This involves faculty meetings, individual meetings with faculty members when they are on campus, as well as virtual, remote faculty meetings. The 'performance' of a faculty member will be addressed yearly, with inputs from each faculty member concerning research outputs and teaching innovations.

A number of junior faculty will be appointed by the institute on a full-time basis to contribute to co-ordination between the several teaching modules, to play active roles in the research through supporting senior faculty, to co-teach various sessions and to interact with the students. Junior faculty will thus function as integrators, bringing an eclectic focus into the institute's programmes.

There will also be a number of leading practitioners on the teaching staff. These are leading experts within particular fields. They possess expertise that is typically found among senior professors in the academic community. The practitioners will function as bridge-builders to the business world, bringing problems, solutions and thought-provoking impulses into the institute's programmes.

A meeting place

New ideas, new thoughts, new propositions are brought forward in the classroom, in debates with executive guests and in the institute's various forums. The institute aims to be a constructive meeting place with propositions being held up against prescriptions in healthy debate, involving listening, learning and give-and-take. This is another way of stating that the institute is fully committed to a Socratian process – two-way learning rather than one-way teaching.

A good mixture of participants further enhances the meeting place through their highly qualified educational backgrounds, diverse professional experiences and varied international origins. Participants bring their own business experience to the institute and cross-fertilise with the faculty, other students and business leaders.

Cutting-edge innovation

All activities aim to be cutting-edge, both when it comes to what goes on in the classroom and to research. All businesses go up and down. The Lorange Institute focuses on examining and discussing these issues rather than 'linear' positive or negative thinking. It takes inspiration from wealth management, shipping and other capital-intensive industries.

Sustainability also plays a central role. This includes more than a focus on renewable issues. A long-term emphasis, probing the critical roles of new technology and stakeholder-based implementation concerns, is key.

Participants take their new insights back to their organisations and 'best practice' is continuously received from them. Hence, we can talk about a partnership between the host organisations where the participants work and the Lorange Institute, which aims at being an innovator for academia in the broadest sense.

Modular programme structure

Classroom teaching is structured in modules so that participants are immediately able to take their learning back to their jobs. Participants tend to be older and to hold full-time corporate positions. It is key that participants keep their full-time jobs while attending our executive programmes. High motivation is a hallmark and being able to continue their growth in their practical daily life is essential today. And after all, good jobs do not come about that easily – who would give up such positions to go back to school?

> Classroom teaching is structured in modules so that participants are immediately able to take their learning back to their jobs.

Programme offerings

There are six areas of focus, each one leading to an Executive Master of Science degree:

- wealth management and management of financial institutions;
- high-value goods marketing (luxury goods);
- shipping, with its emphasis on taking advantage of business cycles;
- human resources management;
- use of information technology and communications science to generate new business revenue;
- sustainable strategies.

The focus is thus on specialisation, though later participants can broaden their experience further to earn an Executive MBA degree by enrolling in additional modules. The living case method involves real-life analysis, recommendations and presentations by student teams for specific companies, represented by senior executives. This gives participants a better appreciation of the managerial point of view based on analysis and an ability to be an effective proponent of his/her recommendations.

So, the guiding principle behind the Lorange Institute of Business Zurich is to offer top academic quality, stimulated by careful 'listening' to the Institute's key prospective users: a modularised set of programme offerings, to encourage participants to maintain their corporate full-time jobs while also attending the Lorange Institute – effective two-way learning (!); to engage the best professors available to cover a given topic from anywhere in the world, rather than rely on one's own permanent staff – network thinking(!); and to be as un-bureaucratic as possible – fast, customer oriented. And, dialoguing with key user groups, on an ongoing basis, is seen as key – cutting-edge innovative ways of approaching academic learning may result from this.

Several programme offerings are also specially tailored to practising executives. There are short modules within each area of specialisation that are open to executives as well as the degree-level participants. There are also executive programmes in areas such as how to create more effective boards, strategy implementation and temporary management.

The business organisation – no bureaucracy

A flat hierarchy in the school's governance guarantees fast decision making. Procedures are codified and standardised and outsourcing is used to the fullest degree.

Integration across axiomatic divides

We attempt to ensure both academic rigour and relevance through teaching modules that tend to be predominantly discipline-based, axiomatic and covering the basic disciplinary foundations. Further, a module will typically attempt to cover state-of-the-art elements of various disciplines. The living case method is central to this – allowing the participants to work with senior executives on real-life problems. Here they must learn how to integrate and use various disciplines in attempting to solve current business problems and cases.

The thesis requirement also adds to the eclectic integration focus in the Lorange Institute's teaching. Various axiomatic disciplines are combined in the analysis, synthesis and write-up of a particular real-life situation.

Summary

The vision of the Lorange Institute of Business Zurich is to develop world-class graduate-level executive education in an alternative way to that followed by traditional business schools. This alternative way is founded on a stable network of part-time faculty with no 'silos', no offices, no tenure, no academic departments. Further, the participants are part-time, with their learning in the classroom complementing their learning on the job. The pace is high – speed is the key. And the focus is on real-life practical approaches.

Making it work

This model presents significant challenges. We know we must attract strong first-tier research faculty, because research is key for cutting-edge teaching. However, we realise that other institutions have cultivated the talents and research skills of these faculty. We do not want to be accused of cherry picking the best talent from other schools so we will ensure that their commitment to their home institutions is fully recognised. We will not only support our part-time faculty members but also compensate their parent institutions for their contributions.

In addition, we will embrace a 'flat hierarchy' where all faculty are involved with the governance of the school so that we can eliminate bureaucracy. We will form a faculty senate, who will be in continuous contact with school leadership regarding curricula design and development. Faculty also will reside on campus to encourage informal, daily interaction with students and other stakeholders.

Our participants will be older executives – typically 35 to 45 years old – with different professional, educational, cultural and national backgrounds. They will bring their real-world experiences into each course and be able to put what they learn to the test almost immediately. We will teach through 'living' case studies, which will be assigned to participants as consulting projects or presented by guest speakers who have lived them. Our EMBA students will complete 'living research projects' that will demonstrate positive impact on them and the companies where they work.

In all respects, we view this new school as a meeting place for ideas. It will be a place where participants and faculty share their immediate experiences.

'Constructive' innovation

Clayton Christensen (1997) talks of 'disruptive innovation'. I do not see my purchase of GSBA as disruptive in the way Christensen describes. Still, what we are doing is different from what one might find as accepted sound practice in most business schools. We aim to make the customer – the participant – the central focus of our attention. We have a culture that allows us do this, to an extent at least, at the expense of the professor (typically the centre-piece in most schools' cultures).

Many might view this approach as controversial. But, I view it as constructive, rather than disruptive, innovation. I argue that we should not be criticising what business schools do or do not do or what they have or have not accomplished. Instead, we should be acting on what our customers need from us – fully integrated education that, at all times, links the curriculum to the workplace. I want to create an alternative to the *status quo* of management education and push it in a new direction.

> We aim to make the customer – the participant – the central focus of our attention.

I think that we might be missing the most critical factor in effective business education: guarded optimism. We must be optimistic that we can change the way we teach business, that we can create new business opportunities for our students and faculty. To do that, we must change our model so that the focus is squarely on participants – rather than on faculty. Good must always be done better!

CONCLUSION

The purpose of this chapter was to stimulate debate about the challenges and opportunities for business schools as they rethink their approaches to management education and choose (and implement) their new models and paradigms. The Lorange model discussed here is certainly a more radical and extreme alternative to the *status quo* – with its constituents of part-time faculty, no silos, no offices, no tenure, no academic departments and a fully integrated education philosophy that links the curriculum to the learning process in the workplace. It provides a clear range of options that should provide insight and guidelines as we assess and discuss the innovative new range of business school models in Chapters 4 and 5.

REFERENCES

AACSB. (2011). *Globalisation of Management Education: Changing International Structures, Adaptive Strategies, and the Impact on Institutions.* Bingley: Emerald.

Bartlett, C. and Ghoshal, S. (1989). *Managing Across Borders: The Transnational Solution.* Boston: Harvard Business School Press.

Cabrera, A. and Bowen, D. (2005). Professionalising global management for the twenty-first century. *Journal of Management Development,* 24(9): 783–91.

Christensen, C. M. (1997). *The Innovator's Dilemma.* Boston: Harvard Business School Press.

Damast, A. (2008, 13 April). In India, MBAs remain in demand. *Bloomberg Businessweek.*

Datar, S., Garvin, D. A. and Cullen, P. G. (2010). *Rethinking the MBA: Business Education at a Crossroads.* Boston: Harvard Business School Press.

De Meyer, A. (2012). Reflections on the globalisation of management education. *Journal of Management Development,* 31(4): 336–45.

Drucker, P. (1989). *The New Realities* (revised edn, 2003). New Brunswick: Transaction Publications.

Durand, T. and Dameron, S. (2008). *The Future of Business Schools*. Houndmills: Palgrave Macmillan.

The Economist. (2005, 10 September). The brains business.

(2006, 7–13 October). The search for talent.

Financial Times. (2006, 20 March). Issue on distance learning.

Fleck, J. (2012). Blended learning and learning communities: opportunities and challenges, *Journal of Management Development*, **31**(4): 398–411.

Friedman, T. L. (2005). *The World is Flat: A Brief History of the Twenty-First Century*. New York: Farrar, Straus and Giroux.

Ghemawat, P. (2008). Reconceptualizing international strategy and organization. *Strategic Organization*, **6**(2): 195–206.

Hamalainen, M., Whinston, A. B. and Vishik, S. (1996). Electronic marketing for learning: education brokerages on the internet. *Communications of the ACM*, **39**(6): 51–8.

Hawawini, G. (2005). The future of business schools. *Journal of Management Development*, **24**(9): 770–83.

Hirsch, E. D., Jr. (1987). *Cultural Literacy: What Every American Needs to Know*. New York: Houghton-Mifflin.

Hoare, S. (2006, 19 January): Focus report on MBA programmes, *The Times*.

Hochberg, J. M. (2006). Online distance education pedagogy: emulating the practice of global business. *Distance Education*, **27**(1): 129–33.

Iniguez, S. (2011). *The Learning Curve: How Business Schools are Re-Inventing Education*. New York: Palgrave MacMillan.

Ivory, C., Miskell, P., Shipton, H., White, A., Moeslein, K. and Neely, A. D. (2006). *The Future of Business Schools in the UK: Finding a Path to Success*. London: Advanced Institute of Management Research.

Livingston, J. S. (1971). Myth of the well-educated manager. *Harvard Business Review*, **49**(1): 79–89.

Lorange, P. (2005). Strategy means choice: also for today's business school. *Journal of Management Development*, **24**(9): 783–91.

(2010). New challenges for value-creation in the modern business school, *Business Leadership Review*, **7**(4): 1–7.

(2012). The business school of the future: the network-based model. *Journal of Management Development*, **31**(4): 424–31.

Lutz, W. (2011). Demographic challenges affecting business schools. *Journal of Management Development*, **30**(5): 463–73.

McCann, J. E. (2006): The next economy. *BizEd*, March/April.

McGee, J., Thomas, H. and Wilson, D. (2010). *Strategy: Analysis and Practice* (2nd edn). New York: McGraw-Hill.

Meister, J. (1998). *Corporate Universities: Lessons in Building a World Class Workforce* (revised edn). ASTD (American Society for Training and Development).

Mintzberg, H. (1973). *The Nature of Managerial Work*. New York: Harper & Row.

(2004). *Managers, Not MBAs: A Hard Llook at the Soft Practice of Managing and Management Development*. San Francisco: Berrett-Koehler Publishers.

Newman, J. H. (1852). *The Idea of the University*. London: Longmans, Green.

Ohmae, K. (1985). *Triad Power: The Coming Shape of Global Competition*. New York: Free Press.

Porter, M. (1990). The competitive advantage of nations. *Harvard Business Review*, March/April: 73–93.

Reynes, R. (1998, 1 October). Motorola University changing with the company. *Meetingsnet*.

Schoemaker, P. J. (2008). The future challenges of business: rethinking management education. *California Management Review*, 50(3): 119–39.

Scrimenti, M. (2010, 16 December). China business schools hit their stride. *Bloomberg Businessweek*.

Sheth, J. N. (2008). *Chindia Rising: How China and India Will Benefit Your Business*. New Delhi: Tata McGraw-Hill.

Sheth, J. N. and Sisodia, R. S. (2004). *Tectonic Shift*. Delhi: Response Books/Sage.

Thomas, M. and Thomas, H. (2012). Using new social media and Web 2.0 technologies in business school teaching and learning. *Journal of Management Development*, 31(4): 358–68.

Vesper, K. H. and Gartner, W. B. (1997). Measuring progress in entrepreneurship education. *Journal of Business Venturing*, 12: 403–21.

Watson, S. R. (1993). The place for universities in management education. *Journal of General Management*, 19 (Winter): 14–42.

4   A framework for re-evaluating paradigms of management education

INTRODUCTION

The previous chapter addressed the many challenges facing the context and relevance of management education and emphasised the importance of re-evaluating and rethinking existing models. This chapter tries to provide some benchmark information and a set of guidelines and general principles for improving management education based on our collective experience. It adds to the Lorange model (see pp. 123–34) with one developed by Professor Jagdish Sheth that outlines an interactive framework detailing the 'bad habits' of business schools and examining how they should then embrace the opportunities provided by the changing business environment.

This is followed in Chapter 5 by an evaluation and analysis of a number of innovative new models of management education using the Sheth framework and the results from a recent study of new MBA models carried out by Professor Datar and his colleagues at Harvard Business School (Datar et al., 2010).

THE SHETH MODEL FRAMEWORK

Since the financial crisis of 2008, business as a capitalist institution has received much criticism, especially with respect to its obsessive focus on creating shareholder value as opposed to shared value (Porter and Kramer, 2011; Currie et al., 2010). By association, business and management education, as indicated earlier, has also come under criticism about its relevance, purpose, mission and curriculum, and about its teaching, research and service outcomes.

Business schools, despite often possessing a strong financial base through record numbers of student applications, good fundraising and solid reserves are now often at a strategic crossroads and at a turning point in their evolution. There is growing mistrust of capitalism as business leaders reward themselves with high salaries and bonuses. They are often not seen as creating greater good for society. Traditional approaches of philanthropy and corporate social responsibility (CSR) are often perceived as 'Trojan horses', paying 'lip service' to CSR and generating undirected debate rather than action. Unfortunately, this has been exacerbated over the past five decades as business leaders have emphasised that creating shareholder value is the only purpose of business using catchphrases such as 'The social business of business is business'.

The new generation of business students are now questioning what companies are doing for sustainability and community when they make their career choices. There are new movements seeking to broaden the purpose of business into a 'triple bottom line' (profit, people and planet) focus – for example, *Conscious Capitalism* (Sisodia et al., 2008) advocated by Raj Sisodia and supported by John Mackey at Whole Foods or *Connected Capitalism* advocated by Neville Isdell, a former chairman of Coca-Cola.[1]

In Europe a number of business schools have increasingly advocated the virtues of stakeholder capitalism. They have been reinforced by management education organisations such as EFMD, EABIS (European Academy for Business in Society) and the GLRI (Global Leadership Responsibility Initiative).

Most business schools seem to be trapped by old paradigms of the role of business education in society. They are either unable or unwilling to change.

Instead of leading this change, most business schools seem to be trapped by old paradigms of the role of business education in society.

---

[1] N. Isdell and S. E. Eizenstat (2011, 16 March). Connected capitalism and the opportunities for the United States. At http://csis.org/event/connected-capitalism-and-opportunities-united-states

They are either unable or unwilling to change. The inability to change arises partly from orthodoxy and partly from accreditation standards. Unwillingness to change may arise from current strong levels of market demand and from the denial of the new realities of the business environment.

Unfortunately, this unwillingness to change and adapt for the future is fuelled by the recent focus on flagship full-time MBA degree programmes whose graduates command extraordinary salaries and signing bonuses primarily from strategy consulting and investment banking industries, where they are high-margin revenue-generators for the partners. This is further reinforced by reputation rankings started by *Businessweek* magazine and more recently developed by the *Financial Times*, which put significant emphasis on the employment and salaries of MBA graduates in their ratings of business schools.

Finally, both the shortage and very high entry-level salaries of faculty with minimal teaching loads (Peters and Thomas, 2011) suggest that business education may likely become another bubble just as we recently experienced the dot.com and real-estate bubbles (Sull, 2005). Indeed, the growth and high valuation of for-profit higher-education corporations and online education companies with no accreditation clearly indicates that market forces are encouraging what Alan Greenspan referred to, in a different context, as 'irrational exuberance'. It will perhaps create a speculative bubble and this may impact even the well-established, highly reputed, high-legacy business schools.

The most insightful question we have been asked by any CEO of a large company has been 'Why do good companies fail?' In Jagdish Sheth's (2007) research on decline in highly respected companies such as the Digital Corporation, Kodak, Sears, Xerox, Sony, HP, A&P and many others, he found that most good companies fail when they are either unable or unwilling to adapt in the face of external forces changing dramatically or disruptively. These forces include capital markets, regulation, technology, competition, globalisation and customers.

In fact, this research on why good companies fail comes to the conclusion that it is due neither to non-traditional competition nor to

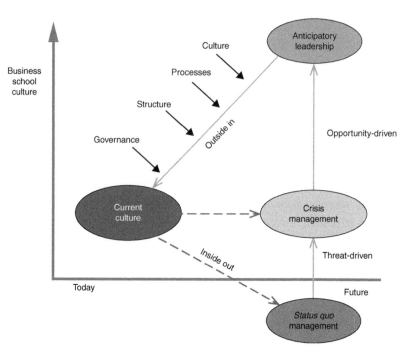

FIGURE 4.1 Threat- versus opportunity-driven transformation

the inevitable cycle of birth and death that is responsible for the decline of great institutions. Rather, it is due to acquiring self-destructive habits. Among the bad habits of good institutions are: denial, complacency, competency dependence, competitive myopia, internal turf wars and volume obsession (Sheth, 2007).

We believe that management education in general, and well-established business schools in particular, also suffer from the same bad habits and especially from denial, complacency, competency dependence and internal turf wars anchored to functional disciplines. Figure 4.1 depicts how business schools will need to go through the transition of crisis management before they embrace change and adapt to a changing environment.

Figure 4.1 suggests that if business schools continue to practise 'status quo' management and take an 'inside-out' perspective they are likely to decline over time. However, a 'wake-up' call occasioned by some crisis such as a drop in enrolments or a decline in reputation rankings will lead to crisis management and probably short-term survival. What is needed, however, is to anticipate drivers of change such as globalisation and technology advances and to adapt the organisation to them by transforming the existing culture, processes, structure and governance. In short, it will require transformation of the business school.

It is important to stress again that adapting to a changing environment will require transforming organisational processes and recipes. This can be achieved more easily only if leadership embraces change as driven by opportunity rather than threat. Unfortunately, transforming an existing institution is a lot harder than building a new one. The failures of trying to change existing culture are abundant, often resulting in non-renewal or resignation of deans and directors beyond one term (normally five years). The best time to change is typically when an organisation is doing well and before it reaches a state of crisis. Regrettably, the need to change is seen as having low priority then. It is only when there is a crisis that managers react and realise that change is needed. Action then is often too late.

BROADENING THE MARKET AND THE MISSION: THE STAKEHOLDER PERSPECTIVE

In our view, the long-term survival and growth of business and management education are only possible if it gains society's respect and relevance. In other words, what can we do to make business education respected and loved by society's stakeholders? It will require a fundamental shift on two dimensions. First, it must broaden its monolithic philosophy of the mission of management education as *creating value for the shareholder*. It must broaden its belief system to include *creating value for all of its stakeholders*. The latter includes not only investors but also employees, customers, suppliers and the community. It means balancing the often-conflicting interests of different stakeholders and developing a balanced scorecard that includes financial performance and profit but expands to include people and the planet or the 'triple bottom line' metaphor. Unfortunately, business disciplines are anchored to trade-offs and win–loss theories and beliefs. It is the dominant 'either–or' mindset and it needs to change to an 'and–and' mindset or what we call oxymoron management.

> The long-term survival and growth of business education is only possible if it gains society's respect and relevance.

Chakravarty and Lorange (2007) show in their research that there is no need to settle for either profits *or* growth – both can easily be achieved together resulting in 'and–and' outcomes. It is too easy to deliver shareholder value at the expense of customers, employees, suppliers and community. But it is a lot harder for business leaders to create a win–win value creation across all of its stakeholders as Lorange (2012) points out in his discussion of the philosophy of the Lorange model in Chapter 3. Business schools must lead in teaching both 'know-what' and 'know-how' to students and create insightful research about shared value.

In fact, in *Firms of Endearment*, Jagdish Sheth's 2007 book (with Raj Shishoda and David Wolfe), he found that companies delivering multiple-stakeholder value consistently outperformed the stock market by four times (46 per cent annualised return) and the *Good to Great* companies (Collins, 2001) by two times over more than fifteen years (1995–2010). Furthermore, none of them sought Chapter 11 bankruptcy protection during the fifteen years in contrast to two *Good to Great* companies and numerous companies in the S&P 500 Index.

Second, we should *broaden our target market to include both public and private sectors* as well as civic non-government organisations (NGOs). All sectors are interrelated today and this premise must be accepted in understanding management. As the market for private-sector businesses becomes very competitive and global, it will become increasingly necessary to grow the total market by extending management education and research to other sectors of the economy. This includes government and NGOs. For example, billions of dollars are now spent on advertising and social media in political elections. Also, large foundations are investing billions of dollars in global health and education issues. In degree programmes this means offering management education that is equally appropriate for for-profit as well as non-profit sectors and for private as well as public sectors.

The two largest non-profit sectors where management education is becoming increasingly relevant and respected are education and healthcare. So, for instance, in many Executive MBA programmes students include medical doctors and hospital administrators. In fact, many schools of public health offer management specialisations in public health. And, of course, there are separate schools of public administration at major universities.

The risk of too narrow an approach can be real. However, it is the examination of the interplay between the private and public sectors that is urgently required. There might be a similar growing need for business education in the government sector, including the defence sector. Managers in large government agencies, as well as regulatory bodies, may have little or no formal business education. Many countries such as India and China have civil service entrance examinations such as the Indian Administrative Service (IAS) or Indian Foreign Service (IFS) tests but regrettably with no formal business education requirement. In many advanced as well as emerging economies, most infrastructure industries are government owned and operated. They may be managed by professionals with non-business education. So there should be little wonder that since economics drives politics and policy there is increasing interest in the government sector for formal business education. It should be pointed out, however, that when Yale University launched its management school, the specific aim of the school was to educate its students in both *public* and *private* business, as was also reflected in the name of the school. Only after several years did Yale drop the word 'public' from its name. So general market perceptions may not (yet) open up for specific recognition of the term 'public'.

> Little wonder that since economics drives politics and policy there is increasing interest in the government sector for formal business education.

Finally, with the growth of large foundations and NGOs, as well as the increasing prevalence of public/private partnerships, there is a growing awareness of formal management education in civic societies and organisations. Business schools, therefore, must actively target students who are interested in working for non-business entities.

This will require a more holistic and integrative curriculum between liberal arts, sciences and business. While this is more common at the undergraduate level in the US and in four-year programmes in countries such as Singapore (e.g. Singapore Management University [SMU]), it is not prevalent in the traditional vocational programmes such as the Bachelor of Commerce (B Com) with specialisations in accounting or personnel management more common in the UK and other countries. In addition, it is extremely uncommon in any MBA degree programme; we are not aware of any MBA programme with strong liberal arts and science in its core curriculum.

In our view, integrative education is similar to integrative medicine. More and more medical colleges are educating their students in alternative medical therapies such as meditation, yoga, acupuncture, and herbal and homeopathic medicine. Similarly, business schools need to require of their students, as part of their non-elective core programme, a significant addition of humanistic sciences as well as natural sciences in their business curriculum. This is, of course, more do-able with the four-year time horizon of undergraduate business degrees and possibly in a five-year hybrid model of combined bachelors' and MBA degrees. It is only with this integrative education that we are likely to develop 'deep generalists' in place of experts for hire. At the University of Pennsylvania's Wharton School – the only 'Ivy League' institution that offers an undergraduate degree programme in business – there are clear requirements that students must take significant course loads in both the arts and sciences in addition to their business-focused courses.

A final aspect of integrated education is the fusion of cognitive and experiential learning. This is similar to the laboratory as part of the course offerings in engineering colleges; clinical practice as part of the course offerings in medical schools; fieldwork in public health; and extension services in agriculture. In other words, we need both the 'theory of knowledge' and 'theory in use' not as two separate complementary parts of the curriculum but as an integral part of each course in business.

Most business schools have summer internships and field studies and especially study-abroad programmes. However, they are generally supplemental to the core curriculum, which is predominantly cognitive and disciplinary in nature. To involve the participants in what might be seen as 'consulting-type' team activities might serve this purpose. At the Lorange Institute, for instance, the so-called living cases approach provides the participants with critical practical issues from a particular business organisation presented by a senior manager. Two weeks later groups of participants present their recommendations to senior management, with much directed discussion about the options. A similar form of interactive group 'consulting' project forms part of IMD's MBA curriculum.

The above discussion is summarised in Figure 4.2, which shows the need to embrace the public, private and voluntary sectors as well as an overarching stakeholder perspective.

Beyond stakeholder and wider management sector perspectives, another major area of market expansion is the rapid economic growth of emerging markets. The demand for business education in global and emerging markets is exploding. For example, India today graduates as many MBA students as the US, and China is not far behind. This is also likely to be the case for undergraduate business degrees as well as for evening and weekend programmes. However, this will be a challenging task because management education in emerging markets has to be affordable.

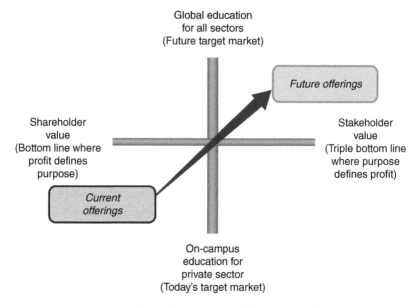

FIGURE 4.2 Broadening the market and the mission of business schools

As Jagdish Sheth has mentioned in *Chindia Rising* (2008), while necessity is the mother of invention, affordability is the father of innovation. Smart business schools will learn how to make their offerings affordable by designing innovative approaches including online MBA and bachelor's degree offerings without sacrificing academic quality and reputation. Some of the most recent examples of online MBA degree offerings in the US are Indiana University and UNC (Chapel Hill), with its 'one MBA' model. However, the one MBA concept was developed much earlier by Erasmus and Warwick in Europe, and schools such as CUHK (China) and ITESM (Latin America). Mention must be also be made of the pioneering efforts of the Open University Business School in the UK (Fleck, 2012; Thomas and Thomas, 2012), with its blended learning models.

> The down-market image of distance learning associated with correspondence schools and satellite-based education, will transform to make it perhaps the preferred medium supplemented by periodic campus visits.

It should be noted that business schools in India often align with local banks to offer student loans that make attendance at one- or two-year MBA programmes more attainable. And, there are grants from the government and non-profit foundations to support and sub-sidise management education if it is targeted toward public-sector enterprises and non-profit professionals.

The third way of broadening the market is through the wider development of *online business education* (*New York Times*, 2012). It is simply a matter of time before the tablet becomes the backpack and all teaching materials including textbooks are downloaded as e-books. (Note the announcement by Apple in January 2012 of its alliances with textbook publishers.) As the internet becomes universal and mobile computing becomes very affordable, online education for both degree and non-degree programmes will transform from a peripheral to a primary medium of education. The internet is a very rich medium capable of converging voice, video and data. It also has global reach. This will provide unprecedented access for well-established business schools with high reputation rankings. In other words, the down-market image of distance learning associated with correspondence schools and satellite-based education will transform to make it per-haps the preferred medium supplemented by periodic campus visits. The sooner schools participate in this opportunity, the better.

BUILDING SELECTION AND DEVELOPMENT VALUE:
HOW TO ENHANCE SELECTION VALUE

As pointed out by Moldoveanu and Martin (2008), what business schools need is to add both *selection* and *development* value in trans-forming human capital, especially in MBA programmes.

Selection value comes from screening and selection (and cru-cially *de*selection) of students who apply to business schools for degree and non-degree programmes. The two most common criteria for selection, based on past research, are general intelligence and conscientiousness. Standardised tests such as SAT and GMAT or GRE have proven to be good surrogates for these two personal traits.

While these have been historically relevant (although many critics of business education are sceptical), they are not sufficient for future selection for several reasons. With the rise of emerging markets (especially India and China) the number of undergraduate and MBA applications are destined to grow astronomically. For example, at the top ten private business schools in India, it is not uncommon to have 100,000 students apply for 1,000 places in full-time residential MBA programmes despite high tuition and living costs.

Good business schools are like a good diamond cutter, who has the experience and skill to cut a diamond and bring out its brilliance. However, a lot still depends on the quality of the rough diamond. This is also true in sport. A good coach (or scout) has a knack of identifying raw talent and then shaping and moulding that talent to become exceptional.

In both analogies, people recognise and admire the brilliant cut diamond and the exceptional athlete but often do not know who the diamond cutter or the coach is. It is not the ranking and reputation of a business school that matters but rather its selection process. This is most evident in India, especially for the Indian Institutes of Technology (IITs) in engineering and Indian Institutes of Management (IIMs) in management. In both cases, what differentiates them is neither their curriculum nor their research but the exceptional quality of their students. In Sheth's own experience in the late 1960s as a visiting professor at IIM-Kolkata, the students were simply outstanding and more motivated than at any institution he has taught in whether in the US or Europe. At the same time, the physical infrastructure, the library and the support staff were less than adequate.

Unfortunately, standardised tests such as SAT and GMAT suffer from both Type I and Type II statistical errors that result in inconclusive outcomes about the development of human capital. We need a selection methodology at both undergraduate and graduate level that goes beyond general intelligence and conscientiousness with several more filtering criteria to identify and select the right talent for generating future managers and scholars.

There are three criteria above and beyond standard assessment tests.

First and foremost is an applicant's *passion*. We have found that without exception, what matters most in any endeavour is passion. It has been the hallmark of great political leaders, great scholars, great thought leaders, great artists and great entrepreneurs. In fact, we believe it is a universal criterion for survival and success in life. Passion is even more necessary in organisations that have hierarchy, bureaucracy and often incompetent or unpleasant bosses. Passion sustains the person despite the organisational constraints. Otherwise, it results in burn-out. In academic and other non-profit institutions we have all witnessed the 'burn-out' of deans, provosts and presidents.

A second filter is an applicant's *purpose*. If the sole reason to get a degree is its earning capability measured by return on investment (ROI), it is likely that we will generate managers who will define their success only in terms of title and monetary compensation. It is even possible, as we have witnessed in recent decades, that they will manage businesses for their own personal gain at the expense of the organisation and its stakeholders, including investors. This has been recently amply demonstrated in the financial services sector and especially in the hedge fund community.

What we need to identify a 'high-quality diamond' is to ensure that the applicant is driven by purpose and not just economic motive. In other words, is the applicant purpose-driven while he/she aspires to be a business manager or leader? We do not believe a course on business ethics can have any long-term positive impact in shaping the values of future managers unless the student applicant comes with a belief in a purpose-driven life and career.

> Unfortunately, in recent years we have moulded many students to ignore or set aside whatever purpose-driven values they had prior to joining business schools.

Unfortunately, in recent years, with an obsessive focus on shareholder value, we have moulded many students to ignore or set aside whatever purpose-driven values they had prior to joining business schools, especially in an MBA programme.

Purpose is likely to become an increasingly necessary filter as many young people today look at an MBA as an investment whose lifetime value over the next fifteen to twenty years is astronomical. For example, a large majority of MBA graduates choose careers in strategy consulting and investment banking. This seems to be due to the higher compensation packages offered by those two industries. We believe this has also made purpose-driven careers less important in business schools. This is especially true of non-business graduates such as software engineers and liberal arts majors who do not see comparable economic returns in their own disciplines.

Purpose matters. It provides a moral compass. It generates good self-governance. It makes a person happy. We have personally mentored successful business leaders who made money without purpose and have observed that money without purpose makes life empty, meaningless and lonely. And we do not think purpose-driven values can be inculcated at an adult age and especially in the case of more mature and work-experienced MBA students.

The final filter is *compassion*. Does the applicant care for others? There is an increasing amount of scientific research today to validate the hypothesis that business leaders who care for others such as employees, customers, suppliers and the community deliver better performance for an organisation. This concept of a caring mindset goes back to McGregor's (1960) observations and experiments at the Hawthorne Works (Western Electric), which demonstrated greater productivity and effectiveness of factory workers if the supervisor was caring, as compared to the old command and control (Theory X) way of managing the workforce.

The key ingredient of caring is respect for others and empathy toward their situations and belief systems. This will become increasingly necessary in the era of cultural diversity for global enterprises.

Is an augmented selection process using the three criteria of passion, purpose and compassion feasible and practical? The answer is yes. It also accommodates worldwide affirmative action initiatives including the controversial reservation system in India. Passion, purpose and compassion are universal traits and recognise no ethnic, religious or gender boundaries.

It goes without saying that paying attention to the input side – that is, admitting high-quality students – is critical. Face-to-face interviews would often be desirable, in addition to tests and, perhaps, written essays meant to throw light upon the prospective student's motivation. In many cases interviews are often seen as both time-consuming and expensive. Nevertheless, several leading business schools insist on such face-to-face admissions interviews. This is the case for the entire admitted classes at IMD, the Lorange Institute and SMU (Singapore), for instance.

HOW TO AUGMENT DEVELOPMENT VALUE

The second aspect of transforming human capital is *development* value. Historically, development has been partly governed by accreditation standards and partly by business school culture. Accreditation is generally treated as an exogenous variable and the business school culture is treated as endogenous.

A business school's culture tends to be shaped by historical roots anchored to a discipline or pedagogy. For example, the University of Chicago, the Wharton School and University of Rochester are anchored to finance and economics. Harvard Business School is anchored to the case method. In general, most European business schools, even at the undergraduate level, are anchored to theory in social and economic sciences. However, their foci have included critical management studies and an emphasis on both humanities and public management.

> A business school's culture tends to be shaped by historical roots anchored to a discipline or pedagogy.

As mentioned in Chapter 1, the original British, German and French business schools were developed to generate specific vocational skills such as accounting and commerce, with no liberal arts education in the curriculum.

In the last century and after the Second World War, business school culture, at least in the US, shifted twice in a very significant way. The first was the development of the two-year full-time MBA following the Ford and Carnegie reports in 1959. While focused on analytical rigour and problem solving, the MBA was primarily designed for newly minted engineers to continue and broaden their education before joining a company. This replaced the traditional discipline-based progression from an undergraduate major in marketing, finance or accounting into graduate degree programmes such as masters' and doctorates in marketing, finance and accounting.

Consequently, Master of Science degrees went out of favour faced with the growth of two-year full-time MBA programmes, part-time evening MBAs for working professionals and weekend Executive MBA programmes (EMBA) for more senior leaders in an organisation.

Since the focus of the MBA was general management, discipline-anchored business school cultures began with a few exceptions to morph into an MBA and non-MBA academic divide. In fact, at the University of Virginia, it became necessary to break up the school of business into graduate (Darden) and undergraduate (McIntire) schools of business. At many other schools of business there is a clear caste system of graduate versus undergraduate faculty.

As the marketability of MBA graduates increased dramatically over time, the undergraduate programmes at many state universities became cash cows to be taught by doctoral students, resulting in an elitist MBA faculty culture. In fact, many private universities phased out or marginalised their undergraduate business degrees. The MBA degree became even more attractive in the 1980s when management consulting firms such as McKinsey and BCG began to recruit MBA graduates. This also transformed the business school culture into a market-driven one. It necessitated actively recruiting potential students and, more importantly, placing them in high-paying consulting and investment banking firms. Placement became more important than the management discipline itself.

A second major change that occurred in the late 1980s was the ranking of business schools by *Businessweek*, quickly followed by other business magazines such as *US News and World Report* and financial dailies. The *Financial Times* Global MBA Rankings have also become an important force as management education has globalised.

The rankings became close to an obsession for many deans. Understandably, perhaps, since renewal of their contracts often depended on enhancing their schools' rankings. This continues even today with the added pressure for rankings of competing non-US schools from Europe, Asia and now from all over the world. Reputation ranking has driven many curriculum reforms and faculty recruiting and retention initiatives. In other words, the market economy approach to development became the norm.

This was further exacerbated by the narrow definition of scholarship specified in reputation rankings. What mattered most was faculty publishing in top-tier academic journals in each functional discipline. The esoteric nature of these journals, often with a strong focus on empirical research, resulted in a 'publish or perish' culture. Faculty began to behave like full-time researchers in research laboratories and began to de-emphasise development value through classroom teaching, personal coaching and counselling outside the classroom. That responsibility often fell on non-tenured adjunct faculty and some business schools invented titles such as 'Professor of Clinical Practice' or 'Professor of Practice'. As a consequence, the schools created another caste system between research and teaching faculty. And, sadly, the fundamental link between research and teaching – two sides of the same coin – was lost (Mokyr, 2002).

In our view, based on nearly 140 combined years of academic experience at different business schools, we think this obsession with the MBA degree and with reputation rankings might have set back the value mission. What we need is to go back to an equal focus on teaching and on undergraduate degree programmes as well as redis-covering graduate degrees such as the Master of Science in different disciplines. It will require a non-linear change in faculty mindset about developing 'deep generalists' instead of just generalists.

ENABLING NON-LINEAR TRANSFORMATION

There are at least three dimensions on which the business school curriculum and faculty need non-linear transformation to adapt to the changing environment. The first and most critical is to incorpor-ate an *emerging markets perspective*.

As pointed out in *Tectonic Shift* (Sheth and Sisodia, 2006) and in *Chindia Rising* (Sheth, 2008), the twenty-first century will be driven by emerging markets with respect to innovation and competition from emerging market multinationals such as Haier, Huawei Tech-nologies, the Tata Group, Mittal Steel, and the Aditya Birla Group in aluminium and carbon black. Also, we might add to the list corpor-ations from newly developed countries such as Groupo Bimbo from Mexico, InBev from Brazil and SAB from South Africa. This will also shape the geopolitics of the world especially by the new trilateral relationships between India, China and the Americas.

Both faculty and students need to immerse themselves to gain a deep understanding of the unique issues of emerging markets. It is not enough for students just to have an international week there. They need to do internships and study abroad – say, for a semester or a year. This might be even more vital for the faculty. We have witnessed the fastest transformation of university cultures with faculty-abroad pro-grammes, even more so than student-abroad programmes. Our sug-gestion is that faculty at all ranks should be encouraged, if not mandated, to learn about emerging markets by teaching and doing research *in* and not *on* emerging markets. This is reverse learning. At one time, faculty from less-developed economies came to advanced countries for a doctoral degree or post-doctoral research and to learn the way these countries taught and researched. Now, it must be faculty from advanced countries undertaking serious visits to study and research in emerging markets.

A second dimension of transformative development is to anchor the curriculum to the three Is of learning rather than the three Rs (reading, writing and arithmetic) of learning. Learning must be *interactive, integrated* and *individualised.*

Research supports the hypothesis that interactive learning (as opposed to rote learning) is superior with respect to knowledge retention, problem solving, creativity and innovation. Integrated learning unleashes synergy and learning across different disciplines. Connecting existing knowledge dots often generates better inspiration than brand new ideas. More importantly, they are more readily implementable.

For example, it is the integration of hardware and software that has made Apple products so popular. Embedded chips and software have made many products smart. Today, a typical automobile has more than 200 sensors, memory chips and microprocessors. It is very possible to have a switch and server integrated and networked in each car. Furthermore, today's cars can easily act as mobile base stations for broadband wireless networks.

Integrated research and learning between the disciplines of economics and behavioural sciences has generated a new area of research called behavioural economics. Similar integrated learning between finance, marketing and operations is not only possible but also desirable. At Emory University, the medical faculty is learning from Tibetan monks how meditation affects the brain; and the monks are learning about how modern drugs alter the mind and body.

Finally, individualised learning is becoming increasingly necessary as the diversity of business students grows each year, especially in MBA programmes. It is also becoming prevalent in undergraduate programmes as students move from the traditional four-year graduation cycle to graduate in as few as three years or as many as seven years.

Fortunately, digital technology is becoming universally afford-able and accessible. It makes the three Is of learning both possible and cost-effective (*New York Times*, 2012).

The third aspect of transformative development is *continuous lifelong education*. The half-life of knowledge is getting shorter. In software, it is down to three years and declining rapidly. Our estimate for the half-life of management knowledge is that it is thirty months at present but will decline rapidly due to technology advances and the growth of emerging markets. Therefore, it will not be sufficient to provide education leading up to graduation. Just as in many certified professions such as accounting and medicine, business schools must think of lifelong education.

Furthermore, it is not a good idea to redefine graduating stu-dents as alumni. It changes our mindset and behaviour towards them. This notion of lifelong education will be disruptive in the way we measure faculty's teaching requirements. It will be also disruptive in the way knowledge is generated, aggregated and disseminated. And it will be disruptive, as the classroom has to go to the students anywhere they are located instead of students coming to the classroom. Finally, the cumulative pool of students will quickly become very large. For example, if a business school graduates 2,000 students a year (1,500 undergraduates and 500 MBAs), it adds up to 20,000 students in one decade. Managing an increasingly large and geographically distributed student population will create its own challenges. Fortunately, this is already done in certified professions, and business schools can learn from them how to scale up.

Web-based online education is now more viable and scalable just like social media and online distribution of academic journals. Investing in online lifelong education will become a necessity.

While offering lifelong education will be challenging, it also represents an opportunity for annuity income on a cumulative base for business schools. A quick analysis of the lifetime value of a student suggests that it may make business schools financially sus-tainable without the need for endowments and, therefore, make deans

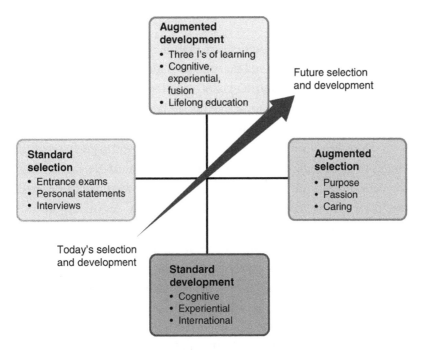

FIGURE 4.3 Augmenting selection and development value

and directors refocus on their education mission and output instead of fundraising and reputation chasing.

These three transformative development initiatives are also compatible with existing accreditation and reputation rankings. In fact, they may become role models; and both accreditation bodies and reputation-ranking assessors are likely to incorporate them for future accreditation and rankings respectively. The above discussion on selection and development is summarised in Figure 4.3.

EXOGENOUS FACTORS IN SELECTION AND DEVELOPMENT

Business schools are influenced by several exogenous factors and the processes of selection and development are subject to changes in them. We have identified six exogenous factors that are important to understand, monitor and adjust; and, if possible, change them.

Accreditation

There are some problems with accreditation. Unfortunately, accreditation usually lags change and the process is too slow. Second, the time interval between accreditation visits is too long for a rapidly changing world. Finally, accreditation standards set benchmarks for an acceptable level of quality and not necessarily for excellence.

However, accreditation can be (and has been) a great agent of change. For example, the field of strategy was mandated by AACSB in the late 1970s and early 1980s. Strategy is now a well-respected discipline in business education and research. Similarly, in the 1960s, the accreditation process transformed personnel management into organisational behaviour and production management into operations management. It is our hope that with the rapid growth of the digital age and global economy, the accreditation bodies can lead rather than lag in both the selection and development processes of transforming human capital in business. Indeed, a key challenge for accreditation bodies (AACSB, AMBA and EFMD) is how to stimulate innovation and encourage experimentation rather than become involved in the cementing of particular practices.

University governance

The autonomy granted to schools of business in the past may be eroding, as university governance is increasingly enforced on them. The often-renegade relationship of the business school within the university may have further pushed the university administration to bring it under university direction. Tenure and promotion decisions are increasingly brought into line with university policies and procedures. Even branding and logo decisions are now standardised to ensure that donor names of schools of business are sub-brands of the university master brand. In our view, the proposed ways forward for selection and development in our model are more likely to bring the business school culture into line with the university culture.

> A key challenge for accreditation bodies is how to stimulate innovation and encourage experimentation rather than become involved in the cementing of particular practices.

External funding

The use of endowed chairs as a way to attract and retain faculty in business schools is less likely to succeed in the future. There are several reasons why. First, many endowments were already committed in the 1990s. Second, the price of endowed chairs has gone up significantly. Third, potential donors are finding better opportunities in emerging markets. Fourth, the donor sees less value in endowing a professorship whose research is esoteric and lacking in relevance. Instead, business school faculty will be increasingly mandated to compete for funded research from industry, large foundations and government agencies such as the Department of Commerce in the US. In fact, following the collapse of communism, many business schools were funded by the US government to start CIBER centres focused on American-type capitalistic education and research in Eastern European countries. We see a similar funding opportunity for the business schools for research and education in emerging markets. This seems to be a clear mandate in Canada and the UK, where most universities are government-funded institutions. It is clearly the message in China and India. Funded research and education will result in starting centres of excellence in different disciplines of business and potentially cross-disciplinary centres of research between business and non-business disciplines.

Technology advances

It is remarkable to think that only a decade ago there was no Google, Facebook, iPad or iPhone. The open-access press is changing the paradigm of the peer review process and the gate-keeping power of well-established academic journals and publishers. The amount of content on YouTube (often user-generated) or in the archived digital content of television networks is enormous. In our view, 'you ain't seen nothing yet!' Most students will get their course syllabi and reading materials on tablets; interactive learning will be mainstream and virtual teamwork will be routine. Our proposition about the three Is of learning will be enabled by technology advances. In addition, most accredited degree education will be online. The internet's two key characteristics (reach and richness) will transform the way we select and develop students. It will also transform the way we do research and not just the way we submit research papers for peer review and publication (*New York Times*, 2012).

Growth of emerging markets

As pointed out earlier, the twenty-first century will be all about the growth of emerging markets, starting with China and India and rapidly moving to Africa and many parts of Latin America. This will require a significant change in what we refer to as the colonial-imperialist mindset of Western countries including Europe, America and Japan. It will require change from 'glocalisation' of business education (as we do it in Executive MBA programmes in China and Singapore) to reverse innovation. It means developing innovative curricula without the legacy of the past. It will give a great competitive advantage to brand new schools of business and universities that do not inherit a culture of orthodoxy.

One key area to understand is the funding of business schools by large business groups or by entrepreneurs as evidenced in India and China. For example, a special act of legislation in the state of Karnataka in India has resulted in the establishment of Azim Premji University (named after Wipro's famous business leader), whose sole focus is to develop world-class teachers and school administrators for more than two million schools. Similarly, another act of legislation in the same state has licensed the Alliance University in India to transform from a business school to a fully fledged university. It will have ten colleges and schools in less than five years with more than 15,000 students in Bangalore. Finally, the Indira Gandhi National

Open University (IGNOU), a government-established higher-education system for inclusive education, has more than 3 million college students in all parts of India who study by distance education. Its breadth of curriculum is astounding, ranging from skill-based certificate programmes to masters and doctorates in sciences and engineering.

Public/private partnerships

A major worldwide trend is the emergence of global public/private partnerships in education. There are cross-border global initiatives between governments and world bodies, foundations (such as the Ford Foundation, McArthur Foundation, Kaufman Foundation and Gates Foundation) and the private sector. While many of these initiatives are focused on poverty and public health (and more recently on science, technology, engineering and mathematics), they are likely to extend to business and management education as a way to make the discipline of business socially relevant and useful. For example, several years ago, the government of Malaysia, in partnership with Manipal University of India (the largest medical college in the world) and funded by the World Bank, set up a medical school in Malaka to ensure that the native Bhumiputras and Chinese Malays also get access to careers in medicine, which were otherwise concentrated among Indian Malays. And, we earlier discussed the effort to bring the public and private sectors more closely together at Yale.

> Business schools that are willing and able to change will not only survive but also thrive in this rapidly changing world of business education and business.

These six exogenous factors will have an enormous impact on the future of business education. And their impact will occur across all internal stakeholders (students, faculty, administration). Business schools that are willing and able to change will not only survive but also thrive in this rapidly changing world of business education and business.

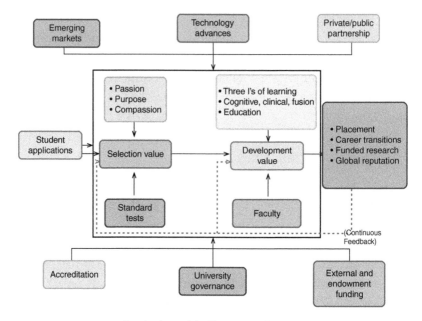

FIGURE 4.4 The Sheth model of business education

Figure 4.4 summarises all the elements of our organising model of business education.

CONCLUSION

Established business schools that are both willing and able to adapt to disruptive drivers of change (especially technology and globalisation) will not only survive but also secure their future. Unfortunately, despite ample warnings and signals, many business school deans and directors will find themselves helpless in transforming their culture and governance due to denial, competency, dependence and internal turf wars among faculty and staff. It is, therefore, not surprising to find so many job openings for business deans and directors. It is much easier to start a new school than transform an existing one.

Business schools that are able to broaden their mission and market will be in a better position. The mission of shareholder value (bottom line) must broaden to that of stakeholder value (triple bottom line). In other words, the business of business is more than business. It is also to serve its other stakeholders including community, suppliers, employees and customers. Therefore, broadening the bottom line to triple bottom line (profit, people and planet) in research and education will become necessary. Similarly, business schools that broaden their markets to serve the research and education needs of both the public and private sectors as well as emerging markets will be in a better position to survive and thrive.

The future of business and management education remains promising. However, the future of business schools as we know them today is doubtful and in crisis. In summary, from the viewpoint of the Sheth model and business school leaders such as Canals (2011), Morsing and Rovira (2011) and De Meyer (2011), who stress humanistic, stakeholder and innovative perspectives, we must embrace the following in our curricula philosophies.

Transformational change

This involves effective innovation and the management of change; lifelong education; interactive, individualised and integrated learning; a global and emerging market focus; leverage of technology in the e-learning domain and an increasing recognition of management needs in public and non-governmental organisations.

A stakeholder perspective

As Howard Thomas (2011: B15) stated, 'business schools must radically reshape their curricula if they want to keep their edge in an age where corporations are being held to account far more in terms of social responsibility. They must also produce humanistic, ethical and morally responsible leaders who focus on the "triple bottom line."'

Student selection

Students must be selected according to a broader set of criteria to encompass emotional as well as cognitive intelligence and to focus on personality characteristics such as purpose, passion and caring (compassion). Before outlining the philosophy of new business school models in the next chapter, it is interesting to re-examine an essay by Nobel Laureate Herbert Simon (1976) on the business school as a problem in organisational design. It provides a set of philosophical, as opposed to Sheth's more normative, guidelines for evaluating new business school models and approaches.

He views the business school as a professional school that should follow the goals of the university, including both the pursuit of knowledge for its own sake *and* the application of knowledge to practical pursuits. It therefore must embrace the world of practice and identify the information and skills (particularly from the social and mathematical sciences) that can improve practice. In linking academic and practical management concerns, the business school must, however, be fundamentally rigorous in research and teaching.

Simon stresses that management is an 'art' and hence this requires the business school faculty to work across boundaries and disciplinary 'walls' to encourage better communication between discipline- and practice-oriented faculty and address solutions to management problems and issues that are interdisciplinary in character.

In essence, following Simon's advice, the research and teaching capabilities of the business school must be directed towards addressing major business problems and issues in an ambiguous, complex and multi-disciplinary world (Schoemaker, 2008) in a holistic manner.

Some questions are appropriate in judging whether business schools understand the nature of changes in the twenty-first century. Have they kept pace with global and technological change? Do they provide multi-disciplinary perspectives in problem solving? And do they really understand the current 'firing line' challenges of managers and entrepreneurs (Gabor, 2008)?

In the next chapter we will, therefore, examine and evaluate a number of new models and approaches to management education using the guidelines offered here as benchmarks for the evaluation process.

REFERENCES

Canals, J. (2011). *The Future of Leadership Development: Corporate Needs and the Role of Business Schools*. New York: Palgrave Macmillan.

Chakravarty, B. and Lorange P. (2007). *Profit or Growth? Why You Don't Have to Choose*. Philadelphia: Wharton Publishing.

Collins, J. (2001). *Good to Great: Why Some Companies Make the Leap ... and Others Don't*. London: Random House.

Currie, G., Knights, D. and Starkey, K. (2010). Introduction: a post-crisis critical reflection on business schools. *British Journal of Management*, **21**: s1–s5.

Datar, S., Garvin, D. A. and Cullen, P. G. (2010). *Rethinking the MBA: Business Education at a Crossroads*. Boston: Harvard Business School Press.

De Meyer, A. (2011). Collaborative leadership: new perspectives in leadership development. *European Business Review*, January/February: 35–40.

Fleck, J. (2012). Blended learning and learning communities: opportunities and challenges. *Journal of Management Development*, **31**(4): 398–411.

Gabor, A. (2008). Lessons for business schools: new books and revisited history illuminate the irrelevance of today's MBA – and ways to make it compelling again. *Strategy and Business*, **50**: 111–18.

Lorange, P. (2012). The business school of the future: the network-based business model. *Journal of Management Development*, **31**(4): 424–31.

McGregor, D. (1960). *The Human Side of Enterprise*. New York: McGraw-Hill.

Mokyr, J. (2002). *The Gifts from Athena: Historical Origins of the Knowledge Economy*. Princeton University Press.

Moldoveanu, M. C. and Martin, R. L. (2008). *The Future of the MBA: Designing the Thinker of the Future*. Oxford University Press.

Morsing, M. and Rovira, A. S. (2011). *Business Schools and Their Contribution to Society*. London: Sage.

New York Times. (2012). On-line learning and digital technology.

Peters, K. and Thomas, H. (2011). A sustainable model for business schools. *Global Focus: The EFMD Business Magazine*, **5**(2): 24–7.

Porter, M. and Kramer, M. (2011). Creating shared value. *Harvard Business Review*, **89**(1/2): 62–77.

Schoemaker, P. J. H. (2008). The future challenges of business: rethinking management education. *California Management Review*, **50**(3): 119–39.

Sheth, J. N. (2007). *The Self-Destructive Habits of Good Companies: And How to Break Them*. Upper Saddle River, NJ: Wharton School Publishing.

(2008). *Chindia Rising: How China and India Will Benefit Your Business*. New Delhi: Tata McGraw-Hill.

Sheth, J. N. and Sisodia, R. (2006). *Tectonic Shift: The Geoeconomic Realignment of Globalizing Markets*. Thousand Oaks, CA: Response Books.

Simon, H. A. (1976). The business school: a problem in organizational design. In *Administrative Behaviour: A Study of Decision-Making Processes in Administrative Organization* (3rd edn). New York: Free Press.

Sisodia, R., Wolfe, D. and Sheth, J. N. (2007). *Firms of Endearment: How World-Class Companies Profit from Passion and Purpose*. Upper Saddle River, NJ: Wharton School Publishing.

Sull, O. (2005). *The Upside of Turbulence*. New York: HarperCollins.

Thomas, H. (2011, 6 June). Working life: doing business for the common good. *The Straits Times*.

Thomas, M. and Thomas, H. (2012). Using new social media and Web 2.0 technologies in business school teaching and learning. *Journal of Management Development*, **31**(4): 358–67.

5 Evaluating new and innovative models of management education

This chapter is devoted to a critical examination and evaluation of a number of new models and interesting new approaches to management education that have been advocated both by deans (e.g. Richard Lyons at Haas, Berkeley, in the US, and before him Laura Tyson, and Roger Martin at Rotman, Toronto, in Canada) and critics (e.g. Henry Mintzberg at McGill, Montreal, Canada). We believe that the organising framework of Figure 4.4, and Simon's careful insights, should provide a basis for our model review and analysis of the philosophy underlying each model. Despite the somewhat unfulfilled promise of management education (Thomas, 2012), there has been considerable investment in new business models for its future development.

Indeed, Professors Datar, Garvin and Cullen (2010) provide an exhaustive review of current curricula trends. Prompted by the growing scrutiny of MBA programmes, they started an ambitious and wide-ranging three-year research project on MBA programmes to coincide with the one-hundredth anniversary of Harvard Business School. They examined a range of secondary data sources, interviewed leading business school deans and corporate executives, and outlined clearly the curricula developments at around a dozen leading schools, focusing particularly on programmes at the Center for Creative Leadership, Chicago, Harvard, INSEAD, Stanford and Yale.

A potential criticism of this research project might be that aspects of what might characterise *smaller* business schools' programmes are not reported or discussed. For instance, one of the authors was extensively interviewed in his capacity as head of IMD – a small, elite MBA programme. This data was, however, left out of the research volume. Could there be at least an implicit revealed preference for larger or case-method-type programmes?

From their research analysis, however, the authors identify a number of important gaps and needs in MBA programmes that should be addressed in their future designs by business schools. They focus on the areas of individual student and management development and skills of leadership and strategic implementation. They suggest that promising innovations should include the following: gaining a global perspective; developing leadership skills; honing integration skills; understanding the roles, responsibilities and purposes of business; recognising organisational realities and the challenges of implementation; thinking creatively and innovatively; thinking critically and communicating clearly; and understanding the limits of models and markets (particularly in the context of non-government organisations and emerging markets).

However, they counsel that these unmet needs should be viewed as useful guidelines since one of the enduring strengths of business schools is the diversity of their approaches, cultures and models. Podolny (2009) similarly offers an alternative set of curricula prescriptions and warns that 'unless America's business schools make radical changes, society will become convinced that MBAs work to service only their own selfish interests'.

We now examine, in detail, a series of interesting educational models. By way of introduction, we map these different experiments and reforms in Figure 5.1.

In subsequent paragraphs we therefore review the following models:

- Mintzberg's IMPM (International Master's Program in Practising Management);
- the Haas/Berkeley dynamic capabilities model;
- the Rotman design thinking model;
- ideas from highly ranked schools (e.g. Yale, Stanford and Chicago);
- the Open University 'blended learning' model;
- the focused innovation model: UC San Diego;
- the 50+20 project: Management Education for the World;

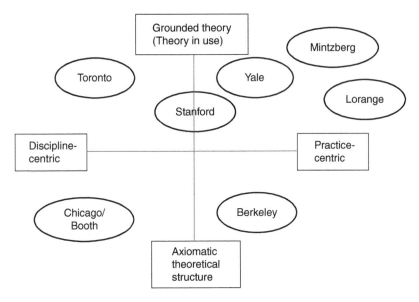

FIGURE 5.1 Different models of management education

- the Starkey knowledge model;
- the network model of Lorange.

THE MINTZBERG IMPM (INTERNATIONAL MASTER'S PROGRAM IN PRACTISING MANAGEMENT) MODEL: A PRACTISING MANAGER'S MODEL

Mintzberg's (2004) book outlines in depth his criticism of MBA programmes, which he regards as far too analytic in orientation and isolated from the context and practice of management. For Mintzberg management is an art and a practice but not a science. Management is a blend of experience, insight and analysis. It is a practice requiring both craft and experience mixed with careful vision and insight and enriched by appropriate analysis of business decisions for decision making.

This IMPM model, developed in partnership with Lancaster University Management School in the UK and other international institutions, such as McGill University in Montreal, Canada, and IIM in Bangalore, India, is his attempt to put his ideas in practice.

Framed around the concept of experienced managers as students, he developed seven tenets by which management education (ME) should be judged (Mintzberg and Gosling, 2002). They are:

Tenet 1: ME should be restricted to practising managers selected on the basis of performance.

Tenet 2: ME and practice should be concurrent and integrated.

Tenet 3: ME should leverage work and life experience.

Tenet 4: The key to learning is thoughtful reflection.

Tenet 5: ME should result in organisational development.

Tenet 6: ME must be an interactive process.

Tenet 7: Every aspect of ME must facilitate learning.

What unites these seven tenets is the proposition that management is a practice that has to be appreciated through experience in context. Professors, in this model, are expected to spend less time lecturing and more time facilitating appropriate discussion about management issues and encouraging students to engage in 'experienced reflection', so that they draw closely on their own experiences in class and group discussions.

In addition, the content of the IMPM involves the study of five cross-cutting, interdisciplinary themes unlike the conventional functional disciplinary MBA model with its 'silos' of marketing, operations, finance and so on that involves little or no thematic integration.

These five themes of the IMPM constitute the five frames, or themes, of the managerial mind – five mindsets – which are linked in the design in a holistic fashion. The five themes are:

• *Managing self: the reflective mindset*

  (involving such topics as the nature of managerial work, leadership, emotional intelligence and ethics);

• *Managing relationships: the collaborative mindset*

  (strategic alliances, teams, knowledge management and conflict management);

• *Managing organisations: the analytic mindset*

(social capital, political dimensions of organisational analysis, complexity theory and approaches to decision making);

- *Managing context: the worldly mindset*

  (looking outward, globalisation, managing conglomerates and international cultural dimensions);

- *Managing change: the action mindset*

  (macro- and micro-change, personal change, managing change and managing growth).

> Five themes address the practice of managing in a holistic way interspersed with modules on operational excellence and value creation.

Together these five themes address the practice of managing in a holistic way interspersed with modules on operational excellence and value creation. The IMPM uses design principles of interactive learning, integrated learning, learning from experience, managerial experience and cross-disciplinary perspectives to understand and develop the process of managing. It is unique in its design and unlike the structure of any existing MBA programme. It treats management as a practical act and stresses the linkage between education and practice.

THE HAAS/BERKELEY DYNAMIC CAPABILITIES MODEL

This model (Lyons, 2012), anchored by Rich Lyons, Dean of Haas, University of California, Berkeley, in the US, proposes that business schools must examine their own cultures, frame their own goals and evolve their unique pathways in order to develop the innovative business leaders of the future.

The overarching intent of the Haas MBA model is to build innovative business leaders by moving from an implicit culture to an explicit culture; from a co-ordinated curriculum to a capabilities-integrated

curriculum and from multiple, independent experiential learning programmes to an integrated experiential learning curriculum.

The cultural change involved four elements:

Questioning the status quo: for example, by advocating bold business ideas
and challenging convention

Confidence without attitude: for example, making analysis- and evidence-
based decisions involving confidence, trust and humility;

Students always; for example, with students exhibiting a constant
curiosity for personal and lifelong learning;

Beyond yourself: for example, through leading firms by stressing larger
longer-term interests in an ethical and responsible fashion.

The culture is, in essence, one of integrity and respect and is
embedded throughout the processes of student admissions and orientation and the design of the curriculum.

The switch to a capabilities-integrated curriculum required the
clear identification by faculty, students and alumni of the dynamic
capabilities of the innovative leader. These capabilities, ten in
number, are categorised under the following three clusters.

Defining opportunities
Problem framing, opportunity recognition, and experimentation;
Making choices
Revenue model identification, valuation of ideas, and risk detection;
Building organisational capacity
*Influence without authority, managing ambiguity and conflict, team
creativity, and adaptive governance.*

The choice of these capabilities rests on two specific criteria.
First, they need to be grounded in the social sciences and be research-
based. Second, they need to be demanded by recruiters and others in
the marketplace.

The culture and the capabilities are then woven into a new
MBA core programme with three new or revised courses (out of
twelve in total), entitled 'Leading People', 'Problem Finding/Problem
Solving' and 'Leadership Communication'.

The third element of the model is that the core has to be implemented, with the electives, in an integrated fashion. Consequently, students are required to choose one of a range of nine experiential learning programmes including Haas@Work – involving a student work team evaluating a business problem with a major firm or an entrepreneurship project in which real business solutions and business plans are developed for small and medium-sized enterprises (SMEs).

> The overall aims of the model are to provide the basic foundations from which new leaders will emerge who have the skills a manager must have to redefine how management takes place.

The overall aims of the model are to provide the basic foundations from which new leaders will emerge who have the courage, characteristics and skills – the dynamic capabilities that a manager must have – to redefine how management takes place in business, government and non-government organisations. Unlike the Mintzberg programme, it is anchored in a research-based, evidence-based social science framework alongside a clear vision about developing ethical, practical, experiential and integrative skills in potential managerial recruits. This design required strong buy-in, clear identification of managerial dynamic capabilities, and faculty involvement during the entire change process.

THE ROTMAN DESIGN THINKING MODEL

Roger Martin (2009), Dean of the Rotman School of Management at the University of Toronto in Canada, is a management thinker who advocates a focus on design thinking in management education. He believes that 'the problem with MBA education is structural, and it runs across three dimensions: where it should be deep, it is shallow; where it should be broad, it is narrow; and where it should be dynamic, it is static' (Martin, 2010). His solution is to encourage an MBA design, the 3D MBA, which is deep, broad and dynamic and encompasses the development of holistic thinkers who will be critical and creative. These thinkers make moral and ethical decisions following the ideals of a 'liberal arts' style MBA.

The goals of the Rotman 3D MBA are depth, breadth and dynamism and we examine each in turn.

First, the idea of 'going deep' is to force the students 'to thoroughly understand the logic structures, assumptions and limitations of the models we teach, even if they don't like it very much' (Martin, 2010). This is done through two courses at the outset of the MBA programme entitled 'Foundations of Integrative Thinking' and the 'Integrative Thinking' practicum. Together, these courses attempt to uncover the underlying logic structure of business models and suggest appropriate revisions or re-engineering of these models. The other aim is to show how models from different areas, such as finance, operations and marketing, should be framed as more integrated business models to address real-life practical business problems. In other words, disciplinary models cannot be seen in isolation from the business problems they seek to solve.

Second, the idea of 'embracing breadth' is to reinforce the understanding that most business problems are 'messy' and beset by ambiguity, complexity and often multiple factors. As a consequence, students must be exposed to a broad suite of models, beyond the standard business disciplines. For example, Rotman has a number of institutes in areas such as prosperity, corporate citizenship and health strategy that expose students to more complex issues. These issues broaden the nature of the academic dialogue so that a range of different viewpoints and a multi-disciplinary set of perspectives and lenses are brought to bear on their resolution.

Third, the idea of 'getting dynamic' is to encourage the creation and development of new and better models for attacking business and management models. Rotman achieves this through a set of electives engineered by the design initiative DesignWorks and the Desautels Centre for Integrative Thinking. The philosophy is that students are taught several fundamental principles. These include:

- To be innovative, an open and exploratory mindset is critical.
- to be action-focused and human focused;
- to remember that where people are involved design is applicable for business (both B2B and B2C). (Leung, Director of DesignWorks)

In summary, the Martin philosophy is to embrace design principles in management education and develop skills in addressing complex management decisions from a broad, critical and dynamic viewpoint.

IDEAS FROM HIGHLY RANKED SCHOOLS: STANFORD, YALE
AND THE JAIN/STOPFORD PROGRAMME FOR A
GLOBAL CURRICULUM

As noted already, Joel Podolny (2009), the former dean at Yale in the US, has asserted in a well-cited *Harvard Business Review* article that unless America's business schools make radical changes, society will become convinced that MBAs work to serve only their own selfish interests. He argues that for business schools to regain society's trust they must, first, stop competing on rankings and must state clearly that 'money gain' is not the only reason to get an MBA. Second, they must withdraw degrees from former students found guilty of violating professional ethical and moral codes of conduct. Third, business school courses must be better integrated across a mix of academic disciplines. Fourth, they must appoint cross-faculty teaching teams – balancing 'hard' and 'soft' disciplines – to ensure that analytic approaches and models are not value-free. Fifth, they must encourage more eclectic and applied research.

> For business schools to regain society's trust they must, first, stop competing on rankings and must state clearly that 'money gain' is not the only reason to get an MBA.

As a consequence, Yale restructured its curriculum to break out of traditional 'silo' teaching based on business disciplines such as finance and marketing to develop a set of courses designed around the different organisational perspectives of customers, competitors, investors and society. This means that there is no such thing as a marketing problem in isolation. Rather, it is typically a much richer business or management problem. Therefore, it also added a course in problem framing that aims to develop critical perspectives about problem assumptions and business models and, thus, encourages students to view management problems using multiple disciplinary lenses and lessons learned from business history.

Similarly, under the leadership of Dean Garth Saloner, the Graduate School of Business at Stanford University in the US has completely restructured its educational process so that it now emphasises multi-disciplinary traditions and increased understanding of cultural and global contexts.

Four key elements characterise this new model: a highly personalised programme; a deeper, more engaging intellectual experience; a more global curriculum; and an expanded vision of leadership and communication development, integrating strategy with leadership development and implementation.

A common programme in the first quarter includes courses designed to build an integrated understanding of management: namely, teams and organisational behaviour, strategic leadership, managerial finance and the global context of management. A second aim is to get students – again in the first quarter – to examine the philosophical issues of management through a 'Critical Analytical Thinking' course involving critical evaluation of such issues as when markets work well and when they do not.

The overarching aim of the new programme, personalised to students, is to develop managers who not only think critically and analytically about important management problems but also make decisions responsibly and with a strong set of compassionate, ethical and moral values.

Although the aims of the Yale and Stanford programmes are different, they share some common goals that are seen in undergraduate 'liberal arts' programmes: namely, critical thinking, multi-disciplinary approaches, global and cultural intelligence, a focus on leadership, ethics and social responsibility, and understanding and learning the lessons from business history.

In a recent article by Stopford and Jain (2009), reporting on the curriculum concerns of a consortium of high-ranking business schools from across the world, they present a globally oriented curriculum that mirrors some of the Yale/Stanford concerns. They report four elements: namely, *insight into business functions* in an integrated fashion; *global perspectives* including culture, history, political and economic issues; *skills* desired by employers including multi-culturalism, communication, leadership, creative thinking, entrepreneurship, innovation and strategic change; *present-day issues* including emerging technologies, sustainability, and emerging markets.

> Chicago's reputation in the business school field is at least in part a function of its academic strength and its production of a large number of Nobel Laureates in economics.

Other elite schools, however, such as Chicago/Booth have retained their strong values and their espoused culture of a discipline-focused and strong social science-based scientific foundation. Chicago's reputation in the business school field is at least in part a function of its academic strength and its production of a large number of Nobel Laureates in economics. It believes that business schools should focus on knowledge and theory development.

THE OPEN UNIVERSITY 'BLENDED LEARNING' MODEL

The UK's Open University (OU) has been a pioneer in educational innovations in distance learning (Fleck, 2007, 2012). James Fleck, a recent dean of the OU Business School (OUBS), points out that there have been two main models of distance learning: the early distributed learning model and the more recent evolutionary model, essentially a practice-based model. The early model involved the construction and use of high-quality distributed learning materials with structured tutorials and some face-to-face teaching while the second is an important development of the early model into a practice-based model.

Thomas and Thomas (2012) discuss each of these models as follows.

The early distributed learning model

As Fleck (2007) points out, this consists of four main elements to achieve distributed learning with structured materials, tutorials and some face-to-face teaching. The first extremely important element involves the design and construction of the university-owned curriculum by a dedicated core faculty team, who produce the teaching materials, textbooks, DVDs and so on that are distributed to students. This is an extremely expensive curriculum investment exercise, costing around $1 million to $2 million per course, but critically important as it is the key to a set of high-quality, rigorous and well-designed courses.

The second element requires face-to-face tutorials (of around twenty students) managed by adjunct faculty overseen by OU core faculty. Tutorials are designed to provide insights, oversee student interactions and explain the distributed course materials.

The third element builds on the second, and leverages student learning by linking workplace experiences to course materials.

Finally, all three elements depend upon the provision of a robust and flexible IT platform that can manage the learning requirements of large numbers of students across national borders as well as within the UK.

The practice-based model

The second model has been developed strongly over the past five to ten years. It is a practice-based model that represents a significant evolution of the basic model. It retains the process of producing and updating core materials by the full-time OU faculty but tutorials now increasingly focus on the world of management practice. They involve the careful design of practice-based experiences and professional practices in the classroom. The focus is on sharing learning experiences across students and making a virtue of action learning and student experience. The emphasis is clearly on student-centred learning. But it involves an important design challenge in understanding how students learn from practical experiences. This practice-based model also requires an extensive upgrading of the IT platform.

While the OU has always been seen as a pioneer and has clearly been an innovator in technology and management, its distance/online learning model has attracted many entrants to the business school 'industry' and a range of competitors offering online management education. Iniguez (2011: 72) ably catalogues the nature and character of the 'industry' entrants. The early entrants (such as U-NEXT) simply developed a basic online delivery model. The later entrants, such as the Apollo Group (University of Phoenix), the DeVry group and Hult International Business School (the former Arthur D. Little Institute), mixed the online model with a tutorial and feedback process.

These later entrants are generally for-profit providers that attempt to achieve a low-cost product of good quality. They do not, however, always possess the depth of faculty resources of a publicly funded school such as the OU. And schools such as Indiana and North Carolina in the US and Warwick and Henley in the UK can afford to invest more core 'cutting-edge' faculty resources in course design and updating content.

An interesting question for all these schools is whether the major accreditation agencies will accredit such blended learning models. To date, the OUBS has been accredited by both AACSB and EFMD, while others such as Hult and Phoenix will probably seek accreditation in due course but may lack the core faculty resources and research focus typically needed to achieve that goal.

However, some schools, such as the Lorange Institute in Switzerland, have chosen not to employ any full-time faculty of their own but instead have chosen to create a stable network of part-time faculty, fully committed to research and research-based teaching. EFMD (EPAS) and AMBA have already accredited the Lorange Institute.

Competition of this kind has certainly provided the stimulus for new innovations and ideas, particularly in blended learning models. In the next section we will focus particularly on the OU and Instituto de Empresa (IE) in Madrid, Spain, of the MBA programme 'blended learning' variants.

'Blended learning' and learning communities: how to incorporate new social and digital media

Both the OU and IE Madrid have talked about 'learning communities' in their future blended learning designs. Learning communities are sometimes called 'communities of practice' (Duguid, 2008) in the information systems/knowledge management literature.

Fleck (2012) outlines the key elements of his learning community model. This stresses the importance of capturing the essence of student-based learning and networking communities as the focal element in the delivery of a blended learning programme. Such a programme, however, must be built around a high-quality and innovative curriculum designed by core faculty. The key elements are:

- creation of a learning community;
- a process orientation;
- use of web resources/TV programmes;
- student-driven learning;
- communication via web and mobile;
- use of social/digital media;
- face-to-face residential schools for networking.

It is clear that this is a strong reinforcement of the practice-/student-centred model. The nature and design of the learning community is still, however, a very fluid element alongside the problem of how to leverage the value of web and social and digital media in building such a community.

> The nature and design of the learning community is still, however, a very fluid element alongside the problem of how to leverage the value of web and social and digital media in building such a community.

Iniguez (2011: 77–9), in his recent book *The Learning Curve*, outlines the philosophy of the blended learning model used at IE (where he is the dean). He argues that managers live blended lives in which their careers, and required skills, regularly change.

THE FOCUSED INNOVATION MODEL: UC SAN DIEGO

Bob Sullivan, the dean at the new business school at the University of California, San Diego, in the US, focuses particularly on the role of innovation in business schools. Sullivan recently chaired the committee that produced the influential AACSB report *Business Schools on an Innovation Mission* (2010). He argues that innovation's impact on business and society must be reflected in the dynamic capabilities of business schools. Drawing on broad definitions of innovation, he stresses the need for a focus on innovatory processes in business schools to drive the change agenda. Such innovatory processes should then lead to a renewed focus on, for example, teaching and research in areas such as management and leadership.

One of Sullivan's colleagues at UC San Diego, Vish Krishnan (Bisoux, 2011: 26) suggests that innovation is a discipline in itself. He points out that in the first year of the MBA programme there is a three-course, year-long sequence that runs in parallel with the other basic core courses. In this sequence, the first course covers methods of 'ideation' (idea generation), research and development, and prototyping. In the next two courses, student teams each develop an idea and write a business plan. Throughout the sequence, students are guided by faculty, practitioners and venture capitalists.

The underlying logic of such an innovation-based MBA is the integration of technology and management skills. It offers a problem-solving orientation involving the combination and application of multiple sources of knowledge. It also emphasises the viewpoint that pluralistic and interdisciplinary thinking leads to creative approaches and solutions to problems. Managing in such environments involves different organisational forms such as network organisations and virtual teams linking complex technologies, continual innovation, and intellectual diversity in the skill and talent base.

> The topics stressed in such an innovation-type MBA include entrepreneurship, innovation, globalisation, leadership and technology.

The topics stressed in such an innovation-type MBA include entrepreneurship, innovation, globalisation, leadership and technology. Business areas studied might be approaches to innovation in such industry environments as information and communication technologies, biotech, healthcare, knowledge-based services and sustainable/environmental technologies.

Clearly, the San Diego area, as well as Silicon Valley in general, is a technology 'hot spot'. Many possible linkages between MBA students and new knowledge-based start-ups involving experiential and experimental learning communities are readily available. These provide the living laboratories and internships that create the applied, practical context for the MBA programme.

THE 50+20 PROJECT: MANAGEMENT EDUCATION FOR THE WORLD

The 50+20 project is a partnership between the World Business School Council for Sustainable Business (WBSCSB), the Global Leadership Responsibility Initiative (GLRI) and Principles for Responsible Management Education (PRME). Its aim is to ensure that business, management and leadership schools of the future provide education and research that is relevant and applied, holistic and integrative, responsible and sustainable, interdisciplinary and multi-level and, of course, learning-oriented.

The project's preliminary global survey of the business school world's view on the future of business education indicated that business schools should develop leaders who drive global problem solving and focus on developing and emerging countries and address key stakeholders, particularly entrepreneurs and SMEs.[1] It argues that successful business schools in the future should be judged on the skills and quality of their graduates. These skills include holistic decision making (including social and environmental factors), entrepreneurship and leadership. The clear priority identified for the future of management education is to enhance student leadership skills involving responsible, sustainable and ethical behaviour as well as critical reasoning.

> The clear priority identified for the future of management education is to enhance student leadership skills involving responsible, sustainable and ethical behaviour as well as critical reasoning.

The main research priorities specified for management research in the future include examination of the ways to make business responsible and sustainable and to create and develop globally responsible leaders through experimental and experiential learning. The project's encompassing stakeholder vision and emerging solutions for management education involve a focus on collaboration where all stakeholders in management education interact and meet to engage, enable and educate globally responsible leaders and, in turn, produce action learning/research on relevant regional and global issues.

THE STARKEY KNOWLEDGE MODEL

Professor Ken Starkey of Nottingham Business School in the UK has been an important scholar, and critic, in the field of management education for the past decade. His influential book *The Business School and the Bottom Line* (Starkey and Tiratsoo, 2007) argues that

[1] www.wbscsb.com

business schools should play a growing and influential role in developing knowledge as a reflective and reflexive site for inquiry about business and management. In the knowledge society, therefore, the business school has a big role to play, particularly in championing new research strategies involving practice-engaged scholarship – the co-production of knowledge – that breaks down the barriers between theory and practice and between rigour and relevance.

Starkey views the business school as a knowledge space in which different stakeholders in management education and different disciplines can interact and learn from each other. For example, this would facilitate scientific and policy debates about business and management and allow greater public awareness of key issues to be created. This knowledge might, in turn, lead to worthwhile improvements in business and management practice. Indeed, Starkey (in Starkey and Tempest, 2004: 1529) quotes the eminent organisational scholar James March as reinforcing the role of the business school as a knowledge space in the following manner: a key role of the business school 'is not in trying to identify factors affecting organisational performance, or in trying to develop managerial technology. It is in raising fundamental issues and advancing knowledge about fundamental processes affecting management.'

In summary, Starkey's view is that the business school must pursue a fourfold knowledge strategy – knowledge *for* management, knowledge *for* society, knowledge *about* management and knowledge *about* society. His link between knowledge, management and society is a theme evident in other models such as the focused 'innovation' and 50+20 models discussed earlier.

THE NETWORK MODEL OF LORANGE

As we have noted in this discussion of new models, the Lorange model outlined in Chapter 3 is only one of several alternatives for developing business schools.

The Lorange Institute of Business Zurich argues that it is following an innovative approach aimed at developing a revised curriculum based on strong modularisation. (Many modules are taught over weekends to make it easier for participants to work.) The focus has been on developing Executive Master of Science specialisations (such as Modern Finance, Modern Marketing, Leadership, and Management in Cycles – such as in shipping), which can then be expanded into an Executive MBA.

> Reputation based on quality is established over time and thus does not necessarily go together with intensive innovation.

In addition, many modules are offered jointly for executives and masters' students. Faculty have been recruited from all over the world, not only those that are leading experts on particular topics but also leading practitioners with unique backgrounds and expertise. The latter group primarily teaches shorter, two-day modules.

The school is now working hard on marketing. It takes time to make the marketplace aware of new types of offerings. And reputation based on quality is established over time and thus does not necessarily go together with intensive innovation.

A further challenge is administrative organisation. Paradoxically, this may represent the greatest challenge. Peter Lorange argues that you can have a reasonably good idea of how to put together programmes based on emerging disciplines and which professors to involve. One can also broadly recognise what is needed when it comes to marketing, based on informing and convincing participants that they are paying for value. But to find effective new team members of such a future-focused organisation might be a more open-ended and, frankly, harder task.

Four things seem clear, however.

(1) A website and its related technology offer unique additional opportunities for communicating with the world and for bonding with prospective and present participants.
(2) Co-ordination across modules and across offerings will be key.
(3) A major problem with a franchising-based network would be that the franchise-holder might be seen as rather dominant, even 'imperialistic'.

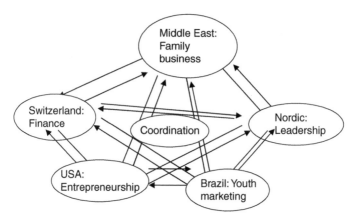

FIGURE 5.2 A global balanced network

Figure 5.2 indicates how a better 'intelligent' network might work. Each of the participating schools would focus on a topic that would represent a natural source of specialisation given its local environment. For instance, a Brazilian school might focus on the young, computer-based consumer, a Middle East school on family business, a Nordic school on entrepreneurship and a Swiss school on finance. Each of these schools would provide a programme on its particular topic of excellence – say, through a two-day module.

(4) One factor that slows innovation is finance. Innovation and change cost money. The established business schools would not be likely candidates to spend financial resources on uncertain, innovative experiments.

SUMMARY OBSERVATIONS ABOUT NEW MODELS AND THE CHANGING CONTEXT OF BUSINESS SCHOOLS

Several factors seem to have changed the context in which business schools operate.

Four factors are particularly important.

- The stable, growth-orientated business environment of the past is changing. There are fewer students, in advanced countries, at undergraduate level as well as graduate level. Even the executive education market, which has been relatively stable so far, seems to be in a recession. Some academic leaders might argue that the difficult market conditions seem to be ending, that the good old days are coming back. Our sense is that we have entered an era with less demand, more turbulence and more market-driven cycles.

What are the consequences for academic leaders? We must further develop our willingness and capability to undertake timing decisions – that is, focus on changes that involve so-called 'in/out' and/or 'long/ short' moves. This refers to when one might enter the market as well as when one might want to exit (in/out), and when to bind oneself up in a long-term contract (long) versus when to stay current ('spot' contract or short).

Speed and agility are becoming more essential than ever and the old stability-based axioms are under attack. This implies that a school might have to be faster and more agile in adapting curriculum and professors to new circumstances – adopting with speed new topics to teach, new research to focus on and even which new competencies professors need – and be ready on a more proactive basis to let the old approaches go.

- Perhaps, at least in part, as a function of more difficult times, our customers – not only our undergraduate and graduate students but also executives – seem to be demanding more emphasis on projects, which, in turn, entails eclecticism. For instance, to develop a new product today involves not only the R&D people but equally the marketing and sales functions, not to mention manufacturing and finance. To enter a new market involves not only marketing and sales but also communications, manufacturing, logistics, legal expertise and so on. This implies co-operation across disciplines and this must be done with speed.

> We may no longer need so many axiomatically focused academic departments or the same emphasis on discipline-focused research.

Thus, the traditional axiomatically based curriculum design is under increasing attack. We may no longer need so many axiomatically focused academic departments or the same emphasis on discipline-focused research. Again, speed in making this shift seems to be key. It goes without saying that this type of change, away from embedded academic traditions to a multidimensional, multi-disciplinary teaching and research approach, can be difficult to pull off.

- Students seem – appropriately – to be more concerned than ever with preparing themselves for the job market, and holding a generalist MBA degree may simply no longer be enough for them. So the tendency towards more job-specific Master of Science degrees seems clear, in line with what was specified in the European Bologna Accord. Examples of more specialised foci might be found when it comes to a master's in, say, banking, high-end marketing, talent management, shipping and sports management. Students may, of course, still demand more general MBAs (in which they might well enrol after having taken a more specialised master's degree). It will be up to each specific academic institution to ensure that both quality and norms for time spent are kept.

- We can say with some certainty that the more traditional business models of many business schools are under attack. Many are struggling with economic problems, given high fixed costs and lower demand. So perhaps the time has come to find other, more cost-efficient business models with an educational technology focus but without losing academic quality. One immediate product of this is that we will probably have to be prepared to utilise our faculty more effectively, to deliver more classroom sessions and have more interaction with students. Again, considering the norms now regarded as essential for academic work this might be a hard change to pull off in many traditional academic contexts.

As we know, a majority of business schools are based on public funding and many are part of public universities. The issue of cash-flow planning, particularly when it comes to the *income* side, may not have attracted sufficient focus. Increasingly, however, we might see a shift. An active focus on how to affect the income side – say, through new programme offerings – *and* how to maintain a keen watching brief on a school's breakeven point will be increasingly important.

We claim that there are ways to meet these challenges, while also maintaining a high level of quality in academic value creation. In the next section, we set out some guidelines to achieve this. They represent *one way* forward but not the only way.

A SET OF GUIDELINES FOR REVISING THE MODERN
BUSINESS SCHOOL'S 'MODUS OPERANDI'

- Why does a business school need an exclusive pool of permanent faculty? Why so at each academic institution? Why do faculty have to give exclusive, earmarked contributions for each particular school setting? Perhaps an answer could be that faculty members might be shared among several academic institutions. Faculty are expensive, so why not share the costs? We are assuming, of course, that each faculty member must be able to and/ or willing to undertake both cutting-edge teaching and research – the two are two sides of the same coin. The receiving institutions must, hence, be prepared to pay for a faculty member's research as well – and indeed insist on contributing to his/her research budget. And why should all faculty come from the pool of academic professors? Why not also include leading practitioners in the teaching (and research)? A combined thematic cutting-edge and practical focus might then more easily be achieved.

It is understood that the concept of a stable network of part-time faculty might also enhance academic performance, both in the class-room and when it comes to research. There will be clear pressure on a faculty member to perform – if not, he/she faces the threat of being asked to leave. This is far away from the cosy situation for faculty members when they have been granted tenure.

> This model leads to a too heavy focus on specialised research rather than on the more relevant business issues of today, such as understanding how to cope in turbulent times through creativity, innovation and attacking new markets.

Most business schools are organised along an essentially similar model. There are academic departments for each major field (finance, marketing and so on). Professors do their research and teaching within the borders set by each field and tend to be promoted based largely on axiomatic research outputs within their specific field; they publish single-authored articles in specialised journals with experts in the given field as referees.

This model is no longer good enough. It leads to a too heavy focus on specialised research rather than on the more relevant business issues of today, such as understanding how to cope in turbulent times through creativity, innovation and attacking new markets. This heavy focus on individual and specialised research leads to a 'me, me, me' culture around the individual professor rather than to a 'we, we, we' culture of teams of professors and students with more focus on cross-disciplinary research and today's practical dilemmas. A good professor must, of course, have authority and self-confidence and believe in what he/she knows. There must be some 'me, me, me'. But today we need a balance – the 'we, we, we' dimension is critical, too – and legitimate. This is a new world for many professors.

There are many other dysfunctionalities with the classical academic model, all reinforcing the 'me, me, me' world of the professor. Let us mention a few.

Specific courses, on well-identified topics, are typically given over a period of a semester by one professor, year after year. The professor typically comes to see this course as 'my course'. Clearly, such a course will be highly shaped by the specific knowledge base of the professor, which may not be necessarily fully relevant in today's setting. And the professor will often essentially re-use the same materials year after year, capitalising on a once-and-for-all 'investment' in course development so that he/she can be free to do more individual research. There is little doubt that such courses easily become boring, irrelevant and at a distance from practical challenges of the day. (Team-teaching might be more realistic instead, might broaden the focus and achieve more cross-disciplinary outcomes.)

On top of this, professors are typically not fully free to innovate. Curriculum changes, at least major ones, must typically be reviewed by a faculty committee, a slow and bureaucratic process. Many professors choose not to go through such a process, which can easily be felt to be rather intimidating. The result is outdated classroom approaches.

- While in many traditional academic institutions there can be a certain tendency towards compartmentalisation, or a 'me, me, me' faculty culture, typically underscored by axiomatically structured academic departments, (tenured) professional chairs and so on the focus on the success of the business school would perhaps call for more of a 'we, we, we' faculty culture. Perhaps, the approach of employing a network of part-time faculty might facilitate this further. Revised procedures when it comes to credits for jointly undertaken/authored research, joint teaching and so on might also help. And so might a bonus system that acknowledges both a faculty member's individual efforts and the overall performance of the school – a reflection of contributions by the team and the individual.

- Many academic institutions have become increasingly bureaucratic, not only with much procedural red tape but also with (excessive) demands on faculty members when it comes to student interaction, evaluations and meetings, leaving little time for the central tasks of a faculty member, which are teaching and research. To decrease the bureaucracy is, therefore, central. Simplified formal structures (fewer departments), streamlined processes, more explicit agendas and leadership in meetings, more purpose-based conclusions in less time all seem to be critical. Many traditional academic departments might be combined, thus reducing the number of silos. And, perhaps, the hierarchy of academic titles might also be reduced or even eliminated – again knocking down a few silos.

- Commonly, full-time study programmes are seen as being of higher quality than their part-time equivalents. This definitely seems to be the case at the undergraduate level but to some extent also when it comes to MBA programmes. This perception is ripe for revision. Ideally, one would learn on the job *and* in business school. It is such a *combined* effort that can enhance a deeper and more practical understanding. This could involve speeding up relevant inputs from both sides: academics would get practical 'living case' inputs and organisations would be able to draw on academia for ongoing innovations. And all of this can take place faster, almost instantaneously.

This also opens up the opportunity for a blend of both senior and junior executives in the same classroom where they can learn from each other. A more youthful perspective can benefit senior executives in understanding such issues as career expectations, consumer trends, IT-based technology and so on. Practice that works is equally critical and here junior executives can learn from their senior colleagues. It is the *blend* of these perspectives – the positive tension – that must be sought.

> Why is the classroom experience so often a one-way communication, where a professor 'talks' to the students?

- Why is the classroom experience so often a one-way communication, where a professor 'talks' to the students? Why cannot the classroom be more of a debating forum, a 'meeting place'? Many leading academic programmes, particularly in the MBA field, are indeed working on this – some have advanced further than others. In an effective 'meeting place' new propositions would be freely launched, often based on a faculty member's research. These ideas would then be 'tested' against existing propositions that have worked well so far, often coming from participants. What follows is debate and broad recognition that we are typically dealing with dilemmas not absolute truths.
- As already noted earlier, students are typically (and appropriately) increasingly concerned about qualifying for jobs. This might mean specialising at first, to gain specific knowledge that might help him/her to get a job – say, through a Master of Science with a focus on banking, talent management or marketing. Then, later, the participant might broaden his/her experience and go for a more generalised MBA education aimed at leadership development and career enhancement.
- Innovation is a key driver. It goes without saying that research that is close to business is an important element in this. Since many faculty members will be able to innovate faster in a business school of the future context than at more traditional schools – with less bureaucracy, fewer silos to contend with, often more managerially focused students – a faculty member might bring such 'proven' innovation back from sabbaticals or leaves of absence to his/her primary academic institutions as examples of something that works.
- While many of us know that speed, increased flexibility, less bureaucracy, fewer silos, and so on are things we would like in our academic institutions, we also know that such institutions tend to be rather conservative. Faculty tend to have a very large say, and this often leads to a rather conservative

culture – a 'bottom-up' dominated culture, one might say. But we also know that many of those positive attributes we have mentioned above only tend to come through when there is true leadership in place at the top. There must be a 'top-down' counterbalance, typically in the hands of the dean. It is this top-down/bottom-up balance that is so critical for success. The likelihood of achieving such a balance might be higher in the business school of the future. Such a balance requires a great many leadership capabilities, yet good leaders will stay away from contexts that cannot be led. It requires a receptive faculty that is prone to endorse a meaningful change agenda and not retreat into 'me, me, me' resistance.

- We might deduce that good governance is critical. Seniority and tenure should not be major determinants when it comes to a faculty member's inputs to governance. It should depend on his/her demonstrated ability, willingness to contribute to teaching, to research, to the establishment and to the maintenance of a 'we, we, we' community. Good governance today implies a lot of 'virtuality', taking advantage of emergent technology.

To meet face-to-face can be hard, impractical and expensive – and it may no longer be necessary. A few face-to-face faculty meetings per year would suffice when combined with virtual meetings. Key value-creating dimensions should dominate, such as: are we innovating enough and how can we do more? Do we have a productive enough learning culture, a 'meeting place', and how can we do better? It is clear that the community of part-time faculty must feel committed and see themselves as a team, a group – even though virtual. Governance is therefore central and must be effective.

- Effective learning is the key driver at the business school of the future; it is its *raison d'être*. We have already discussed the 'meeting place' as a model for two-way dialogue between faculty and participants in the classroom. In fact, there is little difference between these two groups, in that both will be learning. All must have open minds. All persons in the business school of the future are learners – as such, there are no professors/teachers and no students/passive receivers of knowledge. What matters is the equal status of those involved. Technically some are, of course, professors and others are students. But what matters is that all are committed to learning.

In conclusion, this leads us to another central question and our final point in this chapter. What new capabilities must we demand of today's professors? The professor's role becomes similar to that of a conductor of an orchestra and no longer that of delivering monologues. The classroom of today becomes a meeting place for shedding light on critical dilemmas for today's business. The basics can be studied at home, with distance learning an appropriate vehicle. It is surprising, perhaps, that there has been relatively little record of new pedagogical processes (the OU being a strong counter-example). A key question is whether the pedagogy performed in a classroom setting is optimal today.

> Perhaps the major change is that the professor must learn how to listen with respect to the students' points of view.

Let us point out two factors that further underscore the new demand on effective listening capabilities. First, the students/participants will bring with them experiences from real life, including business, which can shed light on specific dilemmas being discussed. Participants learn from each other. Sharing experiences means learning. This can ideally be brought back to a student's own business setting – hopefully rather quickly. Consequently, there is an amalgam of learning in the classroom and learning on the job.

The professor's role involves keeping these discussions on track. His/her own research is critical in this respect, to bring out a prospective view to challenge the prescriptive view from practice. Thus, research continues to be highly important to characterise a good professor but also in leading to a better facilitation in the meeting-place classroom setting.

The room might be 'flat', not the classical horseshoe-shaped auditorium. The students sit around tables, six to seven in each group. The professor walks around the room and gives a 'mini lecture' for twenty minutes. There is no blackboard but he/she can write down key words on a flip chart and hang this on the wall. Each group at each table then discusses this issue or dilemma for, say, twenty minutes. Again, they are free to use flip charts, with key words, if they so wish. Then, there is a twenty-minute plenary discussion, with the professor as the integrator.

Experience drawn from, for example, the Lorange Institute of Business is that with this type of modern pedagogy we can cover in two days what would normally take five days. This is indeed a dramatic improvement and the professor's role has changed totally. We may legitimately ask: why are these changes in academic value creation not happening faster? Why is it so difficult to introduce new pedagogy? Why is it so hard to put the student more in the centre?

Partly, we believe, this has to do with old-fashioned governance models that still exist in much of academia, with their focus on axiomatically based research, publishing single-authored articles in narrow referred journals and tenure. Partly, too, however, it may be hard to retrain our professors for the new roles. Our doctoral programmes should be refocused to cover this. And best practice, when it comes to 'meeting-place-driven classes', should be more widely shared.

REFERENCES

AACSB International. (2010). *Business Schools on an Innovation Mission – Report of the AACSB International Task Force on Business Schools and Innovation.* Tampa, FL: AACSB International.

Bisoux, T. (2011). Re-envisioning the MBA. *BizEd*, **10**(5): 22–30.

Datar, S., Garvin, D. A. and Cullen, P. G. (2010). *Rethinking the MBA: Business Education at a Crossroads.* Boston: Harvard Business School Press.

Duguid, P. (2008). The community of practice then and now, in A. Amin and J. Roberts (eds.), *Organizing for the Creative Economy: Community, Practice, and Capitalism*: 1–10. Oxford University Press.

Fleck, J. (2007). Technology and the business school world. *Journal of Management Development*, **27**(4): 415–25.

(2012). Blended learning and learning communities: opportunities and challenges. *Journal of Management Development*, **31**(4): 398–411.

Iniguez, S. (2011). *The Learning Curve: How Business Schools Are Re-Inventing Education.* New York: Palgrave Macmillan.

Lyons, R. (2012). Curriculum reform: getting more macro, and more micro. *Journal of Management Development*, **31**(4): 412–23.

Martin, R. (2009). *The Design of Business*. Boston: Harvard Business School Press. (2010). Building better decision makers: the 3D MBA. *Rotman Magazine*: 4–9.

Mintzberg, H. (2004). *Managers, Not MBAs: A Hard Look at the Soft Practice of Managing and Management Development*. San Francisco: Berrett-Koehler Publishers.

Mintzberg, H. and Gosling, J. (2002). Educating managers beyond borders. *Academy of Management Learning and Education*, **1**(1): 64–76.

Podolny, J. M. (2009). The buck stops (and starts) at business school. *Harvard Business Review*, **87**: 62–7.

Starkey, K. and Tempest, S. (2004). Rethinking the business school. *Journal of Management Studies*, **41**(8): 1521–31.

Starkey, K. and Tiratsoo, N. (2007). *The Business School and the Bottom Line*. Cambridge University Press.

Stopford, J. M. and Jain, A. (2009). CIBER's first annual Global Roundtable on Advanced Management Education Reform. *UConn Business*, **1**(1).

Thomas, H. (2012). What is the European management school model? *Global Focus*, **6**(1): 18–21.

Thomas, M. and Thomas, H. (2012). Using new social media and Web 2.0 technologies in business school teaching and learning. *Journal of Management Development*, **31**(4): 358–68.

6   Is the business school a professional service firm? Lessons learned

This chapter examines the proposition that business schools have simpler characteristics than professional service firms (PSFs). There are two useful reasons for doing so. First, the process of analysing business schools through a professional services lens sheds new light on the management and leadership challenges for business school deans. Second, the process broadens the range of studies of PSFs that exist outside of the 'core professions' (law, accountancy, medicine and so on; Lowendahl, 1997), enabling closer scrutiny of the characteristics of PSFs.

Business schools, like most higher education institutions and PSFs, are 'loosely coupled' organisations that exhibit a set of distinctive traits and characteristics which lead to a unique organisational form and setting. This presents particular challenges for business school deans since leading a business school is not the same as leading a corporation. In a growing literature that examines business schools and their various constituents, there is only limited coverage of the practice and role of deans (Davies and Thomas, 2009).

A closer inspection of the literature on knowledge-intensive firms (KIFs) and PSFs reveals ambiguity surrounding the term PSF (Malhotra and Morris, 2009; von Nordenflycht, 2010) and too narrow an empirical focus on so-called core professions (Kärreman et al., 2002).

In response to this ambiguity in the field and a lack of studies beyond the core professions, we assess here the case for business

We are extremely grateful to Alexander Wilson (Assistant Professor of Strategy at Loughborough University) for many of the insights in this chapter, which are drawn from current and continuing joint research with Howard Thomas on management education. Fernando Fragueiro (Professor, IAE, Argentina) (Fragueiro and Thomas, 2011) has also contributed strongly to work on PSFs.

schools to be considered as a type of PSF. To guide this process we examine the following set of interrelated issues.

- What is a professional service firm?
- What are the key characteristics of PSFs?
- Are business schools a type of PSF?

The following sections address jointly the first and second issues by drawing on the available literature on PSFs and focusing on the interplay between their distinctive characteristics and organisational opportunities and challenges (cf. von Nordernflycht, 2010). Building on this foundation, we then examine cases of managing business schools together with evidence from business school deans to assess whether their actions are consistent with existing theoretical models of PSFs.

> Business schools have established themselves as relevant, renowned academic institutions whether as part of prestigious universities or as stand-alone management education providers.

INTRODUCTION

The history of business schools has been short but significant. They have established themselves as relevant, renowned academic institutions whether as part of prestigious universities or as stand-alone management education providers. The pursuit of their initial purpose of professionalising management and in the process building up its own body of knowledge, rules and values has shifted from a combination of individual insights shared by savvy veteran managers and practical advice to a more scientific approach that now encompasses several academic disciplines (Fragueiro and Thomas, 2011).

In parallel, the study of professional service and knowledge-intensive firms has made significant contributions to the way we study and manage organisations. Specifically, the research on PSFs (Løwendahl, 2000) and KIFs (Blackler, 1995) reflects the presence of increasingly complex systems of knowledge underpinning organisations and enriches our theoretical capacity to study contemporary organisations. However, scholars in this area have tended to concentrate on a core set of professions – for example, law, accountancy or medicine (Kärreman et al., 2002) – and, where comparisons are made, they tend to be with non-professional organisations.

Therefore, our aim in this chapter is twofold. First, by adopting a definition of PSFs that (a) extends the classification beyond core professions and (b) differentiates between types of PSF our analysis demonstrates that the particular characteristics of business school organisations are consistent with many features of PSFs. Second, if business schools are a type of PSF, there are specific and far-reaching consequences for the leadership, strategic management and competitiveness of business schools. The associated leadership challenges of managing a PSF (business school) should be identified and commonly reflected in the close examination of the accounts and managerial experiences of business school deans.

CONTEXT, CONTROVERSY AND BUSINESS SCHOOLS

Many scholars have identified the pivotal role knowledge plays as the backbone of value creation (DeLong and Nanda, 2003; Newell et al., 2002; Reich, 1991) and competitive advantage (McGee et al., 2010; Teece, 2000). Knowledge is essential in post-industrial economies (Bell, 1974) as the crucial conduit that bonds the network society (Castells, 2000) and as the vital ally of *informatised* society (Kallinikos, 2006).

The central importance of professionals and the knowledge they hold has undoubtedly shaped and repositioned management debate away from control of resources to include the exercise and application of specialist knowledge and competencies (Blackler, 1995: 1022). In this environment of 'headwork' over 'handwork' (Drucker, 1969; cited in Waring and Currie, 2009: 758) the practice of knowledge management entails the accumulation, storage and leverage of knowledge.

For many contemporary organisations the expertise of their workers is at the forefront of value creation. We regard business school academics as professional experts who create value and are actively involved in management training, development and research as part of the management community. We also observe that business schools have diverse models and philosophies. This is reflected in terms of their approaches to management education and research. Antunes and Thomas (2007) contrast the US and European models of management education in business schools, the former exhibiting wide-scale standardisation of programmes and research and the latter adopting more distinctive identities. In addition, we observe differences in the institutional arrangement of business schools where ownership and funding is a continuum ranging from wholly private to fully state-dependent schools. This adds further to the diversity among the global population of schools.

However, business schools face an array of complex and often conflicting demands, perhaps best captured by the tensions between research into management that is academic and rigorous but largely theoretical, and research that promises practical relevance to the management community.

Lively debate surrounds the role of the business school. Critics question the competitive environment of business schools, key stakeholders and the legitimacy of management education and research. In short, there is intense questioning of the role and purpose of business schools and management education.

As we have noted, this has led some commentators to brand business schools as 'schizophrenic' organisations (Crainer and Dearlove, 1998) and an increased questioning of their role and purpose in relation to the needs of the management community, their academic legitimacy as part of a modern university and, in the wake of recent business scandals, their societal value. Lively debate surrounds the role of the business school. Critics question the competitive environment of business schools (Aharoni, 1993; Antunes and Thomas, 2007; Cornuel, 2007; Thomas and Wilson, 2009), key stakeholders

(Brocklehurst et al., 2007; Cornuel, 2007; Grey, 2002; Lorange, 2008; Starkey and Tiratsoo, 2007; Zell, 2005), and the legitimacy of management education and research (Bennis and O'Toole, 2005; Gabriel, 2005; Garvin, 2003; Ghoshal, 2005; Khurana and Nohria, 2008; Podolny, 2009). In short, there is intense questioning of the role and purpose of business schools and management education.

For example, it has been argued that management education needs a system of learning, formal training, an overarching professional body and a code of conduct to produce a model of occupational professionalism comparable to the core professions (Khurana, 2007; Khurana and Nohria, 2008; Reed and Anthony, 1992). Despite frequent comparisons to established professions, management practice is not strictly the sole domain of professional managers (this is one possible contributory factor impeding the emergence of management as a true profession). Management consultancy roles and MBA qualifications are often undertaken by members of other professions; for example, engineers who are also practising managers. Consequently, it is difficult to identify management as a profession in the same sense that law, accountancy or medicine are professions.

Compared to law and medical schools, business schools occupy a controversial space. They lack a legally sanctioned professional body and grapple with the twin forces of academic rigour and practical relevance (Antunes and Thomas, 2007; Pettigrew, 1997). For some commentators business schools have helped to create a rift that prevents management becoming a 'true' profession (Khurana, 2007; Khurana and Nohria, 2008). It is claimed that business schools have abandoned the pursuit of rigorous relevant knowledge in favour of chasing profit (Starkey and Tiratsoo, 2007) and have shunned managerial competencies in favour of technocracy (Ghoshal, 2005; Mintzberg, 2004).

In confronting these criticisms, some argue that business schools should direct their future development towards the unfinished project of professionalisation (Bennis and O'Toole, 2005; Ferlie et al., 2010; Khurana, 2007; Khurana and Nohria, 2008; Pfeffer and

Fong, 2002; 2004). Ferlie and colleagues (2010) suggest a 'public interest school of management' that parallels the role of the medical school. They propose the development of a strong professional identity based on an ethical and societal orientation for managers that fosters an accumulation of knowledge founded on social science and engagement with practice.

It is within this context of controversy and 'schizophrenic' demands that the business school dean undertakes his/her leadership role.

As 'first among equals', deans are expected to act as 'integrators' who reconcile short-term financial needs and long-term academic goals while keeping in sight corporate and private customers' requirements as well as the school's relevant offerings (Fragueiro and Thomas, 2011). The dean must attend to the balance of rigour and relevance (Zell, 2005) and the values associated with academic and professional practice (Grey, 2002). To reconcile these demands, deans must create a persona based on the combination of their scholarly and professional reputations.

Therefore, deans must learn to champion both the academic values of the university/academy and the professional values of their external management constituency without appearing duplicitous (Fagin, 1997; Gmelch, 2004: 78). Baba portrays a dean as 'the Custodian of Intellectual, Social and Reputational Capital'.[1] This has led several deans to compare themselves to partners in PSFs (Davies and Thomas, 2009). They argue that they are promoted on the basis of expertise, knowledge and intellectual capital to leadership/management positions where their subsequent accumulation of political and social capital (Nahapiet and Ghoshal, 1998) combines in a virtuous circle to generate economic and reputational – that is, cultural – capital for the business school.

> Business school deans are confronted with leading not only complex organisational forms but also reconciling diverse stakeholder interests in an era of 'hyper competition'.

[1] Baba, V. V. (2007). Deaning at a BSchool: the generation and deployment of reputation capital. Paper presented at the Canadian Federation of Business School Deans' Meeting, Toronto, 24 November.

In this context, deans need to be able to build consensus and share their vision of strategy. However, they cannot overlook their responsibility to secure the necessary resources to attract the best faculty members, funding adequate compensation schemes and facilitating their research agendas. In this setting, deans have little power to drive change or to introduce bold strategic initiatives that may challenge their schools' *status quo*. Consequently, business school deans are confronted with leading not only complex organisational forms but also reconciling diverse stakeholder interests in an era of 'hyper competition' (Starkey and Tiratsoo, 2007). This forms the context of the leadership challenge for business school deans within which we position business schools as PSFs.

If business schools are faced with these growing social and ideological tensions coupled with mounting global competition then there is an imperative for change. This raises two interrelated concerns for business school deans: *what* needs to be changed and *how* can they instigate change? Undoubtedly, the former is of great importance in the development and future position of business schools as both academic and social institutions. Indeed, the discussion above shows that many of the scholars who highlight the controversies surrounding business schools also propose alternative models for their operation and organisation. However, the central focus of this chapter is on the unique and challenging issues that relate to the latter processes of how business school deans lead their (professional service) organisations.

PROFESSIONAL SERVICE AND KNOWLEDGE-INTENSIVE FIRMS

There is broad and developing scholarly debate surrounding the organisation and processes of KIFs and PSFs. Against the background of knowledge economies, which depend upon knowledge work, there are common elements that suggest similarities between KIFs and PSFs (Løwendahl, 1997; Maister, 1993; Morris and Empson, 1998). Underpinning this argument is the crucial common factor that both depend on expertise held and executed by human capital as a core asset – what differentiates them from capital- or information-intensive firms. We therefore propose an *inclusive* and *integrative* framework for characterising PSFs/KIFs before developing the case for business schools as professional service firms. The framework is inclusive as we draw on literatures on both PSFs and KIFs that extend beyond the core professions such as accountancy, medicine and law (Kärreman et al., 2002; von Nordenflycht, 2010).

The inclusive aspect of our framework addresses the lack of a distinct taxonomy for the structure and practices of PSFs, an issue exacerbated by generalisation from the core professions as representative of other professional organisational forms. We initially explore the central theme of expertise. For example, Starbuck (1992: 717) observes that 'many KIFs are not professional firms' because professions have properties additional to expertise that define their identity. However, Starbuck also underlines the importance that expertise plays in KIFs, which includes firms operating outside core professions:

> Professionals are not the only experts who build their own roles, divide work to suit their own interests, compete for resources, or emphasize autonomy, collegiality, informality and flexible structures. Other occupations share these traditions, and some experts have enough demand for their services that they can obtain autonomy without support from a recognized profession.
>
> *(Starbuck, 1992: 718)*

Furthermore, in sectors where there has been limited or no formal professionalisation of knowledge, there are creative and client-led organisations that closely resemble PSFs (Løwendahl, 2000). Whether or not a professional body exists, Løwendahl argues '[it is] more meaningful to talk about professional services as a type of service rather than to attempt to classify the people delivering the services' (19).

Starbuck (1992) conceptualises knowledge as an input and proposes that 'knowledge intensive' signifies the primary importance knowledge holds for a firm; those who possess and utilise knowledge are viewed as crucial for the success of a KIF. This is echoed by Blackler (1995: 1022) who observes that KIFs are 'organisations staffed by a high proportion of highly qualified staff who trade in knowledge itself'. Alvesson (2004) defines KIFs as companies where most work can be said to be of an intellectual nature and where well-educated, qualified employees form the major part of the workforce.

Mintzberg (1989) also refers to PSFs and KIFs in an inclusive way. He considers the following establishments to be either PSFs or KIFs: universities, general hospitals, accounting firms, law firms and engineering firms, among others. Teece (2003) also emphasises that PSFs are firms that primarily engage in the delivery of expertise to their clients. This signals that the delivery of professional services extends beyond the umbrella of the traditional (and institutionalised) core professions and that expertise holds primary importance in the study of PSFs.

Morris and Empson (1998) assert that PSFs (in their terms, accounting firms and consulting firms among others) can be considered KIFs. However, they are conscious that the role knowledge plays in PSFs has received little research attention and that it might be important in the future to consider it as an objectively definable and key resource for PSFs.

> PSFs are knowledge intensive by virtue of their dependence on the expertise of employees. KIFs, by contrast, experience different levels of professionalisation.

We therefore conclude that PSFs are certainly knowledge intensive by virtue of their dependence on the expertise of employees. KIFs, by contrast, experience different levels of professionalisation. Again, this resonates strongly with the calls for building the theoretical capacity to differentiate between types of PSF.

As well as endorsing an inclusive definition of PSFs, we propose an integrative understanding of the systems of knowledge work that underpin them. This asserts that 'there is an interactive relationship between dominant knowledge types and organisational forms. Further, the extent to which tacit knowledge constitutes the knowledge base of the firm, and how it is formed and used are powerfully shaped by the broader institutional context' (Lam, 2000: 487). This has implications for professional knowledge to the extent that '[it] is not fixed but situated in a recurring set of unstable conditions, in a variety of localised circumstances' (Gleeson and Knights, 2006: 283). Therefore, it is not only the 'stock' of knowledge or expertise held by an organisation that makes it effective; it is the combined dynamic processes of formal training, membership selection and application of expertise that operate and interact in an institutionalised context (Lam, 2000; Robertson et al., 2003). This reinforces the notion that firms that depend on expertise will experience differing levels of professionalisation yet exhibit similarities to traditional core professions.

Business schools may be assessed as being PSFs across three broad indicators.

- First, in terms of indicators from the literature (i.e. whether and in what sense business schools have been included in accounts of PSFs).
- Second, organisation structure indicates how resources (including knowledge) are co-ordinated and arranged to provide goods and services within the business environment. This reflects upon how organisations are structured for the co-ordination of expertise in order to deliver professional services.
- Third, an alternative analytical lens is applied that enables differentiation between types of PSF. We draw on a recent framework by von Nordenflycht (2010), which elicits distinctive characteristics and their related organisational challenges in order to differentiate distinctive forms of PSFs.

These three arenas provide the criteria for positioning business schools as a type of PSF.

Is the business school a professional service firm?

Henry Mintzberg's important work on patterns in strategy formation provides a framework for the examination of the business school as a professional organisation.

In his work *The Structuring of Organizations* (Mintzberg, 1979) he proposes four types of organisation: entrepreneurial, machine, adhocracy and professional, of which the latter two most closely resemble a business school and are defined as follows:

> *Adhocracy organisations*: (characterised by a dynamic external environment and decentralised internal power) organised around teams of experts working on projects to produce novel outputs, generally in highly dynamic settings;
>
> *Professional organisations*: (characterised by a stable external environment and decentralised internal power) dependent on highly skilled workers who work rather autonomously, subject to professional norms, mostly providing standardised services in stable settings.

Mintzberg also studied the strategic development pathways over time of both McGill University as an organisation and Mintzberg himself as a researcher, professor and faculty member in McGill. This involved identifying their actions and investigating their origins and the patterns in their decisions and strategy formation.

Mintzberg described McGill University as the classic professional organisation, with a highly trained professoriate that interpreted the organisation's mission of teaching and research individually with little or no collective strategic planning or collective strategic learning. These individual professors carried out their research in a well-established and consistent fashion. Their academic strategies were shaped both by academic colleagues and by the norms of professional bodies such as the US Academy of Management, which sets standards of practice in the management and organisational behaviour arena.

Typically, their individual strategies tended to dominate those of the organisation (the business school), whose overall leadership with regard to strategy formation is found to be somewhat weaker than in the 'adhocracy' organisation of its professionals.

Table 6.1 shows the configurations of the organisational form and the strategy formation process, contrasting the adhocracy

Table 6.1 *Configurations of organisation form and strategy formation process*

	Adhocracy organisation	Professional organisation
Conditions	Innovation High technology Dynamic environment	Skilled workers Stable environment
Power vested in	Project teams	Each professional
Integration	Loosely coupled	Decoupled
Favoured strategy process	Collective learning (and venturing)	Individual venturing
Strategies	Emergent positions and perspectives	Portfolio of individual positions (deliberate and emergent)
Pattern of change	Cycling in and out of focus	Frequent shifts of position within overall stability
Environment leadership organisation	Environment takes the lead	Professionals in the organisation take the lead
Key strategic issue	Collective mind?	Strategic management in question

Source: Adapted from Mintzberg (1979). See also Fragueiro and Thomas (2011: Table 2.1)

organisation with the professional organisation (which is most likely to resemble a business school).

Mintzberg's work on patterns of strategy formation and strategic processes clearly establishes the business school as typical of the professional organisation form since its professors operate individually and in an idiosyncratic, decentralised fashion managed through relatively weak leadership involving tacit co-ordination and supportive mentoring management styles. This is consistent with Maister's (1993) view of the university structure as conforming to the PSF structure (a problem-solving, creative organisation) in which academics tend to work independently of each other. Bryman's (2007) important study of leadership in higher education indicates that academics expect their leaders to be supportive managers by ensuring the maintenance of faculty autonomy, consultation over important decisions, the creation of collegiality (both in democratic decision making and mutual co-operation) and by fighting the faculty and department's position with senior university managers and in university committees.

He also points out that academics would react against a directive style of leadership since it would interfere with their autonomy. Instead, a minimalist leadership style is preferred. Mintzberg (1998) suggests that professionals expect little direct supervision from managers and require a subtle, more nuanced and covert form of leadership consisting of 'protection and support' and co-ordination that creates legitimacy and reputation for their department. Raelin (1986) also emphasises that 'management of autonomy' is central to the leadership of academics. He points out that collegiality, in terms of critical debate and open examination, and persuasion should dominate bureaucratic control if processes of strategic change are to be successful in the management of professional academics.

ORGANISATIONAL STRUCTURE

Building on an inclusive, expertise-led classification of KIFs/PSFs, Løwendahl (2000) argues that there are three generic organisational types: client relation organisations, problem-solving and creative organisations, and solution and output organisations. She argues that there is a structural balance to be reached between the type of professional service provided and how organisational resources are controlled (see Table 6.2). Crucially, this differentiates between types of PSFs and also alludes to how they are structured as organisations.

There is a core dilemma involved in structuring PSF organisations, which Newell et al. (2002) describe as 'structural constraints on knowledge work', where standardised rules or routines compromise the innovative capacity of knowledge workers. Indeed, Mintzberg's

Table 6.2 *Three generic types of professional firms*

External focus	Clients	Problems/ creative solutions	Standardised/ branded solutions
Internal focus			
Organisationally controlled			Solution and output organisations
Individually, team and organisationally controlled		Problem-solving and creative organisations	
Individually controlled	Client relation organisations		

Source: Aadapted from Løwendahl (2000: 115)

adhocracy appears best suited to the accommodation of expertise and creative activity because of its flat hierarchy, self-organisation of work tasks, minimal formalisation, normative control, decentralised decision making, co-ordination and highly organic form (Mintzberg, 1979; 1993; Newell et al., 2002). However, there is a tension between autonomy and control that is heightened by the size and scope of an organisation and which becomes more acute as firms grow (Løwendahl, 2000; Mintzberg, 1993; Newell et al., 2002; Starbuck, 1992). Our inclusive definition of KIFs and PSFs covers organisations that are not configured as adhocratic enterprises and use more central-ised mechanisms of control to organise expertise. Table 6.2 examines the generic types of PSF according to the services they provide.

The three generic configurations shown in Table 6.2 differen-tiate between firms' output and services in relation to their internal resource base and external focus. This implies that certain organisa-tional forms are likely to be better suited to facilitating the appropriate level of professional autonomy (client relation organisations) or control (solution and output organisations) over expertise.

Using Løwendahl's typology a business school or university department would probably be categorised as a problem-solving/creative organisation because of the complex mixture of individually and organisationally controlled expertise. This duality of control between professional and organisational expertise produces a profound challenge for strategy formation and leadership in PSFs, including business schools.

Although business schools may be run as private institutions (e.g. INSEAD, IMD, Lorange Institute), university-based departments (e.g. WBS, LSE, Judge, Saïd) or a hybrid of these two positions (Cass, LBS), they share few characteristics with the 'creative' adhocracy structure.

For example, university-based schools are embedded within the heavily institutionalised system of university bureaucracy yet academics are expected to pursue and co-ordinate individual or team-led research, deliver and support teaching, and undertake administrative duties. Teece (2003: 907) provides an inclusive (extends beyond core professions) and expertise-centred depiction of academia: '[E]xperts, be they medical doctors, professors [...] desire high autonomy and can be self-motivated and self-directed because of their deep expertise. The university environment caters for this magnificently with the tenure system – requiring the discharge of teaching, research and considerable discretion as to whether and when (other than meeting class) tasks are performed.'

By this description, academics have a high degree of autonomy and are self-motivated experts, consistent with the knowledge-intensive characteristics of PSFs. In terms of organisational structure, business schools have a core of expertise that distinguishes them from machine bureaucracies (Greenwood et al., 1990; Hall, 1968; Mintzberg, 1993; Montagna, 1968), yet provides mechanisms for both co-ordination and autonomy among academics.

While we have been critical of the lack of consensus about what constitutes a PSF and a general preoccupation with core professions, our inclusive approach opens up the substantial body of existing

Table 6.3 Key features of PSFs

Key features Important authors	Individual professionals	Professional competencies	Shared power	Intangibility	Standardisation/customisation	Trust
Løwendahl (2000)	X	X		X		
Bartol (1979)	X	X				
Bucher and Sterling (1969)	X					
Montagna (1968)	X		X			
Hall (1968)	X		X			
Scott (1965)	X					
Kerr et al. (1977)	X					
Hinings et al. (1991)	X					
Friedson and Rhea (1965)	X					
Goode (1960)	X					
Hrebiniak and Alutto (1972)	X					
Empson (2000)	X	X		X		
Paulin et al. (2000)		X				X
Pettigrew and Fenton (2000)		X		X	X	X

Reference				
Maister (1993)		X	X	
Aharoni (1997)		X		
Liedtka et al. (1997)		X		
Mintzberg (1989)	X		X	
Greenwood et al. (1990)	X			
Mills et al. (1983)	X	X		
Greenwood et al. (1994)	X			
Winch and Schneider (1993)		X		
Larson (1977)		X		
Nachum (1999)		X		
Morris and Empson (1998)			X	
Sharma (1997)				X
Thakor (2000)				X
Bloom (1984)				X
Hill (1988)				X
Hill and Motes (1995)				X

Source: Adapted from Chapter 3 in Fragueiro and Thomas (2011)

research on both PSFs and KIFs to identify some of their key organisational challenges. These aspects have been termed 'challenges' because of their implications for the leadership and management processes of PSFs. This combination of organisational characteristics and challenges presents a complex leadership scenario for business school deans. Drawing on the combined wealth of literature surrounding PSFs and KIFs, Table 6.3 identifies six recurring organisational features and challenges: namely, individual professionals, professional competencies, shared power, intangibility, standardisation/ customisation and trust.

Our discussion and literature review indicates that there are two interrelated levels that are distinctive elements of PSFs: organisational characteristics and organisational challenges. PSFs face the structural conundrum of allowing sufficient flexibility to professionals combined with standardised control mechanisms to direct the firm. PSFs are therefore a compromise between the preference for autonomy and the co-ordinating efforts of managers and leaders, 'requiring as they do organizational structures that can facilitate both decentralization and integration' (Boussebaa, 2009: 830), and growth strategies can therefore be particularly problematic as scale often requires greater co-ordination (Løwendahl, 2000).

For leaders of PSFs there is a series of challenges that arise from both the structural and operational demands of a professional organisation. In Figure 6.1 we combine the organisational characteristics (inner circle) and challenges (outer circles) to produce an integrated overview.

RESEARCH INSIGHTS

This chapter argues that business schools are a variety of PSF, which sets specific kinds of organisational challenges on the strategic options available to the business school dean. In most academic institutions and PSFs, leadership roles are not viewed as career aspirations unlike the coveted CEO position in most businesses. Rather, professional and academic career paths tend to revolve around building and consolidating a specific expertise and reputation – for example, as

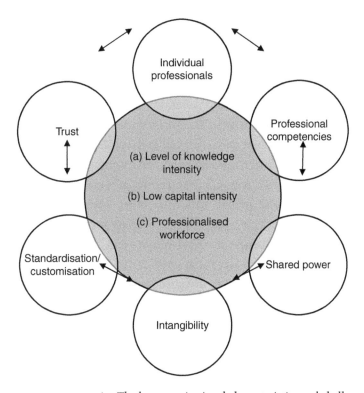

FIGURE 6.1 The key organisational characteristics and challenges of PSFs

an academic by securing tenure, succeeding as a scholar, conducting ground-breaking research and publishing relevant findings. Business school deans are sometimes seen by their internal constituencies as 'first among equals' as they are elected directly or indirectly by the faculty to serve for a specific term, eventually rejoining the faculty when their term concludes.

The dean is rarely viewed as the boss; rather, he/she is regarded as more of a colleague. As the bridge between expert academics and the demands of strategic leadership, business school deans possess unique in-depth insight into the organisational challenges and are thus highly informed subjects for this research.

> The dean is rarely viewed as the boss; rather, he/she is regarded as more of a colleague.

We now develop insights from a dataset covering five business school case studies: IMD (Switzerland), INSEAD (France), LBS (UK), WBS (UK) and IAE (Argentina) (see Fragueiro and Thomas, 2011). The studies of IMD, INSEAD and LBS cover the period 1990–2004, WBS 2000–10 and IAE 1995–2008. We also draw on an array of recent case studies featured in the 'How to Fix the Business School' *Harvard Business School Review* debate series, as well as the studies included in Datar et al. (2010). Accordingly, the dataset comprises primary data from interviews, documentary sources and records from personal experience and is supplemented by secondary data from other leading business schools and their deans. This study therefore spans the contrasting US–European models of business schools (Antunes and Thomas, 2007) and their constituent research areas (e.g. Grey, 2010). The cumulative dataset presents a rich illustration of business school organisations with which to compare evidence from research on PSFs and KIFs.

KNOWLEDGE INTENSITY

PSFs are first and foremost knowledge-intensive organisations. Indeed, PSFs provide innovative problem-solving services based on a high degree of professional expertise and individual judgement. The core resource base of such organisations is present in the expertise and problem-solving abilities of their employees (Løwendahl, 2000: 41) and it is this that differentiates PSFs from other organisational types (Løwendahl, 2000; Starbuck, 1992; Teece, 2003). The knowledge-intensity component of PSFs produces particular organisational challenges (see Figure 6.1). Specifically, our literature review and data indicate that *professional competencies, intangibility* and *trust* pose key organisational challenges in the leadership of PSFs.

Professional competencies include professional knowledge, skills and attitudes that enable employees to develop the required ability to comprehend and analyse the diverse problems faced in new projects and situations (Morris and Empson, 1998).

Three broadly defined characteristics of professional individuals are important elements: (1) the need for autonomy; (2) career development focused on professional expertise; and (3) a stronger link to professional standards and values than to the PSF that employs them.

The first characteristic, the professional's need for *autonomy*, is the perceived right to make decisions about both the means and the goals associated with one's work (Bartol, 1979). This implies that professionals require the independence to define problems and generate solutions without pressure from clients, non-members of the professions or their employing organisation (Hall, 1968; Raelin, 1984; Scott and Scott, 1965).

Hinings and colleagues (1991) identify *professional expertise*, the second characteristic, as the main source of power in PSFs. This may be a reason why a professional's career development is more focused on the level and quality of professional expertise than on progress in an administrative or management hierarchy.

Finally, professionals demonstrate a *stronger link to their professional standards and values than to the PSF that employs them*. This can be seen in the importance professionals attribute to their reputation among their peers, to their professional standards and to their ethical values (Bucher and Sterling, 1969: 12; Goode, 1960). This strong link to the profession is particularly relevant for PSFs since it provides a network and helps its professionals to keep up to date. Professionals' expertise, experience, skills in building and maintaining relationships with clients and peers, their professional reputation and network of peers are the strategic resources that PSFs must access from their workforce (Løwendahl, 2000) in order to overcome the intangible nature of the services they deliver.

> Professionals demonstrate a stronger link to their professional standards and values than to the PSF that employs them.

As these resources are inextricably tied to the individual professional, their ownership and control resides with (or within) these key individuals. There are therefore inherent organisational challenges in building and maintaining knowledge intensity. The combination of a preference for autonomy, career development based on expertise

and strong ties to professional values creates difficulties in the retention and direction of professionals for those leading and managing
PSFs – a phenomenon that is likened to 'cat herding' (Løwendahl,
2000: 62; von Nordenflycht, 2010).

The only half-humorous reference to 'cat herding' captures
the managerial challenges of retaining and directing professionals.
The high knowledge intensity in PSFs means that professionals are
in a strong bargaining position relative to the firm (von Nordenflycht,
2010: 160) and are often highly mobile as their expertise is easily
transferable to other firms (Teece, 2003). These conditions, coupled
with a strong desire for autonomy, limit the capacity for formal
control through management authority (Kärreman and Alvesson,
2004; Lorsch and Tierney, 2002; Løwendahl, 2000; Teece, 2003;
von Nordenflycht, 2010). For this reason, managing PSFs is often
typified by the conflicting pressures of professionalisation versus bur-
eaucratisation (cf. Hall, 1968) that underlies the combined challenge
of keeping and managing a highly skilled professional workforce.

Following Mintzberg's (1989, 1993) work on management and
structure, it is apparent that, through different co-ordinating mechanisms, 'the locus of control is moved from outside of the worker to
the inside: to consensual approval (mutual adjustment)' (Kärreman
and Alvesson, 2004: 152). As such, PSFs tend to employ alternative
strategies for rewarding and retaining professionals, including
performance-related bonuses, deferred incentives or providing an environment of informality and autonomy for professionals (Greenwood and
Empson, 2003; Greenwood et al., 1990; von Nordenflycht, 2010).

> It is clear that knowledge intensity and the intangibility of professional
> services create management challenges in retaining and directing
> individual professionals.

It is clear that knowledge intensity and the intangibility of
professional services create management challenges in retaining and
directing individual professionals. This typically involves internal

organisational strategies about how to structure and reward professional work. However, the high knowledge intensity of PSFs also affects the professional–client interface, emphasising further the interrelated organisational challenges from intangibility and trust. The idiosyncracy of professional activity, together with the intangibility of assets such as reputation and credibility, create the additional need to signal client service quality. PSFs, therefore, have to generate client trust, build and maintain their reputation, and uphold ethical codes and professional standards (Løwendahl, 2000; Maister, 1993).[2] PSF organisations can signal quality through mechanisms including 'bonding, reputation, appearance and ethical codes' (von Nordenflycht, 2010). Table 6.4 summarises the mechanisms available to PSFs to signal quality and build trust with clients and the professional community.

Bonding refers to formalised means that are introduced to protect clients by penalising low-quality output; for example, professional firms structured as unlimited liability partnerships that serve to dissuade partners from exposing others to risk (Greenwood and Empson, 2003; von Nordenflycht, 2010). Bonding captures the organisational and institutional arrangements used to safeguard and maintain quality in the services of PSFs and that accompany the signals from reputation, appearance and ethical codes, which are also key indicators of service quality. All four signalling mechanisms are essential elements in building trusting relationships between PSFs and their clients.

For PSFs it is crucial to build trusting relationships, networks and reputational capital both internally with professionals and externally with customers. 'Moreover, these reputations are built up over time and are not replaceable or imitable in the market place', and '[trust is] the basis of most social and professional relationships [...]

---

[2] Empson, L. (2000). The triumph of commercialism: mergers between accounting firms and the transformation of the professional archetype. Preliminary draft of a paper presented at the Academy of Management annual conference, Toronto, 6 August.

Table 6.4 *Mechanisms for signalling the quality of professional services*

Type of quality signal	Signalling mechanisms
Bonding	Formalised organisational systems that penalise low-quality production: for example, profit share, organisational arrangements such as limited liability partnerships that expose professionals to shared risk
Reputation	Good reputation and standing generates positive signals of high-quality professional services and social capital
Appearance	Symbolic and observable characteristics of both professionals and their services: for example, social and personal traits of experts in their dress and interaction with clients (Starbuck, 1992)
Ethical codes	Professional associations are founded on ethical codes to protect clients' interests. Ethical codes are becoming evident outside of arenas governed by professional associations: for example, in leading MBA courses (see Khurana and Nohria, 2008)

Source: Thomas and Wilson (2011)

[T]rust is hard to build but easy to lose.'[3] Pettigrew and Fenton also note that reputation is critical in reducing behavioural uncertainty and that it provides the basis for the development of trust.

The relevance of 'trust building' is directly related to the following factors. First, the intangible nature of the PSFs assets, such as 'reputation', 'professional knowledge' and 'professional competencies'. Second, the close interaction between professionals and clients requires trust building through appearance and ethical codes of conduct; moreover, the increasing demands for efficiency require

---

[3] Pettigrew, A. M. and Fenton, E. (2000). Becoming integrated global networks: transforming four professional service organizations. Paper presented at the Academy of Management annual conference, Toronto, 5 August.

fluid communication and excellent co-ordination among PSF members, and therefore internal trust building is also a key issue. Third, the professional's respect for the norms of the profession implies certain common ideas about how the job should be done. Fourth, 'information asymmetry' between professionals and clients might lead to professionals applying their discretionary judgement with unclear purposes, such as experimenting with new tools or selling solutions that are not actually necessary to solve the client's problem. And finally, client firms might require 'confidentiality' from the PSF and disregarding this issue could be fatal for the PSF's reputation. Therefore, trust building towards clients also implies managing confidentiality. Here again, ethical codes help to build trust between professionals and clients.

In the context of business schools, a current controversy surrounding the role and value of the MBA offers a vivid illustration of how intangibility places an onus on PSFs to develop the means to indicate the quality of their services. For example, the question 'do MBAs make better managers?' brings the intangibility of professional services to the fore. Perhaps, for a variety of stakeholders, the intangibility of business school outputs has fuelled critics' assessment of their quality.

For business schools, there are also formalised bonding mechanisms that signal quality; however, these tend to be constituents of a broader business school constituency rather than at the level of individual schools. We therefore extend the types of bonding quality indicators to include institutions outside the PSF. Bonding elements in the academic community are ingrained in both teaching and research practice. Having expert external examiners who act as authorities of quality for both teaching and examination in business schools is one such example. The institutionalised process of academic peer review of research also serves as a bonding mechanism designed to ensure its quality. (However, see Starbuck, 2005, for a discussion of the effectiveness of peer review.) Additional constituents include accreditation bodies that outline formal criteria to determine whether business schools meet quality standards.

Table 6.5 *Managing the challenges from knowledge intensity*

Institution (dean)	Data	Organisational challenges
INSEAD (Antonio Borges)	By the end of the decade, INSEAD recruitment efforts focused on faculty candidates with outstanding research performance to bring 'a new wave of more academic-oriented people that provided a lot of renewal'	Professional competencies
INSEAD (Antonio Borges)	To help attract and retain research-oriented professors, a number of systems and incentives were introduced or changed. Chairs, professorships and research support were granted to faculty members who showed an interest in developing relevant, world-class research work.	Professional competencies, intangibility
INSEAD (Philippe Naert)	The main thrust was to secure a better balance between 'the *transfer* and the *production* of knowledge'.[1]	Professional competencies
INSEAD (Philippe Naert)	Naert explained what he viewed as INSEAD's lingering weaknesses: its inadequate per capita research output and its poor standing in the academic community. He advocated a 50 per cent faculty increase and the creation of a doctoral programme.[2]	Professional competencies, intangibility
LBS (George Bain)	'If I deserve any credit, it was probably to have picked some very good people to be champions of products, of policies ...'	Professional competencies
IAE (Fernando Fragueiro)	'An[other] area that calls for deans' attention revolves around the overall academic performance of	Professional competencies, intangibility

Table 6.5 (*cont.*)

Institution (dean)	Data	Organisational challenges
	the school – namely, the rigour of its research, the relevance of its programme contents, its faculty's output, and the quality perceived by students and course attendants.'	
IMD (Peter Lorange)	'Recruitment is one of the school's topmost strategic priorities. There are two key aspects to faculty recruitment: attracting experienced individuals who raise the average quality of the school's faculty on account of their superior teaching and focus on relevant research, and recruiting people who can develop a sense of belonging to the school and cohesiveness towards its faculty in order to lead IMD into the future with its unique organisational model.'	Professional competencies

[1] *Financial Times*, 9 November 1987, in Barsoux (2000: 179).
[2] Minutes of the board meeting, 10 March 1986 in Barsoux (2000).
Source: Fraguiero and Thomas (2011)

The findings from previous research on PSFs suggest that if business schools are professional service firms then there will be evidence of 'cat herding' and quality signals as a consequence of the knowledge-intensive nature of the organisation. Indeed, academics have been included as examples of professional experts and reflect the characteristics of a knowledge-intensive workforce as depicted throughout the previous paragraphs. Table 6.5 examines evidence on how business school deans engage with the organisational challenges of professional competencies, intangibility and trust.

The series of quotes displayed in Table 6.5 indicate that the management of professional competencies and strategies for dealing with intangibility of expertise are paramount in deans' leadership thinking. There is a clear indication that the ability to recruit the best academic expertise is at the heart of each dean's strategy initiative.

There is, therefore, compelling evidence that business schools are knowledge-intensive enterprises and that deans face the leadership and managerial challenges that accompany high knowledge intensity.

A second feature of PSFs is that they tend to have a low capital intensity (von Nordenflycht, 2010). In combination with the challenges that arise from knowledge intensity, the capital structure of PSFs serves to reinforce the distinctive competencies and the bargaining power of employees and diminish the attractiveness of outside ownership. The key asset in a PSF/business school is, hence, the high quality and intellectual capital possessed by each individual.

LOW CAPITAL INTENSITY

In the so-called 'knowledge economy' a firm's knowledge and how it is leveraged need to be at the core of the theory of the firm (Hitt et al., 2001; Spender, 1996), especially as PSF production hinges on human capital. But though they may depend on knowledge intensity, PSFs tend to rely less on non-human assets such as specialist manufacturing technology or complex data handling systems as might high-technology or information-intensive firms. Inevitably, this low capital intensity brings a further set of organisational challenges to managers of PSFs.

> Though they may depend on knowledge intensity, PSFs tend to rely less on non-human assets such as specialist manufacturing technology or complex data handling systems.

As von Nordenflycht (1996) argues, these challenges stem from the increased bargaining power of professionals given a reduced or non-existent need for external capital for the firm. Low capital intensity means the skills of professionals are the main means of production, a fact that is difficult to overcome. Individual professional experts are highly mobile in the labour market and quite prepared and able to join competitor organisations or to set up their own professional practice. To protect themselves, PSF offer incentives such as preferential rewards and conditions (pay, autonomy, informality) to these 'gold-collar workers' (Kelley, 1990; Lorsch and Tierney, 2002) to secure their loyalty. The situation where high knowledge intensity is accompanied by low capital intensity therefore amplifies employee bargaining power, creating the organisational challenges of retaining professionals (academics).

Another additional factor is that low capital intensity provides conditions where a PSF is unlikely to require capital from external investors who would expect not only some return on their investment but also mechanisms to control their stake. This means that where capital intensity is low PSFs, rather than concentrating on producing shareholder value, have the flexibility to employ alternative incentives to align the interests of professionals with the organisation. For example, deferred financial bonuses or equity in the firm can be used both to retain professionals and to align them with organisational goals.

Additionally, without the imperative to structure the firm to the needs of external investors, there is the increased flexibility to accommodate professionals' preferred conditions of autonomy and informality (von Nordenflycht, 2010). Von Nordenflycht argues that as firms become more capital intensive they have a greater need to secure external investment, which in turn reduces the ability to provide conditions of informality and autonomy to its professionals. This has strong resonance with the literature on 'regulated PSFs' (Greenwood and Empson, 2003) and also 'neo-PSFs' such as management consultancy firms (Løwendahl, 2000). Because professional campuses are reliant on both a knowledge-intensive workforce and forms of traditional capital, this would imply the possibility of outside ownership.

As an example, von Nordenflycht (2010) refers to hospitals as professional campus PSFs. This form of PSF implies a degree of capital intensity alongside knowledge intensity and a professionalised workforce that is likely to diminish, rather than exclude, the organisational consequences of low capital intensity such as 'outside ownership' (162, 169). Continuing with the example of hospitals in the US it is shown that there is a mixture of ownership between publicly traded, non-profit and state ownership: 'This suggests that distinctive ownership outcomes are driven more strongly by workforce professionalization than by low capital intensity' (169).

The mixture of ownership is mirrored across the business school sector, with a similar blend of state, non-profit and private schools. In terms of ownership, however, we argue that in conjunction with workforce professionalisation, the national, historical and institutional contexts (Robertson et al., 2003) have been highly influential in shaping the profile of business school organisations.

For example, Antunes and Thomas (2007) observe the contrasting characteristic features of European and US business schools – both of which face the challenges of organising a professionalised workforce. The professional campus type of PSF reflected in the examples of hospitals and business schools indicates that low capital intensity is not a necessary consequence of knowledge intensity. However, knowledge intensity does not preclude other forms of capital from playing a role in the PSF.

Clearly there are types of PSF that require both knowledge- and capital-intensive configurations. These include biotechnology research laboratories, hospitals (von Nordenflycht, 2010) and, we argue, business schools. Indeed, these 'professional campuses' require that other particular forms of capital are brought successfully together with the expertise of a professional workforce to provide professional services.

> Clearly there are types of PSF that require both knowledge- and capital-intensive configurations. These include biotechnology research laboratories, hospitals and, we argue, business schools.

A hospital must have the expertise of specialist surgeons and anaesthetists; it must also have the surgical tools, operating theatres and administrative core in order to treat patients, and hence there is partial dependence on traditional forms of capital.

In the case of business schools, the provision of teaching facilities, libraries (including subscriptions to a wide array of journal materials), scholarly database services, alumni networks and an arsenal of student support services must accompany faculty expertise. Certainly, in the global and distributed nature of higher education the processes of teaching and research are dependent upon a vast ensemble of information technologies and strategic financial investments, particularly if distance and blended learning experiences are being delivered.

The dependence of business schools on both knowledge (expert academics) and capital (campus facilities, endowments and ICT), coupled with professional and institutional ties (e.g. accreditation and links to the higher education system and ideology), serve to create significant barriers to entry. Indeed, as Willmott (1995: 1001) argues, the extensive barriers to entry create conditions 'that fall considerably short of the full commodification of academic labour'. In this sense, academic labour is governed more comprehensively by professionalised norms than by free market conditions, providing a degree of protection from outside ownership. The implication of this scenario for the business school dean becomes the pursuit of demonstrable increases in school performance to secure valuable resources: 'performance measures provide an approximation of market discipline by making departments and institutions compete with each other for rankings that are linked to the provision of valued material and symbolic resources' (1001).

These conditions reinforce the need for deans to:

- attract, direct and retain the best academic expertise;
- engage mechanisms that enhance the standing of every school through various rankings, accreditation criteria and socially driven reputational effects, including strong endowments and fundraising that provide quality signals;
- foster conditions of informality and autonomy among faculty, consistent with the expectations of a professionalised workforce. (This is discussed in the following section.)

From our dataset we can see evidence of how business school deans attempt to develop strategies that simultaneously retain and align faculty with the strategic agendas of the school and the preferences of professional workers (see Table 6.6).

Using what could be described as a strategy of differentiation, Peter Lorange instituted an alternative incentive mechanism for faculty in an attempt to strengthen the bond between academics and the school. The logic was that by stepping outside the tenure system of other business schools, faculty members would have to

Table 6.6 *Strategies for managing challenges from low capital intensity*

Institution (dean)	Data	Organisational challenges
IMD (Peter Lorange)	'The fact that IMD does not offer tenure affects new candidates' careers. Driven out of the mainstream system, they must consider IMD as a place to stay for quite some time.'	Individual professionals
WBS (Howard Thomas)	[The school's strategic vision, articulated by the dean] 'To be in the top echelon of European business schools by 2015, through strong innovation and a positive step change in investment, encompassing academic and professional expertise, new teaching programmes, physical and IT infrastructure and international profile-raising.'	Individual professionals, professional competencies, intangibility

Source: Fraguiero and Thomas (2011)

regard IMD as a long-term career choice. At the same time, IMD provided a flexible and lucrative platform for its workforce to undertake executive teaching alongside their degree teaching and research duties. This alternative incentive mechanism feeds individual professionals' desire for autonomy while building and rewarding loyalty to the business school organisation.

The discussion so far has shown instances where high knowledge intensity and low capital intensity align business schools as exemplars of 'professional campus' forms of PSF. Finally, we examine the role, regulation and control of professional knowledge and examine the ideology of applied professional knowledge as embedded within the characteristic practices of a professionalised workforce.

PROFESSIONALISED WORKFORCE

The third organisational characteristic that differentiates PSFs from non-PSFs concerns the practice of expertise. This is reflected by three factors that constitute a professionalised workforce: *a particular knowledge base, regulation and control* and *ideology* (von Nordenflycht, 2010).

The knowledge-intensive nature of PSFs implies that there is, *de facto*, a particular knowledge base, and the organisational implications of this were discussed earlier in the chapter. A professionalised workforce is knowledge intensive yet a knowledge-intensive workforce might not be professionalised. The professionalisation of a workforce forms the third source of differentiation between types of PSF. The additional factors of *regulation and control* and the *ideology* of business school professionals thus form the additional basis for gauging the professionalisation of the workforce and its organisational challenges.

Regulation and control is a controversial issue where management as a profession is concerned. There is no single professional body that has a monopoly over a particular management knowledge base or presides over its use. This is compounded by certain constituents, particularly management consultancies, which have impeded professionalisation by not joining industry associations and not supporting licensing efforts (Løwendahl, 2000; von Nordenflycht, 2010: 163). Consequently, management education has been criticised for its failure to realise its original aim of recreating management as a profession (Khurana, 2007; Khurana and Nohria, 2008).

But what of the numerous organisations that accredit, monitor and allocate resources to business schools? Davies and Thomas (2009: 1399) observe that 'business school deans must pay attention to professional bodies (such as the Association of Chartered Certified Accountants, Chartered Institute of Marketing, Chartered Institute of Personnel and Development), business school accreditation bodies (AACSB, AMBA, EQUIS), government quality assurance and the kind of dysfunctional behaviours that the UK research assessment/ excellence frameworks generate' (Piercy, 2000).

Perhaps, rather than having failed to emerge as a 'true' profession, management is better perceived as being in stasis as a developing profession – a partly professionalised entity. Certainly, there is evidence in the case of business schools that various proxies and stakeholders serve to regulate and control knowledge and, furthermore, are emphatic and vocal in instilling ideologies into management education (which parallels the role of traditional professional bodies).

At the level of professional practice, the expectations of academics are to be able to pursue their own agendas and strategies, to be given autonomy and consultation with preference for a 'minimalist' leadership style offering 'protection and support' for their endeavours. Therefore it is expected that the consequence of a professionalised workforce is that there is evidence of a trusteeship norm and self-regulation as well as alternative incentive mechanisms to accommodate academics' preference for informality and autonomy.

Table 6.7 captures some of the responses by business school deans in relation to leading a professionalised workforce.

SUMMARY AND CONCLUSIONS

The analysis, and case evidence, in this chapter has confirmed that the business school has many of the characteristics of the

Table 6.7 *Strategies for managing challenges from a professionalised workforce*

Institution (dean)	Data	Organisational challenges
INSEAD (Antonio Borges)	To help attract and retain research-oriented professors, a number of systems and incentives were introduced or changed. Chairs, professorships and research support were granted to faculty members who showed an interest in developing relevant, world-class research work. A strong programme of sabbaticals was instituted to further promote research. This bold shift towards a more research-oriented profile caused unrest among incumbent faculty members, who had devoted themselves to the superior teaching that had made INSEAD a top-ranking institution.	Professional competencies, individual professions, trust
INSEAD (Ludo Van der Heyden)	Internally, the arrival of new, more research-oriented professors led to the development of two distinct groups within the school's faculty.	Professional identities
IMD (Juan Rada)	'There were two radically different cultures [...] I realised this during the merger process. IMI had been founded by Alcan, a business that focuses on long-term return on	Professional identities

Table 6.7 (*cont.*)

Institution (dean)	Data	Organisational challenges
	investment and, therefore, is interested in geopolitics and social stability [. . .] IMEDE was founded by Nestlé, which is a business of short-term cash flow, with an interest in management functions – and marketing in particular.'	
IMD (Peter Lorange)	As IMD President, Lorange's formal authority was robustly established but he realised having the faculty on his side was crucial. 'He said quite clearly, "I cannot do the job alone. I need the faculty."'[1] Lorange was also determined to bring different perspectives and experience to the table so he drew on key faculty members from IMI and IMEDE to create IMD's 'Management Committee'.	Trust
IMD (Xavier Gilbert)	Its deteriorating finances called for an urgent turnaround and its faculty was divided as to what the school ought to be and do. A group of professors, known as 'the farmers', concentrated on teaching the IMD regular curricula, while another group, 'the hunters', ventured outside the school, working with companies and delivering their own programmes.	Customisation/ standardisation

Table 6.7 *(cont.)*

Institution (dean)	Data	Organisational challenges
IMD (Peter Lorange)	To attract and retain the best faculty, an academic institution has to be an eminently attractive and interesting place. Lorange adapted the workload system in order to develop more transparency among IMD's professors. Faculty workload was allocated to three broad categories: teaching, research and citizenship. Transparency was a key feature: 'Everybody knew what the other was teaching. That immediately meant that we got a lot more capacity built.'[2]	Trust

[1] Fred Neubauer, former IMI faculty.
[2] Peter Lorange, IMD President.
Source: Fraguiero and Thomas (2011)

professional service firm. There, the key organisational characteristics and challenges of business schools tend to follow those of PSFs and are illustrated powerfully in the descriptions of deans' strategies for managing knowledge intensity, low capital intensity and a professional workforce. These short descriptions clearly indicate that there are strong similarities between managing and leading a business school and a PSF.

In leading and managing business schools, the relentless creation of new knowledge and new dynamic capabilities reinforces and enhances the 'path-bending' leadership capabilities that business school deans or senior managers must address in directing the future pathways for their business schools or organisations. How such dynamic capabilities can be identified, learned and leveraged in leading and managing business schools is, therefore, examined in the next chapter.

REFERENCES

Aharoni, Y. (1993). *Coalitions and Competition: The Globalization of Professional Business Services*. London: Routledge.

(1997). Management consulting, in *Changing Roles of State Intervention in Services in an Era of Open International Markets*. State University of New York Press.

Alvesson, M. (2004). *Knowledge Work and Knowledge-Intensive Firms*. Oxford University Press.

Antunes, D. and Thomas, H. (2007). The competitive (dis)advantages of European business schools. *Long Range Planning*, **40**(3): 382–404.

Barsoux, J.-L. (2000). *Insead: From Intuition to Institution*. New York: St Martin's Press.

Bartol, K. M. (1979). Professionalism as a predictor of organizational commitment, role stress, and turnovers: a multidimensional approach. *Academy of Management Journal*, **22**: 815–21.

Bell, D. (1974). *The Coming of Post-Industrial Society*. London: Heinemann.

Bennis, W. G. and O'Toole, J. (2005). How business schools lost their way. *Harvard Business Review*, **83**(5): 96–104.

Blackler, F. (1995). Knowledge, knowledge work and organizations: an overview and interpretation. *Organization Studies*, **16**(6): 1021–46.

Bloom, P. N. (1984). Effective marketing for professional services. *Harvard Business Review*, **62**(5): 102–10.

Boussebaa, M. (2009). Struggling to organize across national borders: the case of global resource management in professional service firms. *Human Relations*, **62**(6): 829–50.

Brocklehurst, M., Sturdy, A., Winstanley, D. and Driver, M. (2007). Introduction: whither the MBA? Factions, fault lines and the future. *Management Learning*, **38**(4): 379–88.

Bryman, A. (2007). Effective leadership in higher education: a literature review. *Studies in Higher Education*, **32**(6): 693–710.

Bucher, R. and Sterling, J. (1969). Characteristics of professional organizations. *Journal of Health and Social Behavior*, **10**: 3–15.

Castells, M. (2000). *The Rise of the Network Society* (2nd edn). Oxford: Blackwell.

Cornuel, E. (2007). Challenges facing business schools in the future. *Journal of Management Development*, 26(1): 87–92.

Crainer, S. and Dearlove, D. (1998). *Gravy Training: Inside the World's Top Business Schools*. Oxford: Capstone.

Datar, S., Garvin, D. A. and Cullen, P. G. (2010). *Rethinking the MBA: Business Education at a Crossroads*. Boston: Harvard Business School Press.

Davies, J. and Thomas, H. (2009). What do business school deans do? Insights from a UK study. *Management Decision*, 47(9): 1396–419.

DeLong, T. and Nanda, A. (2003). *Professional Services: Text and Cases*. Boston: McGraw-Hill/Irwin.

Drucker, P. F. (1969). *The Age of Discontinuity: Guidelines to Our Changing Society*, London: Heinemann.

Fagin, C. M. (1997). The leadership role of a dean. *New Directions for Higher Education*, 98 (Summer): 95–100.

Ferlie, E., McGivern, G. and De Moraes, A. (2010). Developing a public interest school of management. *British Journal of Management*, 21: s60–s70.

Fragueiro, F. and Thomas, H. (2011). *Strategic Leadership in the Business School*. Cambridge University Press.

Freidson, E. and Rhea, B. (1965). Knowledge and judgment in professional evaluations. *Administrative Science Quarterly*, 10(1): 107–24.

Gabriel, Y. (2005). MBA and the education of leaders: the new playing fields of Eton? *Leadership*, 1(2): 147–63.

Garvin, D. (2003). Making the case: professional education for the world of practice. *Harvard Magazine*, 106: 56–65.

Ghoshal, S. (2005). Bad management theories are destroying good management practices. *Academy of Management Learning and Education*, 4(1): 75–91.

Gleeson, D. and Knights, D. (2006). Challenging dualism: public professionalism in 'troubled' times. *Sociology*, 40(2): 277–95.

Gmelch, W. H. (2004). The department chair's balancing acts. *New Directions for Higher Education*, 126 (Summer): 69–84.

Goode, W. (1960). A theory of role strain. *American Sociological Review*, 25(4): 485–96.

Greenwood, R. and Empson, L. (2003). The professional partnership: relic or exemplary form of governance? *Organization Studies*, 24(6): 909–33.

Greenwood, R., Hinings, C. R. and Brown, J. (1990). 'P²-Form' strategic management: corporate practices in professional partnerships. *Academy of Management Journal*, 33(4): 725–55.

(1994). Merging professional service firms. *Organization Science*, 5(2): 239–57.

Grey, C. (2002). What are business schools for? On silence and voice in management education. *Journal of Management Education*, **26**(5): 496–511.

(2010). Organizing studies: publications, politics and polemic. *Organization Studies*, **31**(6): 677–94.

Hall, R. H. (1968). Professionalization and bureaucratization. *American Sociological Review*, **33**(1): 92–104.

Hill, C. J. (1988). Differences in the consumer decision process for professional versus generic services. *Journal of Services Marketing*, **2**(1): 17–23.

Hill, C. J. and Motes, W. H. (1995). Professional versus generic retail services: new insights. *Journal of Services Marketing*, **9**(2): 22–35.

Hinings, C. R., Brown, J. and Greenwood, R. (1991). Change in an autonomous professional organization. *Journal of Management Studies*, **28**(4): 375–93.

Hitt, M. A., Bierman, L., Shimizu, K. and Kochhar, R. (2001). Direct and moderating effects of human capital on strategy and performance in professional service firms: a resource-based perspective. *Academy of Management Journal*, **44**(1): 13–28.

Hrebiniak, L. G. and Alutto, J. A. (1972). Personal and role-related factors in the development of organizational commitment. *Administrative Science Quarterly*, **17**(4): 555–73.

Kallinikos, J. (2006). *The Consequences of Information: Institutional Implications of Technological Change*. Cheltenham: Edward Elgar.

Kärreman, D. and Alvesson, M. (2004). Cages in tandem: management control, social identity, and identification in a knowledge-intensive firm. *Organization*, **11**(1): 149–75.

Kärreman, D., Sveningsson, S. and Alvesson, M. (2002). The return of the machine bureaucracy? Management control in the work settings of professionals. *International Studies of Management and Organization*, **32**(2): 70.

Kelley, R. E. (1990). *The Gold Collar Worker: Harnessing the Brainpower of the New Work Force*. Reading, MA: Addison-Wesley.

Kerr, S., Von Glinow, M. A. and Schriesheim, J. (1977). Issues in the study of 'professionals' in organizations: the case of scientists and engineers. *Organizational Behavior and Human Performance*, **18**(2): 329–45.

Khurana, R. (2007). *From Higher Aims to Hired Hands: The Social Transformation of American Business Schools and the Unfulfilled Promise of Management as a Profession*. Princeton University Press.

Khurana, R. and Nohria, N. (2008). It's time to make management a true profession. *Harvard Business Review*, **86**: 70–7.

Lam, A. (2000). Tacit knowledge, organizational learning and societal institutions: an integrated framework. *Organization Studies* **21**(3): 487–513.

Larson, M. S. (1977). *The Rise of Professionalism: A Sociological Analysis*. Berkeley: University of California Press.

Liedtka, J. M., Haskins, M. E., Rosenblum, J. W. and Weber, J. (1997). The generative cycle: linking knowledge and relationships. *Sloan Management Review*, **39**(1): 47–58.

Lorange, P. (2008). *Thought Leadership Meets Business: How Business Schools Can Become More Successful*. Cambridge University Press.

Lorsch, J. W. and Tierney, T. J. (2002). *Aligning the Stars: How to Succeed When Professionals Drive Results*. Boston: Harvard Business School Press.

Løwendahl, B. (1997). *Strategic Management of Professional Service Firms*. Copenhagen: Handelshøjskolens.

——— (2000). *Strategic Management of Professional Service Firms* (2nd edn). Copenhagen: Handelshøjskolens.

McGee, J., Thomas, H. and Wilson, D. (2010). *Strategy: Analysis and Practice* (2nd edn). London and New York: McGraw-Hill.

Maister, D. H. (1993). *Managing the Professional Service Firm*. New York: Free Press.

Malhotra, N. and Morris, T. (2009). Heterogeneity in professional service firms. *Journal of Management Studies*, **46**(6): 895–922.

Mills, P. K., Hall, J. L., Leidecker, J. K. and Margulies, N. (1983). Flexiform: a model for professional service organizations. *Academy of Management Review*, **8**(1): 118–31.

Mintzberg, H. (1979). *The Structuring of Organizations: A Synthesis of the Research*. Englewood Cliffs, NJ: Prentice Hall.

——— (1989). *Mintzberg on Management*. New York: Free Press.

——— (1993). *Structure in Fives: Designing Effective Organizations*. Englewood Cliffs, NJ: Prentice Hall.

——— (1998). Covert leadership: notes on managing professionals. *Harvard Business Review*, **76**(6): 140–7.

——— (2004). *Managers, Not MBAs: A Hard Look at the Soft Practice of Managing and Management Development*. London; Pearson Education.

Montagna, P. D. (1968). Professionalization and bureaucratization in large professional organizations. *American Journal of Sociology*, **74**(2): 138.

Morris, T. and Empson, L. (1998). Organization and expertise: an exploration of knowledge bases and the management of accounting and consulting firms. *Accounting, Organizations and Society*, **23**(5): 609–24.

Nachum, L. (1999). *The Origins of the International Competitiveness of Firms: The Impact of Location and Ownership in Professional Service Industries*. Cheltenham: Edward Elgar.

Nahapiet, J. and Ghoshal, S. (1998). Social capital, intellectual capital and the organizational advantage. *Academy of Management Review*, **23**(2): 242–66.

Newell, S., Robertson, M., Scarbrough, H. and Swan, J. (2002). *Managing Knowledge Work*. Basingstoke: Palgrave.

Paulin, M., Ferguson, R. J. and Payaud, M. (2000). Business effectiveness and professional service personnel Relational or transactional managers? *European Journal of Marketing*, **34**(3/4): 453.

Pettigrew, A. M. (1997). The double hurdles for management research, in T. Clark (ed.), *Advancement in Organizational Behaviour: Essays in Honour of Derek S. Pugh*: 277–96. London: Dartmouth Press.

Pfeffer, J. and Fong, C. T. (2002). The end of business schools? Less success than meets the eye. *Academy of Management Learning and Education*, **1**: 78–95.

(2004). The business school 'business': some lessons from the US experience. *Journal of Management Studies*, **41**(8): 1501–20.

Piercy, N. (2000). Why it is fundamentally stupid for a business school to try to improve its research assessment exercise score. *European Journal of Marketing*, **34**(1/2): 27–35.

Podolny, J. M. (2009). The buck stops (and starts) at business school. *Harvard Business Review*, **87**: 62–7.

Raelin, J. A. (1984). An examination of deviant/adaptive behaviors in the organizational careers of professionals. *Academy of Management Review*, **9**(3): 413–27.

(1986). *The Clash of Cultures: Managers and Professionals*. Boston: Harvard Business School Press.

Reed, M. and Anthony, P. (1992). Professionalizing management and managing professionalization: British management in the 1980s. *Journal of Management Studies*, **29**: 591–613.

Reich, R. B. (1991). *The Work of Nations: Preparing Ourselves for Twenty-First-Century Capitalism*. London: Simon & Schuster.

Robertson, M., Scarbrough, H. and Swan, J. (2003). Knowledge creation in professional service firms: institutional effects. *Organization Studies*, **24**(6): 831–57.

Scott, W. A. and Scott, R. (1965). *Values and Organizations: A Study of Fraternities and Sororities*. Chicago: Rand McNally.

Scott, W. R. (1965). Reactions to supervision in a heteronomous professional organization. *Administrative Science Quarterly*, **10**(1): 65–81.

Sharma, A. (1997). Professional as agent: knowledge asymmetry in agency exchange. *Academy of Management Review*, **22**(3): 758–98.

Spender, J.-C. (1996). Making management the basis of a dynamic theory of the firm. *Strategic Management Journal*, **17** (Winter Special Issue): 45–62.

Starbuck, W. H. (1992). Learning by knowledge-intensive firms. *Journal of Management Studies*, **29**(6): 713–40.

(2005). How much better are the most-prestigious journals? The statistics of academic publication. *Organization Science*, 16(2): 180–200.

Starkey, K. and Tiratsoo, N. (2007). *The Business School and the Bottom Line*. Cambridge University Press.

Teece, D. J. (2000). *Managing Intellectual Capital: Organizational, Strategic, and Policy Dimensions*. Oxford University Press.

(2003). Expert talent and the design of (professional services) firms. *Industrial and Corporate Change*, 12(4): 895–916.

Thakor, M. V. (2000). What is a professional service? A conceptual review and bi-national investigation. *Journal of Services Marketing*, 14(1): 63–82.

Thomas, H. and Wilson, A. (2009). An analysis of the environment and competitive dynamics of management research. *Journal of Management Development*, 28(8): 668–84.

(2011). Business school and PSFs. Working paper. Singapore Management University (SMU).

von Nordenflycht, A. (2010). What is a professional service firm? Toward a theory and taxonomy of knowledge-intensive firms. *Academy of Management Review*, 35(1): 155–74.

Waring, J. and Currie, G. (2009). Managing expert knowledge: organizational challenges and managerial futures for the UK medical profession. *Organization Studies*, 30(7): 755–78.

Willmott, H. (1995). Managing the academics: commodification and control in the development of university education in the UK. *Human Relations*, 48(9): 993–1027.

Winch, G. and Schneider, E. (1993). Managing the knowledge-based organization: the case of architectural practice. *Journal of Management Studies*, 30(6): 923–37.

Zell, D. (2005). Pressure for relevancy at top-tier business schools. *Journal of Management Inquiry*, 14(3): 271–4.

7 Enhancing dynamic capabilities in the business school: improving leadership capabilities in curricula and management

INTRODUCTION

In Chapter 3 we questioned the existence of a 'theory of managing' and examined the issue of what necessary capabilities and qualities management educators should develop in their students. We initially focused on Mintzberg's ten managerial roles, which we clustered into *interpersonal, informational* and *decisional* skills.

We then reinterpreted them to suggest that management education should cover:

- the intellectual skills of *analysis, criticism* and *synthesis*;
- the study of the *domain of management knowledge* (i.e. knowledge skills about the structure and functioning of organisations, including process skills about the interactions and interfaces between the different functions);
- the range of Mintzberg's *interpersonal skills*, including imagination, vision and leadership capabilities;
- the multi-disciplinary nature of the managerial skill set required to develop the broader skills of global and cultural intelligence. (Here managers must learn to be sensitive to ethical and socio-cultural differences and take an holistic view of the enterprise in global networks.)

As Thomas (2007: 13) has pointed out elsewhere, it is quite clear that corporate 'recruiters increasingly require higher-level candidates who possess complex interactive skills (i.e. the ability to link things together and frame complex problems) involving an enhanced judgemental mindset'. He goes on to indicate that the challenge for business schools is 'to produce students who have the skills, flexibility and training to compete in the new economy defined by globalization and technological change'. In other words, the curriculum must increasingly embrace a cross-disciplinary, holistic and interactive form of education with a strong focus on global exposure, ethics and social responsibility.

Teece, a leading pioneer of the concept of dynamic capabilities and dynamic capability research (2009; 2011), argues that this strategic management paradigm may be helpful in developing such a curriculum since it 'can assist faculty and students alike in linking things together, framing complex problems, helping identify value-enhancing strategies and achieving better business decision-making. It can also bring a higher degree of order and integration to management education, enabling students to see how courses and subject matter interrelate' (Teece, 2011).

Therefore, in this chapter we will undertake the following:

(1) a brief review of the logic of existing capability review models and processes that attempt to frame the key management skills and capabilities;
(2) a more thorough examination of Teece's writings on dynamic capabilities and management education;
(3) an examination of how it has influenced the MBA models at UC Berkeley and Toronto;
(4) a discussion of the implications of the dynamic capability approach for enhancing leadership capabilities and models. Specifically, we shall also discuss what might be the implications for capability development at business schools.

CAPABILITY REVIEW (CR) MODELS AND PROCESSES

Introduction

There are many capability models that seek to identify and assess key managerial capabilities. Although many writers, including Herbert Simon (1955), argue that we do not have a theory of managing, the philosophy of capability review (CR) approach is to examine managerial capabilities in terms of continuous organisational regeneration and change. The top management team – CEOs and boards – then has overall responsibility for both delivering and demonstrating organisational improvement.

CR models: overall design and structure

Capability is an elusive and complicated concept. Therefore, it is important to define terms clearly. The theoretical literature (McGee et al., 2010; Teece, 2009) defines capabilities as 'the organization's capacity to deploy resources, usually in combination, using organizational processes to effect a desired end' (Teece, 2009). In this context capabilities may include leadership expertise, strategic expertise, innovation expertise, behavioural (people management) expertise and delivery/customer service expertise. In essence, capabilities are clusters of skills, organisational systems, routines and so on. 'Unlike resources, however, capabilities are based on developing, sharing and exchanging information through the organisation's human capital – as information-based assets they are often called invisible or intangible assets' (Teece, 2009).

Thus 'dynamic capabilities enable business enterprises to create, deploy, and protect the intangible assets that support superior long-run business performance' (Teece, 2009: 3).

> Competitive success, whether in the public or private sector, depends on transforming key business processes into strategic capabilities that consistently provide superior value to the customer.

Competitive success, whether in the public or private sector, depends therefore on transforming key business processes into strategic capabilities that consistently provide superior value to the customer and are typically championed by the top management team. They should also provide the basis for superior organisational performance.

In practical terms, a full range of capabilities – the exact balance will vary between organisations – would involve a combination of effective, efficient and reliable current operations (i.e. meeting delivery and efficiency targets), the ability to develop evidence-based, implementable policies, and the following, more dynamic capabilities:

- continuous improvement in effectiveness (as perceived by the customer/citizen) and efficiency;
- more robust systems and processes and improved risk management to reduce the likelihood of future crises;
- a more flexible, adaptive organisational culture and systems, seeking both to improve the response if a crisis does occur and to support and deliver new or reprioritised policies;
- the ability to deliver more radical innovations, increasingly in collaboration with other organisations (delivery or alliance partners, etc.).

Most CR models focus particularly on what are specified as the most crucial areas of capability – leadership, strategy and delivery (performance). These managerial capabilities include the following.

LEADERSHIP

The main elements of leadership are the ability to:

- see, frame and communicate the big picture and be committed to working corporately, across boundaries and organisations, to deliver the right strategic outcomes;
- be a role model, promote great teamwork, foster innovation and creativity, and reflect on how to improve and drive the development of others;
- lead others through the complexities of change by creating a shared vision of the future that all can understand and help deliver;
- to be open, honest and courageous and not flinch from delivering tough messages to colleagues;
- pose tough questions and encourage dialogue about their resolution.

The sub-elements of leadership are therefore:

- setting direction, intent and vision;
- igniting passion, pace and drive;
- taking responsibility for leading organisational change;
- building organisational capabilities.

Note that the leadership area focuses primarily on managerial and problem-framing skills. In addition, creating strong organisational performance and delivery is an important leadership outcome from a balanced scorecard viewpoint.

STRATEGY

Strategy is a contested concept in the literature but is here defined as the ability of an organisation to:

- optimise outcomes in support of the organisation's objectives within the constraints of time and resources;
- make choices about what is best offered in terms of products and services and to whom, through which processes and which partners, in order to create public and customer value;
- act upon these choices.

The sub-elements of strategy are therefore:

- focusing on outcomes;
- basing choices on evidence;
- building common purpose.

In the strategy area, strategic capabilities, including questions of problem identification, policy development, strategic prioritisation and so on, are identified as important. As a consequence, the evidence about, and analysis of, options needs to be drawn from a broad set of people in the organisation and not just the top management team.

PERFORMANCE DELIVERY

Performance delivery is defined as:

- the ability of the leadership team to lead the implementation of agreed strategy through the collective action of a network of people and organisations.

The sub-elements are therefore:

- to plan, resource and prioritise;
- to develop clear roles, responsibilities and business models;
- to manage performance.

Similarly, the top team performance delivery capabilities involve issues of performance management, problem solving and managing delivery across business units. The resulting higher-level capability judgements, however, may require insights and evidence from an even wider set of participants, including those at the centre, various delivery and distribution channels and so forth.

Model evaluation: strengths and weaknesses

An important comment is that the construct of capability in the CR model may be too narrow because it is often anchored around top team board-level leadership and strategic capabilities, despite the need to 'drill down' to various management levels in an organisation to answer strategy and delivery questions. Further, it is not much concerned with delivery, behaviour, culture and innovation capabilities – all of which have an important influence on outcomes and organisational capability formation.

> Existing capability models are seen on balance to be a good starting point for assessing key strategic execution skills. The focus on leadership, strategy and delivery capabilities sets out clearly the organisational change agenda.

The broad weaknesses of existing models concern issues of the definition of capability and the overall purpose of the CR model. Capability is often viewed as a 'soft concept' that is somewhat difficult to understand. In addition, there is particular concern about whether the model is intended to focus on capability in order to tackle organisational sub-goals (such as delivery) or to attack system-wide organisational goals.

There is also confusion about the causal linkages between capability and performance; in other words, should good capability skills lead to good departmental performance? And there is some uncertainty about the ultimate purpose of the CR model; namely, is it about seeking to improve organisational capability or improving service performance delivery?

In summary, though, existing capability models are seen on balance to be a good starting point for assessing key strategic execution skills. The focus on leadership, strategy and delivery capabilities sets out clearly the organisational change agenda. The models may also help to identify common themes and capability gaps across organisations in areas such as resource utilisation, talent management and delivery/outcome assessment. Nevertheless, the question remains as to whether identifying common capability gaps will subsequently lead to the development of dynamic capabilities.

Therefore, in the following section we examine the theoretical framework of dynamic capabilities exemplified in the writings of Teece, and its potential applications to management education.

DYNAMIC CAPABILITIES AND MANAGEMENT EDUCATION

Introduction to resource-based and dynamic capabilities approaches

The intellectual origins behind the concept of dynamic capabilities lie in Schumpeter's (1994) concept of creative destruction and Cyert and March's (1992) behavioural theory of the firm. However, the primary influence has been the resource-based view (RBV) of the firm (Barney, 1991; Penrose, 1959; Peteraf, 1993; Prahalad and Hamel, 1990).

Unlike market-based strategy analyses such as Porter's (1980) well-known five forces model, which focuses on industry factors and influences on the firm's strategy, RBV's fundamental idea is that the success or failure of an organisation, in terms of sustainable long-term competitive advantage, is determined largely by its internal characteristics. These consist of its unique resources and skills.

The purpose of firm-level strategy is first to identify the firm's set of unique resources, capabilities or core competencies, which may include tangible assets (such as financial capital or intellectual property) or intangible assets (such as business models, brand equity, reputation or innovative abilities). The manager's role is then to leverage these organisational assets alongside appropriate organisational structures and processes and, in so doing, build the skills, expertise and organisational capabilities to generate competitive advantage. Capabilities, which are essentially bundles of resources, are developed and nurtured over a long period and evolve as the vision, strategy and intent of the organisation changes.

Strategy (according to Teece et al., 1997) is about 'choosing among, and committing to, long-term paths or trajectories of competence development'. This dynamic capabilities approach has evolved in Teece's writings and, according to Helfat and colleagues (2007: 12), the original definition of dynamic capabilities referred to 'the firm's ability to integrate, build and reconfigure internal and external competences to address rapidly changing environments'. Helfat and colleagues reviewed subsequent work and produced a revised definition stating that 'a dynamic capability is the capacity of an organization to purposefully create, extend or modify its resource base' (4).

> What is distinctive about the dynamic capabilities approach is that it addresses the ability of firms to develop *new* capabilities.

Thus, 'capabilities' and 'competencies' are essentially 'resources' in terms of the RBV. Resources, however, must be valuable, rare, inimitable and not easily substitutable for them to be a basis for stimulating and achieving sustainable long-term competitive advantage. In other words, the RBV (Penrose, 1959) could easily be retitled the 'capabilities-based' (Teece, 2009) or 'competence-based' (Prahalad and Hamel, 1990) theory.

What is distinctive about the dynamic capabilities approach, however, is that it addresses the ability of firms to develop *new* capabilities, adding to their strategic capabilities resource base as a source of sustained long-term competitive advantage. This is very important in fast-paced technological and constantly changing global environments that place a premium on the quality of organisational and managerial skills and the exploitation of innovative and creative capabilities in finding new market spaces and products. Hence, 'dynamic capabilities are high-level competences that determine the firm's ability to integrate, build and reconfigure internal and external resources/competences (including its intangible assets) to address and shape a business environment' (Teece et al., 1997; Teece, 2010).

DYNAMIC CAPABILITIES AND CURRICULUM CHANGES IN BUSINESS SCHOOLS

In a recent paper, David Teece (2011) argues that in the current business environment old ways of viewing competition and the functions of management are inadequate. He believes that firms must recognise the complexity and the evolving nature of the business ecosystem (see Figure 7.1) in which they operate.

In particular, he points out that the business school curriculum needs to explain the interactions and interdependencies between the elements of this ecosystem. The exploitation of these interactions is important in valuing, creating and reinforcing intangible assets and organising cross-disciplinary managerial skills and capabilities. This means that the context of existing functional courses in business schools and the narrow discipline-oriented structure of the typical MBA curriculum must change dramatically.

Teece believes the dynamic capabilities perspective with its emphasis on managing the 'soft assets' needed for orchestrating

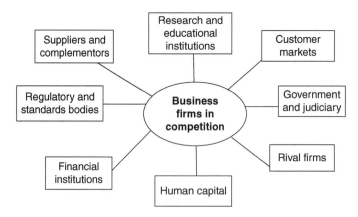

FIGURE 7.1 The business ecosystem. *Source*: Based on Teece (2011)

resources inside and outside the firm can provide a framework for business school curricula. He suggests that the interactive aspects of managing across functions and the wider business ecosystem should be recognised and that three key elements (or clusters) of dynamic capabilities can form the anchors for the new curriculum.

These three clusters are:

- *sensing* – the identification and assessment of a business opportunity;
- *seizing* – the mobilisation of resources to address an opportunity and capture value from doing so;
- *transforming* – continued renewal.

The micro-foundations for each of these capability clusters are shown in Figure 7.2 and comprise problem frameworks and analytical systems for sensing opportunities, processes and designs for seizing opportunities, and alignment processes for transforming necessary strategic change.

Sensing opportunities implies the formation of a set of entrepreneurial capabilities involving the ability to imagine new markets and technological opportunities by bringing into the managerial mind things not currently present or immediate to the senses. It requires managerial insight and vision and a knowledge of problem framing, scenario development and analytical approaches that can enhance the set of insights and ideas that processes of imagination and creativity can suggest. The key question here is: how do we teach the essence of creativity that is at the heart of all the work we do?

Seizing opportunities requires capabilities that develop processes and business models that can create value from new opportunities. It will also require capabilities to understand how to collaborate with suppliers, 'complementors' and customers in order to leverage assets within the ecosystem. The key issue here is to encourage diversity and breadth in the curriculum and encourage a culture of innovation.

Managerial behaviour must change and organisations and their leadership must be more adaptive and far less rigid in their thinking.

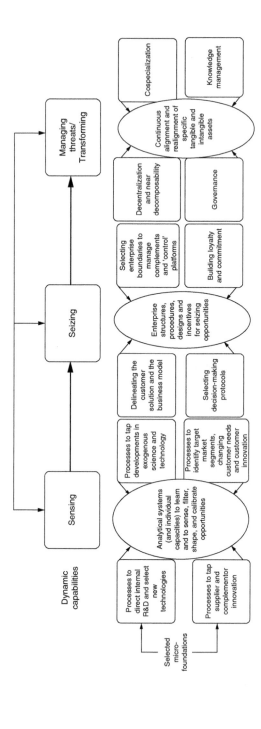

FIGURE 7.2 Dynamic capabilities and their micro-foundations. *Source:* Based on Teece (2007; 2011)

Transforming opportunities and putting ideas into practice involves capabilities of adapting and realising assets continually to maintain a strong 'fit' between the firm and its broad ecosystem and its internal organisation structure and external processes, such as the alliance processes with suppliers and complementors. These are the elements of transformational change.

The key curriculum question here is how to generate flexibility and openness to change. Managerial behaviour must change and organisations and their leadership must be more adaptive and far less rigid in their thinking.

Teece (2011) uses Apple as an example of a paradigmatic practitioner of dynamic capabilities as it has successfully created and transformed a series of markets. Figure 7.3 is Teece's explanation of Apple's development in terms of the three elements of dynamic capabilities and its transformational strategic change in identifying and orchestrating new asset combinations.

From a business school perspective, therefore, the important issues for curriculum design are the following.

- How do you make organisations creative?
- How do you make new ideas systemic?
- How do you run organisations that are creative and innovative?
- How do you run organisations that can respond and adapt quickly?

CURRICULA DESIGNS IN PRACTICE: THE DYNAMIC
CAPABILITIES APPROACH

As we noted in earlier chapters criticisms of business schools and doubts over their value continue unabated. And in Chapters 4 and 5 we examined a number of alternative curricula models and approaches for management education. These newer models have generally focused on linking the analysis of the various management disciplines – the current dominant business school model – with an approach involving cross-disciplinary integration of the curriculum.

The curriculum pioneered by Joel Podolny when he was dean at Yale resulted in an MBA core curriculum with a number of

	Sensing	Seizing	Transforming	Result
iPod	Existing mp3 players were too 'geeky'	Create an aesthetically appealing portable device with a simple interface over an accelerated product development cycle; later: improve appropriability with exclusive FairPlay DRM in the iTunes Music Store	Port iTunes software to rival Windows platform; expand into content distribution with the iTunes Music Store; shift company emphasis from computers to consumer electronics	Domination of the portable digital music player market; expansion to video capabilities (playback and distribution)
iPhone	Existing 'smart phones' retained an awkward interface too close to their cell phone roots	Create a multimedia phone with a large screen and an intuitive interface; promote complementary asset creation with the App Store infrastructure	Develop telephony capabilities; enter the regulated telephony market	One of the few companies making money with smart phones
iPad	'Netbooks' provide an unsatisfying computing experience and 'E-readers' provide limited functionality	Scale up the iPhone interface to provide a richer multimedia platform without phone functionality	Extend the 'simple interface' aesthetic to a computing platform	Domination of the tablet market and associated App structure

FIGURE 7.3 Dynamic capabilities at Apple. *Source*: Based on Teece (2011)

team-taught cross-disciplinary courses involving themes such as leading and managing across boundaries, values and creative problem solving. Yet, these are not fully integrated in a coherent manner or framework.

Teece (2011) argues that the dynamic capabilities model offers such a coherent and theory-grounded framework and provides appropriate rigour in the absence of a credible general theory of management.

Teece, as a faculty member at Haas, University of California, Berkeley, was heavily involved in the intellectual reframing of the MBA curriculum at the school. While the macro-end of the curriculum is pinned down with a leader archetype (that of an innovative leader), the micro-end is anchored with a set of ten capabilities that are extended and integrated throughout the curriculum (e.g. problem framing). Figure 7.4 illustrates the ten capabilities of an innovative leader as proposed by Richard Lyons (2012). This seems to be the basic logic behind the MBA curriculum at Haas.

Teece's (2011) dynamic capabilities are clearly evident in this model and identified as follows.

- *Sensing capabilities* equates with defining opportunities.
- *Seizing capabilities* equates with making choices.
- *Transforming capabilities* equates with execution.

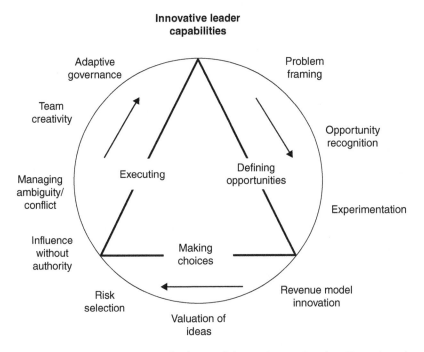

FIGURE 7.4 Innovative leader capabilities. *Source*: Based on Teece (2011) and Lyons (2012)

These ten capabilities were chosen based on two criteria: first, they had to be grounded in the social sciences and research based using models such as the dynamic capabilities approach; second, they had to be demanded by recruiters and others in the marketplace. They also are identified as developing capabilities consistent with the macro-image of an innovative leader.

A criticism of this model is that it leans toward individual learning and does not involve significant collaborative learning as advocated by Henry Mintzberg in his discussion of managerial mind-sets. However, the Berkeley curriculum includes an experiential learning course, and a team performance and training module is included elsewhere in the curriculum.

LEADERSHIP AND DYNAMIC CAPABILITIES

In a 2010 *Financial Times* column Richard Lyons argued that leading in complex environments, involving fast-paced technological change and global economic uncertainty, requires what the famous sociologist J. D. Thompson (1967) described as 'inspirational leadership'. He refined this concept in framing the major curriculum revision at UC Berkeley, introducing the archetype of a 'path-bending' leader who breaks the mould from a philosophy of incremental strategic adaption to a more innovative, anticipatory strategic leadership. Lyons states that 'path-bending leaders are not just CEOs, but people working at all levels in all kinds of organisations. Path-bending leaders need to know the fundamentals etc. ... They also need a set of skills of knowledge that are targeted to produce this type of leader, such as problem-framing, experimentation, influence without authority, managing ambiguity and other capabilities.'

Path-bending leaders need to have courage and capabilities that produce 'innovating' rather than 'adaptive' behaviours.

In essence, path-bending leaders need to have courage and capabilities that produce 'innovating' rather than 'adaptive' behaviours.

LEADERSHIP CAPABILITIES IN THE BUSINESS
SCHOOL CONTEXT

With his usual perception and insight Charles Handy (1995) noted in a reflective essay that: 'It is odd, to say the least, that the education which we have devised for the best of our managers has so little in it about personality theory, what makes people what they are, or about learning theory, how people grow and develop and change; or political theory, how people seek power, resist power and organize themselves; or moral philosophy, how they decide between right and wrong.'

His remarks are perhaps even more important and appropriate in the extremely uncertain environment that has followed the global economic crisis. Leaders must reflect on the historical lessons of leadership and their future implications. The process-based model of the strategic leadership process (Fraguiero and Thomas, 2011) stresses that key strategic decisions emerge from an interactive process involving internal and external constituencies. Having an awareness of personality theory, learning theory, political theory and moral philosophy can only enhance the understanding of how decisions result from internal and external contexts and from individuals (in particular, deans) in the context of organisational (business school) processes and bureaucratic (university, institutional) politics (Allison and Zelikow, 1999). Similarly, high levels of self-awareness and empathy are also great assets.

Lorange (2010: 20) draws on the work of Peter Drucker and further stresses that 'leaders grow, they are not made and the way they grow is by learning (whether formally in the classroom or on the job) through good and bad times'.

Leadership is, therefore, an innate skill but it also involves a set of skills that can be learned, or acquired through formal training or from on-the-job experience.

In summary, three elements of strategic leadership therefore need a much closer focus in future research: first, leadership and leadership characteristics; second, the roles leaders play in the strategic change process; and third, the development of both formal and experiential leadership training.

The logic of the strategic leadership process is further confirmed in the writings of the prominent leadership scholar Manfred Kets de Vries (2006). He points out that 'leadership never happens in isolation. There can be no leaders without followers and all leadership activities take place in context' (111).

He puts forward an 'interactionist' model of leadership that involves not only the personality characteristics of the leader (the dean or the leadership team) but also the characteristics of followers (faculty, corporate advisors etc.) and the details of the context (business schools' university positioning, culture and growth) of the leadership situation. Figure 7.5 outlines the key elements in this

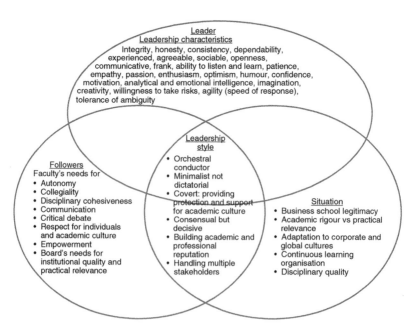

FIGURE 7.5 An interactionist model of business school leadership and leadership characteristics

model, which is an adaptation of the 'interactionist' model to the business school context (Thomas and Thomas, 2011).

Mintzberg's metaphor of the style of the academic leader as an 'orchestral conductor' is important in examining the elements of this model. An academic leader is an innovative and insightful organiser/co-ordinator who must possess and exploit a wide range of personal characteristics. These include self-awareness, confidence, motivation, empathy, social skills and intuition in order to cope with a range of tasks, including those of strategist, implementer, human capital developer and talent manager. The leader must be able to set the overarching strategic intent of the business school, build trust and respond to such issues as 'What are we?' and What are we doing?' It is also vital to specify the core competencies of the school and provide a clear orientation for the faculty, the followers and the university in terms of the speed, simplicity and broad development necessary to execute the school's strategy effectively.

A dean (leader) thus must create a style of strong, stable, supportive and consistent leadership while recognising the pressures and stresses faced in addressing political, bureaucratic and organisational processes (i.e. the faculty, the university, the board and the wider economic and management environment). The dean must also be able to leverage the range of the school's dynamic capabilities in order to build a learning organisation and a strong reputation in the academic and business marketplace.

> The dean must also be able to leverage the range of the school's dynamic capabilities in order to build a learning organisation and a strong reputation in the academic and business marketplace.

There are relatively few detailed studies specifically relating to the leadership characteristics and styles of deans and this might be an area for useful future research. Such research may also result in a refinement and narrowing of the characteristics indicated in Figure 7.5.

Kets de Vries (2006: 263), who writes prolifically about leadership, offers four key leadership characteristics: hope, humanity, humility and humour. Lorange (2010: 63) focuses on integrity, agility, a broad stakeholder focus and pragmatic optimism. These clusters of leadership attributes are conjectures about critical leadership features that may act as a catalyst for future studies of leadership. It will also be interesting to explore whether common characteristics emerge or distinctive patterns become apparent.

A few preliminary observations may be made.

- The effective leader must probably be willing to expose a good sense of a top-down holistic vision. He/she represents the entire school and the top-down vision must help in 'putting it all together' – a centripetal force to counterbalance the messy bottom-up visions of individual faculty members, which tend to be highly oriented towards 'what's in it for me?'
- To be an effective path-bender the dean must focus on one, or a few, tasks – that is, 'strategy means choice'. Simplicity is key and his/her message must be repeated over and over again. For instance, one such message might be to focus in the classroom on discussions of key dilemmas rather than on covering the basics, which are easily acquired by individual background readings and distance learning.
- A good dean must be able to bond with the relevant outside communities, above all with business executives. It is from this market that many of the impacts for dynamic change and innovation might emerge. This requires openness, listening skills and willingness to spend energy.
- The dean must solve internal conflicts in terms of 'what is best for the school'. He/she must not depend on building up his/her own popularity by 'siding' with particular individuals on changes. The dean must be seen to be fair!
- An effective dean must be prepared to spend a lot of time and energy on the job. It is not a '9 to 5' job for five days a week. It is critical, however, that a good dean stays away from 'battles' that he/she cannot win but without creating the feeling that he/she is 'avoiding' key issues.

LEADERSHIP ROLES, STYLES AND CHANGE

Leaders have to balance the requirement for continuous improvement and regular day-to-day incremental changes with the need to reshape the organisation quickly when opportunities arise or competitive forces threaten the *status quo* (Kets de Vries, 2006; McGee et al., 2010). Competitive change may often be met with a sense of organisational inertia and resistance to change expressed in terms such as 'Why do we need to change – things are going well?' or 'If it isn't broke, why fix it?' Organisational culture must therefore embrace openness to change, continuous learning, speed and entrepreneurialism. However, change involves uncertainty and is frequently unsettling. One of the important questions facing any leader is how to frame these changes and 'bend' the organisation's attitude to change.

There are clearly two roles for leadership in such change situations. First, as Goffee and Jones (2000) point out, leaders establish a creative mindset for change through establishing vision, energy, authority and strategic direction – they highlight and press the need for change through signalling changing environments and benchmarking competitive threats. Second, as Kotter (2001) notes, while leaders press for change, managers promote stability, and both sides of the equation are needed in turbulent times. Leaders must, therefore, build the rational architecture and structure of change (organisational roles, culture, design and structure) as well as imagining and championing the mindset, vision and need for change.

> Leaders must build the rational architecture and structure of change as well as imagining and championing the mindset, vision and need for change.

Indeed, Zaleznik (1992) specifically emphasises the creative and visionary aspects of leadership in the following terms: 'Vision, the hallmark of leadership, is less a derivative of spreadsheets and more a product of the mind called imagination. And vision is needed as much as strategy to succeed.' He also notes that leaders are able to cope with situations involving uncertainty. 'Leaders also tolerate chaos and ambiguity and are prepared to keep answers in suspense thus preventing closure on key issues.'

In common with other leading writers in the leadership field, Zaleznik emphasises a set of enabling leadership characteristics that promote change. Rather like Mintzberg, he views the skills of creativity and imagination as critical. In addition, as Goleman (1998; 2000) points out, effective leaders are alike in one crucial way: they all have a high degree of emotional intelligence, possessing self-awareness, self-regulation, motivation, empathy and social skill.

Goffee and Jones (2000) amplify this theme of creativity and inspiration by emphasising four other qualities of leaders: they selectively show weaknesses; they rely heavily on intuition to gauge appropriate timing and course of actions; they manage employees with tough empathy; and they reveal their differences.

Kotter (2001) summarises leaders as those who set direction, align people and motivate people in order to lead change effectively. Dean Antonio Borges demonstrated strong strategic leadership at INSEAD in France in the late 1990s and early 2000s when he implemented two critical and radical breakthrough strategic change initiatives (Fraguiero and Thomas, 2011). He turned the school into a research-oriented institution – when most of the faculty had a different background – and later spearheaded the drive to open a new campus in Singapore in order to globalise the school. The globalisation move could easily have conflicted with the earlier initiative, sidetracking INSEAD's effort to make its research capabilities competitive with leading elite US business schools. However, Borges' ability to sell his initiatives to key faculty and board members, effectively engaging them as initiative sponsors, made it possible for INSEAD to overcome a multitude of obstacles and difficulties in both pursuits.

LEADERSHIP TRAINING

In a recent study of leadership in universities (Goodall, 2009) it was noted that the leading elite universities and business schools (the top 100 in each case) were led by scholars – that is, high-quality academics. While both presidents (vice-chancellors) and deans had prior administrative experience in universities either as deans or departmental heads, few had received any formal training. They had learned and developed their skills primarily through their on-the-job experiences.

Lorange (2010) points out that learning can be achieved through formal training *and* experiential learning. Goleman (2000) points out that emotional intelligence can be taught, learned and acquired through a variety of techniques. Feedback can be provided by leadership inventories (such as those developed by Kets de Vries and the Center for Creative Leadership) and through personality inventories such as Myers-Briggs, Campbell 360® and other methods.

There is now greater openness to the idea of individual coaching and mentoring for leaders. There is also a growing interest in exploring such issues as work/life balance, the benefit of heightened self-awareness and reflection, greater empathy, strong interpersonal skills, relationship building and the development of better communication styles. Equally, students can benefit from courses that draw their attention to these areas.

The role of training for leadership within an academic environment remains under-researched and is another area that could benefit from further study. As business schools and universities adapt to an increasingly financially constrained world, coupled with the ongoing growth of the 'communication age', the design of leadership programmes for educational administration also needs critical attention. The challenge is significant but, as others have argued, leadership skills can be taught as well as acquired and refined through on-the-job experience.

It seems clear, however, that participants' engagements in certain types of practical activities might enhance such leadership capabilities. Let us discuss one example: namely, the so-called Zurich Living Case approach of the Lorange Institute. Here the participants are presented with a set of key managerial issues from the senior management of a specific company. The participants then work in small teams (four to five individuals) to come up with ideas about how to 'solve or resolve' these issues. They then present their solutions to senior management. At least three leadership capabilities are created:

- the ability to set priorities and to work out recommendations within a team setting;
- the skills to present recommendations in such a way that senior management might be convinced, so that they 'buy in' to the advice. Effective leadership is to convince others strongly. This is path-bending behaviour in practice;
- the ability to work under heavy time pressure, which is also a critical dimension of effective leadership. The key capability here is to cope with deadlines in an energy-efficient manner.

SOME EMERGING DYNAMIC CAPABILITIES OF THE BUSINESS SCHOOL OF THE FUTURE

We have discussed how business schools must focus on the dynamic capabilities phenomenon in at least two ways.

First, business schools should contribute to the development of relevant dynamic capabilities for their students and the companies they come from. Therefore, we have noted that the school's curriculum must reflect this concern. We have closely examined recent examples of curriculum redesigns that have refocused their content and structure to be better able to 'deliver' relevant dynamic capabilities.

Second, it is also clear that a thorough examination of the dynamic capabilities of the business school itself should be undertaken. This issue has been partially reviewed in our prior discussion of the dynamic capabilities and leadership strengths of the dean.

We now take this analysis a step further by examining the emerging dynamic capability requirements for the business school of the future. We particularly focus on these areas:

- the need to identify relevant dynamic capabilities to attract and develop greater differentiation among faculty members so as to better address pressures for relevance and impact;

- the importance of developing dynamic capabilities to monitor new competitors and to respond to these competitive challenges. The key capability here is the ability to act decisively and dynamically in contrast to the more stable reality in which many business schools see themselves today;
- dynamic capabilities to deal with the funding and fundraising requirements of the future in the face of diminishing willingness of the government sector to fund business schools and tighter economic situations for corporations and students alike to contribute to funding.

We now explore each of these issues in turn.

Greater faculty differentiation

We anticipate a need for a wider range of faculty, above all to meet the increasing demands from business for practical relevance. This calls for drawing not only on faculty members who have classical academic training (PhD) and careers (full-time professor at an academic institution) but also on teaching practitioners.

To achieve continuous improvement in efficiency and effectiveness, and increase instructional quality, a school might need to develop a range of dynamic capabilities such as:

- creating an effective network of available 'affiliated' faculty both from practice and from various leading business schools;
- developing an ability to attract and nurture 'affiliated' faculty by integrating them into programme offerings and linking them to core faculty;
- promoting continuous training in new pedagogical approaches involving both technology and experimental learning options;
- revising its organisational culture to encompass the management of faculty 'networks' of core and affiliated faculty. This might involve the creative use of communication by social and digital media;
- stimulating the delivery of more radical innovations by demobilising old bureaucratic routines and fostering an open-minded attitude to experimentation in instructional approaches by changing the role of a professor from a communicator of knowledge in a 'linear' fashion to that of a 'facilitator'.

New competitors

It is clear that there is an abundance of new sources of competition coming partly from the academic sector itself, partly from our customers (e.g. corporate universities) and partly due to new 'blended' learning technologies. In order to carefully monitor and respond quickly to these competitive forces many business schools require new dynamic capabilities.

First, there are capabilities associated with concerns from customers and students about the efficiency, value, quality and effectiveness of our teaching. This calls for the following:

- the ability to deliver programmes in a more cost-efficient manner involving such capabilities as outsourcing, blended learning, simpler pedagogy and creative, innovative designs for programme-learning effectiveness.

Second, there are clearly risks arising from new competition that require further capability development. These developments include:

- the dynamic capability to act faster and to come up with new, innovative responses against well-funded 'for-profit' competition such as the Apollo Group and Hult International Business School. Business schools in universities must continue to invent new approaches rather than sticking with the *status quo*;
- the capability to offer customers, and students, both value for money and a creative menu of options so that appropriate personal customisation of learning can be achieved;
- the willingness to implement alternative instructional approaches and adapt the organisational culture to embrace change.

Finances

The continuing tightness in funding models for business schools certainly requires creative capabilities in designing *new business models*. We have already examined Lorange's new business model in the Lorange Institute, which involves both a high-quality delivery focused on practical concerns but simultaneously cost efficiencies through the lower fixed faculty costs (i.e. no core faculty but 'networked' part-time faculty) and associated overheads. In Porter's (1980) terms, this is both a 'cost leadership' and a creative differentiation strategy.

This model by Peter Lorange is a clear example of a creative attempt to address the concerns of Howard Thomas and Kai Peters (2012) about the continued long-term sustainability of many current rather 'luxurious' business school models.

Other innovative business models may involve creative co-sponsoring of specific research projects with corporate clients and other practical funding partnerships requiring deep immersion with corporate and public-sector organisations.

In summary, the creative design of joint ventures and alliances with both academic and managerial institutions will be an important capability set. It clearly requires new capabilities. These include co-ordination abilities, open-mindedness, continued communication and an atmosphere of trust in order to deliver quality outputs at high performance levels.

REFERENCES

Allison, G. T. and Zelikow, P. (1999). *The Essence of Decision: Explaining the Cuban Missile Crisis*. London: Longman.

Barney, J. (1991). Firm resources and sustained competitive advantage. *Journal of Management*, **17**(1): 99–120.

Cyert, R. and March, J. (1992). *A Behavioral Theory of the Firm*. Oxford: Blackwell.

Fraguiero, F. and Thomas, H. (2011). *Strategic Leadership in the Business School: Keeping One Step Ahead*. Cambridge University Press.

Goffee, R. and Jones, G. (2000). Why should anyone be led by you?. *Harvard Business Review*, **78**(5): 62–70.

Goleman, D. (1998). What makes a leader? *Harvard Business Review*, **76**(6): 93–102. (2000). Leadership that gets results. *Harvard Business Review*, **78**(2): 78–90.

Goodall, A. H. (2009). *Socrates in the Boardroom: Why Research Universities Should be Led by Top Scholars*. Princeton University Press.

Handy, C. (1995). Editorial, in *Training the Fire Brigade*. Brussels: EFMD Publications.

Helfat, C., Finkelstein, S., Mitchell, W., Peteraf, M., Singh, H., Teece, D. and Winter, S. (2007). *Dynamic Capabilities: Understanding Strategic Change in Organizations*. Oxford: Blackwell.

Kets de Vries, Manfred F. R. (2006). *The Leadership Mystique: Leading Behavior in the Human Enterprise*. New York: Prentice Hall/Financial Times.

Kotter, J. (2001). What leaders really do. *Harvard Business Review*, 79(11): 85–96.

Lorange, P. (2010). *Leading in Turbulent Times: Lessons Learnt and Implications for the Future*. Bingley: Emerald.

Lyons, R. (2010, 25 October). Richard Lyons: leading in a complex world. *Financial Times*.

—— (2012). Curriculum reform: getting more macro, and more micro. *Journal of Management Development*, 31(4): 412–23.

McGee, J., Thomas, H. and Wilson, D. (2010). *Strategy: Analysis and Practice* (2nd edn). New York: McGraw-Hill.

Penrose, E. T. (1959). *The Theory of the Growth of the Firm*. New York: John Wiley.

Peteraf, M. (1993). The cornerstones of competitive advantage: a resource-based view. *Strategic Management Journal*, 14(3): 179–91.

Porter, M. (1980). *Competitive Strategy: Techniques for Analyzing Industries and Competitors*. New York: Free Press. (Reprint edn, 1998).

Prahalad, C. K. and Hamel, G. (1990). The core competence of the corporation. *Harvard Business Review*, 68(3): 79–91.

Schumpeter, J. (1994). *Capitalism, Socialism and Democracy*. London: Routledge.

Simon, H. (1955). A behavioral model of rational choice. *Quarterly Journal of Economics*, 69(1): 99–118.

Teece, D. (2007). Explicating dynamic capabilities: the nature and microfoundations of (sustainable) enterprise performance. *Strategic Management Journal*, 28(3): 1319–50.

—— (2009). *Dynamic Capabilities and Strategic Management*. Oxford University Press.

—— (2010). Alfred Chandler and 'capabilities' theories of strategy and management. *Industrial and Corporate Change*, 19(2): 297–316.

—— (2011). Achieving integration of the business school curriculum using the dynamic capabilities framework. *Journal of Management Development*, 30(5): 499–518.

Teece, D., Pisano, G. and Shuen, A. (1997). Dynamic capabilities and strategic management. *Strategic Management Journal*, 18(7): 509–33.

Thomas, H. (2007). An analysis of the environment and competitive dynamics of management education. *Journal of Management Development*, 26(1): 9–21.

Thomas, H. and Peters, K. (2012). A sustainable model for business schools. *Journal of Management Development*, 31(4): 377–86.

Thomas, H. and Thomas, L. (2011). Perspectives on leadership in business schools. *Journal of Management Development*, 30(5): 526–40.

Thompson, J. D. (1967). *Organisations in Action*. New York: McGraw-Hill.

Zaleznik, A. (1992). Managers and leaders: are they different?. *Harvard Business Review*, 70(2): 126–35.

8 Afterword: business school futures

As mentioned in the Preface, this book is a sort of freeze-frame view of business schools and the management education industry at a moment in time – we cannot be sure yet if what follows will be an inelegant pratfall or a graceful recovery.

The book contains some suggestions both for how to avoid the former and embrace the latter, but the result will be in the hands of the business schools themselves and, in particular, their deans and senior faculty.

There are two key issues (among others, of course) that they will need to address:

- the business model of business schools;
- the impact of a globalised world.

How they handle them will have a huge influence on their future.

BUSINESS MODEL

We have pointed out here and elsewhere that the current somewhat luxurious business model employed and enjoyed by many leading business schools is potentially unstable and possibly unsustainable in the longer term.

The key is funding – where it comes from and where it is spent.

The largest percentage of business school funding has traditionally come from the state. Schools are directly funded to educate students and to produce research. The state perceives education as a public good that produces an educated workforce, which eventually should produce returns to the state through higher productivity and taxes. Equally, research is seen as generating innovation that also creates long-term public benefit.

However, note the word 'traditionally'.

European governments (with the UK well in the lead) are already questioning the philosophical basis for the state funding of (at least some kinds of) education. In other regions, such as some parts of Asia and Latin America, education has always been seen as a more or less private affair with little role for the state. In any case, no one is particularly keen to be seen transferring funds to business schools *per se* given their unfortunate links to big business and the financial sector (both anathema to the public at present) at a time of economic stringency.

So, if the state cannot or will not pay then the money will have to come from students themselves. And indeed tuition fees for degree programmes and executive education courses are rising impressively around the world.

In the US, tuition fees are very high, with over 100 institutions charging over $50,000 a year for fees, room and board. Fees for four-year undergraduate degree programmes could well reach $330,000 by 2020. The top twenty MBA programmes in the US already ask tuition fees of around $100,000 while Executive MBA programmes (usually paid for by corporations rather than individuals) can cost up to $172,200.

Even traditional state funders are beginning to move towards asking students to contribute at least some of the cost of their education, with the UK again acting as pacemaker. Although historically students have judged the return on investment as not unreasonable, the increasing costs of tuition and living expenses combined with foregone income may well lead to numerous candidates concluding that a tipping point will soon be reached where the costs outweigh the benefits. Indeed, in the UK there have been recent signals that the country's relatively high undergraduate tuition fees are starting to depress university applications.

The real problem comes when we discuss how this diminishing amount of money – like a water butt in a drought – is being spent. Most is going on permanent and (some) part-time faculty. This is not unexpected given that faculty are the main, possibly only, asset of a business school. However, how that faculty is rewarded is key.

Kai Peters and Howard Thomas have argued (2011) that business schools tend to be either teaching-intensive or research-intensive. In many of the newer universities in the UK and elsewhere (which in the UK have tended to emerge from old-style polytechnics and are strongly teaching-intensive), they say, there is an anchor at about 300 teaching hours a year, which tends to produce a teaching cost of about €270/hour. At the other, research-intensive end of the spectrum, fully loaded salaries can be considerably higher than those in a newer university and the teaching load much reduced, leading to an hourly teaching cost of €2,200. In comparison, secondary school teachers in middle-income and developing economies cost, on average, €8/hour and in the OECD €34/hour.

Realistically there are only two ways to deal with this situation: teach less (and undergraduates across the world are becoming used to dwindling contact hours) or teach more students (ditto).

Peters and Thomas propose a third way: increasing teaching loads. They suggest that many institutions are using a faculty model that is very luxurious, allowing their main human capital directly to generate income for less than 10 per cent of their annual time at one end of the spectrum or only about 30 per cent at the other. Instead, they say, 'the consequent strategic options, including part-time and on-line education, should encourage deans and directors of business schools to reflect genuinely on the long-term financial viability of their business models and focus on refreshing such models in the future'.

GLOBALISATION

As pointed out in Chapter 3, middle managers and college graduates from Latin America and Asia used to come to a business school in the US or the UK if they wanted to gain an MBA. Now, graduate education is becoming more local. In 1991, for example, there were nine graduate business schools in China; now there are some 250 programmes and over 30,000 MBA graduates per year. Within China alone over the next decade business will require an additional 75,000 MBAs able to speak English. And, just as foreign students sought entry into American or European business schools for much of the twentieth century, some Western students are now applying to Chinese, Asian and Indian business schools.

Emerging markets need huge numbers of business professionals and leaders. Thanks to rapidly improving and accessible technology, online and distance learning MBAs are one of the fastest-growing segments in business education – servicing a niche of professional students thirsty for a degree that allows them to stay within their region of the world.

As we said in Chapter 3, universities and business schools must seize this opportunity to educate a growing crop of emerging market business leaders. No university is too large or too prestigious not to do so. It will lose its size, scale, budget reserves and influence if it is not willing to change and adapt to the current status of the world. Lack of activity is the danger educational institutions face today, especially since the 'half life' of knowledge (i.e. software, social media, supply chain and energy) is decreasing. Much of what we teach in the business arena today will be obsolete in eighteen months or less.

The global marketplace is being refreshed by emerging technologies and investments in infrastructure by their governments. Thus more and more working professionals are demanding MBA programmes that offer expertise, connectivity and flexibility.

Schools must prepare business managers and leaders with the ability to compete in the global marketplace. This preparation includes addressing the business and social issues around energy, transportation, food and water, technology, healthcare and the environment. Social consciousness and stakeholder awareness will also prove to be very significant considerations in the marketplace.

Just as MBA programmes need to adapt to global demands, so too must business professionals not be content with obtaining a single degree or certification. They must participate in lifelong learning, which provides endless opportunities for universities to develop more programmes.

Whether or not business schools (for which, read deans) have the stomach and expertise to drive through reforms and changes that are needed must remain a moot point. But the outcome will be crucial.

REFERENCE

Peters, K. and Thomas, H. (2011). A sustainable model for business schools. *Global Focus: The EFMD Business Magazine*, **5**(2): 24–7.

Index